St Mary's Abbey and the King's Manor, York:
The Pictorial Evidence

By Barbara Wilson and Frances Mee

Published by York Archaeological Trust — 2009

St Mary's Abbey

... one of the bewties of this realme to al men and strangers passing threw the same
(Robert Aske, under interrogation in 1537, cited in Fletcher 1968, 133–4)

When perfect it must have been very beautiful and almost a rival to the Minster
(Brady 1854)

That after such repeated and extensive spoliations one stone should be left standing upon another, to mark the spot on which this once splendid establishment flourished, is a matter of pleasing astonishment; that no more remains must ever be deeply regretted by all who are capable of forming any just conception, from the little that violence and time have spared, of the exquisite taste and unrivalled elegance that distinguished the original structure ... the ruins of the conventual church of St Mary have afforded a favourite subject for the pencil of the artist, and gratified even the most fastidious lover of the picturesque.
(Allen 1829, 454–5)

The King's Manor

... the most complex and confusing though not the most beautiful of York's secular buildings
(Hutchinson and Palliser 1980, 149)

We may rejoice that this interesting edifice, dignified as it is by so many stirring associations, has suffered but little injury in its external aspect from the many changes it has experienced, and that it still exists to adorn our venerable city.
(Davies 1883, 17)

Contents

List of Figures v

Acknowledgements xi

Preface xii

A brief history of monasticism and the Benedictine Order in England 1

St Mary's Abbey
    Foundation 5
    The Romanesque church 7
    Historical development 1088–c.1500 8
    The Gothic church 15
    The claustral buildings 27
    The outer precincts 35
    The precinct walls 43
    Decline and dissolution 55
    History of the archaeology of St Mary's Abbey 60
    Abbots of St Mary's Abbey (1082–1539) 61

The King's Manor
    History 63
    Architectural development and layout 68
    Selected architectural features 76

Illustrations
    St Mary's Abbey 83
    The King's Manor 111
    Maps and plans showing the entire site 121

Sources 123

Select Index of Artists 125

Glossary 131

Bibliography 133

List of Figures

St Mary's Abbey

1	Fourteenth-century ink drawing in the margin of a manuscript, showing York from the south-west with the Minster and St Mary's Abbey	xii
2	Detail from 'The Gardens of the Yorkshire Philosophical Society' by J. Storey, c.1860	xiii
3	Detail from 1545 plan of York	xiv
4	Detail from Speed's plan of York, 1610	xiv
5	South-east view of the remains of St Mary's Abbey by F. Nash, showing excavations in progress	xv
6	Scale plan of the abbey by William Richardson, 1843	xvi
7	Thirteenth-century manuscript illustration of Stephen and the abbey church	5
8	Plan of the Norman church from *The Charm of St Mary's Abbey* by Edwin Ridsdale Tate, 1929	6
9	Outline plan of the Norman church	7
10	View from the south-east showing the inner sides of the north and west walls of the nave by Joseph Halfpenny, 1807	10
11	The north wall and west end of the nave, with the north-west pier of the crossing, by W. Richardson, 1843	11
12	Compartment of the inner face of the north wall of the nave aisle based on a measured drawing by R.H. Sharp	12
13	A rare view of the exterior of the nave north wall by F. Nash, clearly showing the solid standing buttresses	13
14	The ruins of St Mary's Abbey church from the south, c.1678, by William Lodge, looking through the arches of the six bays of the nave to the ruins of the north wall	14
15	View of the abbey church from the south-west by J. Haynes, 1735	15
16	William Lodge's view of the abbey church from the south-west, c.1680, with both north and south aisle arcades still standing, each surmounted by its triforium	16
17	The western front of the church, F. Nash, 1829	16
18	A reconstruction drawing of the west front before the dissolution, based on standing remains and architectural fragments, by E. Ridsdale Tate, published in 1929	17
19	Detail, probably of the inner side of the north-west corner of the church, by S. Prout, 1821	17
20	Francis Bedford's semi-coloured lithographic view of the church from the south-west, showing clearly the west front, part of the north nave wall and crossing pier, 1843	18
21	View of the west front by W. Richardson, c.1843	19
22	Detail from an ink drawing in the margin of 14th-century manuscript. St Mary's Abbey is shown with west towers and a central spire	20

23	East end of the nave, by J.S. Prout	21
24.	View of the north-west pier of the crossing from west-south-west, with clear detail of the stonework, by John Sell Cotman, dated 1810	21
25	Photograph of the foundations of the church choir uncovered in excavations of October 1912	22
26	Photograph of the south arcade pillars rebuilt in February 1913 with fragments of stone found during excavation	22
27	Edwin Ridsdale Tate's reconstruction of the south elevation of St Mary's Abbey before 1377	23
28	Fragment of painted glass showing an angel playing a gittern	24
29	Round ventilator grille used in a window in the abbey to provide fresh air	24
30	Two floor tiles from St Mary's Abbey	24
31	Wooden rood screen originally from Jervaulx Abbey, repainted to give an idea of the original colour and splendour of English abbeys	25
32	Excavation of the foundations of the chapter house vestibule, looking east with the King's Manor and the Minster in the background, by F. Nash, 1829	26
33	Illustration from a lecture by Gilbert Scott showing a reconstruction of the probable appearance of the vestibule entrance to the chapter house, based on architectural fragments	27
34	View from the south-east by J.S. Prout, 1840, showing the remains of the chapter house some ten years after excavations, with the abbey church in the background	28
35	Photograph of the pillar which was part of a pier at the entrance to the chapter house	28
36	Statues discovered in excavating a part of the south aisle of the nave of the church, from Wellbeloved 1829	29
37	Engraving from Drake's *Eboracum* of two figures on the churchyard wall of St Lawrence, York	30
38	Fragments of St Mary's Abbey in the Yorkshire Museum, J.S. Prout, 1840. The material includes carved figures of some apostles. The museum opened in 1830.	30
39	St Mary's Abbey drain uncovered during excavation in 1984 to the south-east of the Yorkshire Museum	32
40	Another drain in the same area incorporated re-used architectural fragments in its arched roof	32
41	Reconstruction drawing of the east end of the south cloister walk by Ridsdale Tate	33
42	Detail from Wellbeloved 1829 showing the fireplace from the warming house and a carved head from the fireplace	34
43	Detail from Wellbeloved 1829 showing a roof boss with the Virgin Mary and vine-branches, and a roof boss with a musician, both from the warming house	34
44	Detail from Wellbeloved 1829 showing a roof boss from the warming house depicting two monsters or sea creatures intertwined and biting each other	34
45	Detail from Wellbeloved 1829 of the centre knot from the warming room showing the Lamb of God, with a staple and ring for a hanging lamp	34

46	Medieval green-glazed pie dish made to look like a pie crust with an animal in the centre, found near to the Multangular Tower	36
47	Memorial cross slab found under the hospitium, drawn from a rubbing by D.A. Walter in 1874	37
48	An imaginative reconstruction of all the buildings in the abbey precincts by R.H. Sharp, c.1836	38
49	The Abbey Grounds, York, by J.S. Prout, 1840	39
50	Granary (hospitium), St Mary's Abbey, 'after Twopenny', 1832	40
51	Columns supporting the granary floor, St Mary's Abbey, by William Twopenny, 1832	40
52	View of the south-east end wall of the hospitium by W. Moore, Jr, 1886	41
53	Hospitium steps and water gate, by W.J. Boddy, 1897	42
54	The archway adjoining the hospitium, from the inner (eastern) side, by E. Harper	42
55	West view of the abbey by W.H. Toms, reproduced in *Eboracum* (published 1736)	43
56	Outline plan of the abbey precincts and walls	44
57	Photograph of abbey walls exterior after removal of houses in Marygate, c.1900	46
58	Photograph of inner side of abbey walls with terraced houses, c.1933	46
59	Marygate water tower by Henry Cave, 1813	47
60	St Mary's Abbey gatehouse and lodge, F. Place, c.1700	48
61	Watercolour painting of St Mary's Abbey gateway, T. Rowlandson, 1801	48
62	Entrance to St Mary's Abbey, J. Halfpenny, 1807, showing the gateway and lodge from the outer side	49
63	St Mary's Tower by H. Cave, 1813	49
64	Detail from 'The Gardens of the Yorkshire Philosophical Society', J. Storey, c.1860, showing the north-eastern wall running along Bootham from within the abbey precinct	50
65	The precinct walls from Marygate Tower to Queen Margaret's Arch, parallel to Bootham. Ridsdale Tate produced this drawing in 1915 to show how the walls had originally appeared and should look in the future after clearance	51
66	Ancient gateway to the Yorkshire School for the Blind, F. Bedford, 1843	52
67	Photograph of men working on the inner side of the abbey precinct wall in Exhibition Square, probably in the 1890s	52
68	Detail from an engraving by William Lodge, showing (from left to right) the still crenellated Marygate water tower, the abbey precinct wall running parallel to the River Ouse, the hospitium with the adjacent water gate behind, and Lendal Tower.	53
69	Detail from west view of the abbey by W.H. Toms, showing a small part of the southern precinct wall between the hospitium and river bank	53
70	Photograph of part of the southern precinct wall between the hospitium and the river after excavation in the 1980s	54

71	House incorporating parts of the abbey, by John Browne	57
72	The Yorkshire Museum, H. and W. Brown, 1836	59
73	Gateway to the Yorkshire Museum, H. and W. Brown, 1836	59

The King's Manor

74	The King's Manor and its grounds in relation to the abbey precinct and the river: plan by Jacob Richards, 1685	63
75	The south, or main doorway on the east front, 1610, by Joseph Halfpenny	65
76	Entrance to Huntingdon Room by A. Buckle, 1883	67
77	Plans showing the development of the King's Manor over time	69
78	Watercolour of 1840 by Harper showing the main (south) entrance on the east front with the initials of James I and the arms of Charles I	70
79	Palace of the Stuart Kings by Piper, 1895, showing the two doorways in the east front	71
80	Rodwell's engraving shows some of the south side of the western courtyard, with part of the former hall and kitchen below	72
81	Halfpenny's engraving of an inner doorway, 1807	72
82	Detail of Richards' plan, 1685	73
83	Francis Place's sketch (1718) of a ruined wall with the archway of a gate, possibly part of the warming house or kitchen of the monastery	74
84	Another sketch by Place, showing the view towards the river with part of a bay window and detail of a frieze	74
85	The Yorkshire School for the Blind by Monkhouse, c.1840	75
86	John Browne's view of the main entrance, 1817	76
87	The eastern courtyard by Cave, c.1822	78
88	The Huntingdon Room by A. Buckle, 1883	78
89	Monkhouse's 'Palace of the Stuarts': the inner doorway of the central range, with steps leading up to the Huntingdon Room	79
90	Nicholson's view of the south-east front, along the lane now leading from Exhibition Square to the Museum Gardens, August 1813	80
91, 92	The vaults under the outer west range, etched by Halfpenny (1807)	80, 81

Figures appearing with the list of illustrations

93	Abbey from near the present Museum Street entrance to the Museum Gardens by John Varley	84
94	The west front of the abbey church with the King's Manor in the background, by Joseph Halfpenny, 1782	87
95	Wash drawing by Henry Cave (1801) showing the interior of the church nave from the south-east	88
96	John Browne's study, probably made in the 1820s, of the inner face of the nave north wall	90
97	West end of the nave, by J.S. Prout, 1840	91
98	West end of the abbey church by Francis Bedford, 1843	92
99	The ruins of St Mary's Abbey, York, c.1850, by Louis-Jules Arnout	93
100	St Mary's Abbey, York, c.1906, by W. Boddy	96
101	Abbey from the south-west, E. Ridsdale Tate, 7 July 1906	95
102	Detail from Wellbeloved 1829 showing a voussoir, possibly depicting the Marriage at Cana	97
103	Parts of the buildings of St Mary's Abbey, F. Nash, 1829	97
104	Details of Moses and the apostles, bosses from the warming house and some windows by W. Richardson	98
105	This rather enigmatic drawing by Nicholson, simply entitled 'At St Mary's', probably shows the water gate alongside the hospitium	101
106	Early 20th-century photograph of the interior of the lower room of the hospitium by George Benson	102
107	York Esplanade, showing St Mary's Tower, by W. Boddy, 1895	103
108	Inner view of the lodge and part of the entrance arch by George Nicholson, 17 June 1825	104
109	Old Tower, Marygate, by H. Waterworth	107
110	The Yorkshire Museum and Roman Multangular Tower, by H. and W. Brown, 1836	110
111	Place's 1717 view looking north-east from the King's Manor towards Bootham Bar; part of the abbey wall is still standing	112
112	Wash drawing of the south-west front by Edward Abbot (1776)	113
113	John Sell Cotman's view of the main entrance, probably drawn on his visit to York in 1803	114
114	H. and W. Brown's wood engraving of the eastern courtyard in 1836	115
115	This 1836 wood engraving by H. and W. Brown gives a wider view of the east front and puts the main entrance in context	115
116	The doorway at the foot of the steps leading to the Huntingdon Room by A. Buckle, 1883	116
117	The King's Manor and Minster by Rodwell, 1887	117
118	A wide-ranging view of the Manor from the north-west side by Ridsdale Tate, 1889	117
119	Boddy's watercolour of the King's Manor Blind School Entrance	119
120	The King's Manor from the abbey by Boddy, 1906	119

121	Ridsdale Tate's 1906 view of the north range, with the foundations of the abbey church choir in the foreground	120
122	Detail from 'Plan de York', 1650	121
123	Drake's plan of 1736 shows the King's Manor in the context of the abbey ruins	122

Folded sheets in back pocket

124 Plan of St Mary's Abbey, showing the 13th-century (Gothic) church and 13th/14th-century claustral buildings, with the outline of the Norman (Romanesque) church superimposed in red

125 Plan of the King's Manor (ground floor)

Acknowledgements

The authors owe a huge debt of gratitude to many individuals and organisations: to Dominic Tweddle and Peter Addyman without whom the Pictorial Evidence series would never have been conceived; to Paul Harvey, Gordon Forster and Richard Hall for helpful comments on the text; to those people who have helped so willingly with picture research and supplying illustrations (Sarah Riddick and Jenny Alexander of York City Art Gallery; Sue Rigby of York Reference Library, now retired; David Main of York Reference Library Local Studies Collection; Melanie Baldwin, Registrar of York Museums Trust; Jackie Logan, Collections Management Co-ordinator of York Museums Trust; Katherine Bearcock, Assistant Curator of Archaeology at the Yorkshire Museum; Mike Andrews, Lesley Collett and Christine Kyriacou of York Archaeological Trust; Mary Matthews, Cultural Officer at Wakefield Art Gallery; Frances Chambers and Veronica Wallace of the Yorkshire Philosophical Society; Wood and Richardson, printers; staff at the Bodleian Library and the British Library). The authors are also grateful to Lesley Collett for her careful draughtsmanship and considerable skill in designing this book.

The publication could not have come to fruition without the financial support of the following institutions, to which the authors and York Archaeological Trust would like to express their thanks: the Friends of York Archaeological Trust; the Marc Fitch Fund; the Sheldon Memorial Trust; York Common Good Trust; and Yorkshire Architectural and York Archaeological Society.

Illustrations are reproduced by courtesy of the following: York Archaeological Trust collection of maps and topographical views (Figs.3, 4, 35 and 111); York City Library, Local Studies Collection, Imagine York, © City of York Council (Figs.57–58, 67 and 106); Simon I. Hill and other YAT photographers, © York Archaeological Trust (Figs.39, 40 and 70); Lesley Collett (Figs.9, 56, 77, 124 and 125); York Reference Library (Figs.5, 6, 11–13, 17, 20–21, 32, 36, 41–45, 47, 53, 72–74, 79, 82, 98, 100–104, 107, 110, 114–115 and 119–122); York Museums Trust (York Art Gallery) (Figs.14–16, 19, 24, 33, 50–52, 54, 60–61, 65, 66, 68, 71, 78, 80, 83–87, 89–90, 93–96, 99, 105, 108–109, 113 and 117–118); York Museums Trust (Yorkshire Museum) (Figs.28–30 and 46); Yorkshire Philosophical Society (Figs.2 and 64); British Library (Figs.1 and 22); Bodleian Library (Fig.7); Wakefield Art Gallery (Fig.112); Derek Mee (Fig.31).

Preface

This fourth volume in the series on the Pictorial Evidence for the Medieval Buildings of York deals principally with two buildings, linked in origin but with very different histories. St Mary's Abbey church, its life effectively ended in 1539, is now little more than a dignified backdrop to the picnickers and pigeons enjoying the Yorkshire Philosophical Society's gardens. In contrast, the King's Manor, originally the Abbot's lodging, developed after the Dissolution of the Monasteries, becoming successively headquarters of the King's Council in the North, residence of the city's military governor, the home of the Manor School and the Yorkshire School for the Blind, and is now a part of the University of York. Consequently, while the abbey remains slowly dwindled, the Manor has alterations and additions from every century, even incorporating stonework originally from the abbey. Thus the student might well complain that there is too little of the one and too much of the other.

St Mary's was the richest and most powerful abbey in the North of England, and the remains reflect this. The church, built all of one style, would have been one of the finest examples of 13th-century architecture; the series of statues discovered in 1829 and now in the Yorkshire Museum represent 12th-century art of the highest order, and the

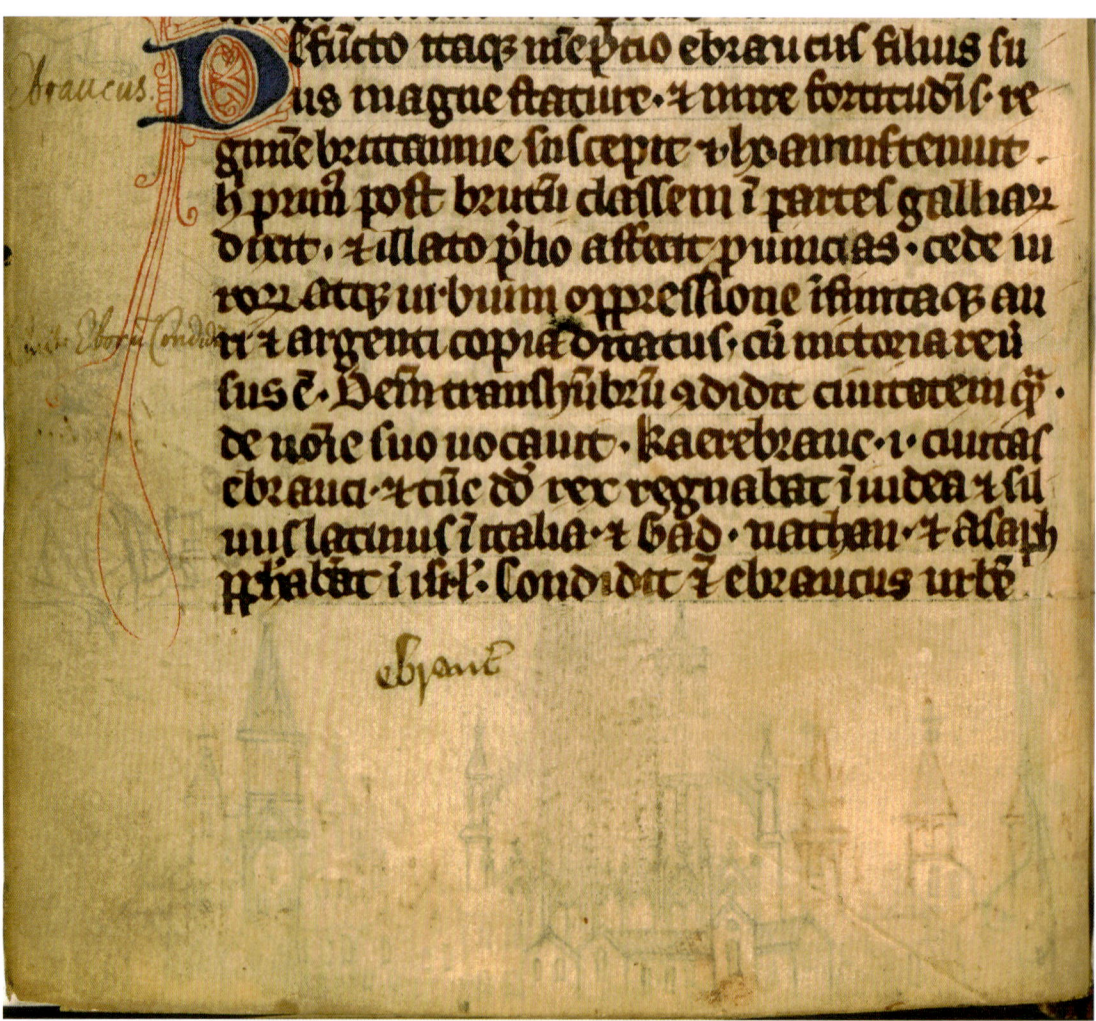

Fig. 1 Ebrauc, c.1320 (© British Library Board. All Rights Reserved. MS Royal, 13.A.III fo.16v). Ink drawing in the margin of the manuscript copy of Geoffrey of Monmouth's History of the Kings of Britain, *dated from internal evidence to c.1320. Possibly the earliest view of York, it shows the city from the south-west with the Minster in the centre, towers partly erased, and St Mary's Abbey on the left.*

Fig. 2 Detail from 'The Gardens of the Yorkshire Philosophical Society', J. Storey, c.1860. Storey made the lithograph of Nathaniel Whittock's Bird's-Eye View of York, and his own view of the Gardens is similar, but it is not an exact copy. It shows the 3-acre abbey site leased by the Yorkshire Philosophical Society for its new Museum in 1829 and some of the further 5 acres added a little later and turned into botanic gardens. The print gives a clear indication of the precinct walls and puts the abbey ruins into context chronologically as well as spatially, as buildings here range from Roman to mid-Victorian. The Museum, opened 1830, is in the centre, with the King's Manor behind and the observatory (1833) in front; to the left are the abbey ruins and St Olave's Church. Below is the 14th-century hospitium fronted by a recreated Elizabethan knot-garden. The Manor Shore has been developed as the Esplanade between Marygate and Lendal towers. Much of the precinct wall is still obscured by houses, but the lodge, gateway, towers and Queen Margaret's arch are visible.

precinct walls, though now incomplete, are probably the finest in the country. Antiquarian interest in these remains developed principally during the 17th century, and two artists, Francis Place (who lived in the Manor) and William Lodge, produced valuable sketches of parts of the abbey that were later dismantled. The 'ingenious Mr Place' also 'took pains to trace and measure out the remains of the abbey church', thus allowing production of the first 'ichnography', or ground plan (Drake 1736, 576, 577), and his views also included the abbey gatehouse and parts of the Manor. Francis Drake himself contributed to monastic study by copying and printing numerous manuscripts relating to the abbey (Drake 1736, 582–627). His own writing is lively and sometimes opinionated (he starts his account of St Mary's with its dissolution, and only after venting his spleen on that does he return to the abbey's history). There was, however, a lull in artistic interest until the end of the 18th century, when again York produced two topographical artists of note: Joseph Halfpenny and Henry Cave. Both expressed their intention of recording York's ancient and possibly endangered buildings, so they both aimed at accuracy, though each achieved it in a different way. Halfpenny's work is clear and crisp, if rather stiff, showing what the structure should look like. Cave, who taught art to the young ladies at the Manor School, preferred the quick impression, showing something a little more ruinous and romantic.

During this period the city was visited by artists of national repute, though in general they showed more interest in the Minster, the bridge or the city walls than in the abbey or Manor, which appear only in general views. Turner made a rough sketch of the west end of the abbey church, but never

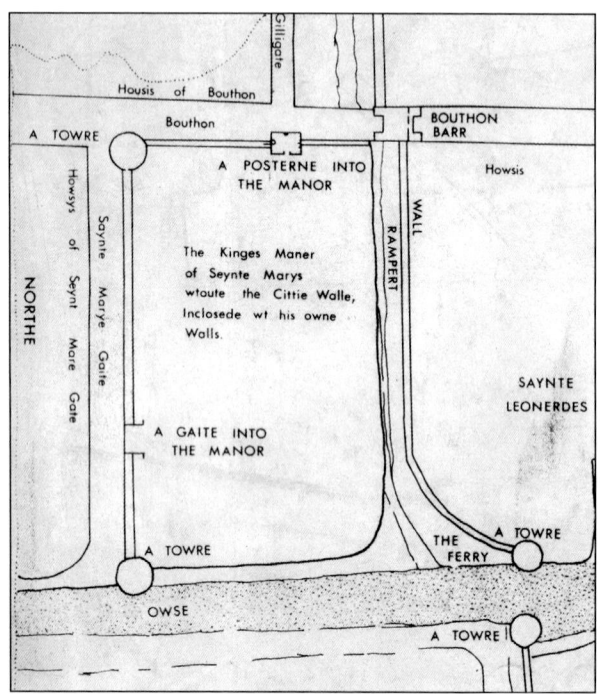

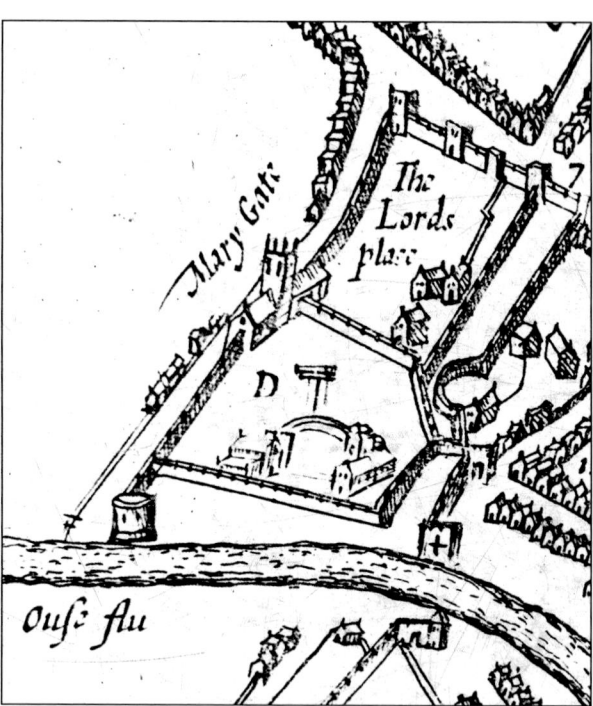

Fig. 3 *Detail from 1545 plan of York. This very early plan of York shows the abbey precincts 'inclosede wt his owne Walls'. A path can be seen between the city walls with their ramparts and the abbey precinct walls.*

Fig. 4 *Detail from Speed's plan of York, 1610. This somewhat confusing map shows St Olave's Church on Marygate but the abbey precincts have been divided by a wall. The King's Manor is clearly shown above the wall but there is no realistic representation of the abbey ruins. The building below D may represent the hospitium but the arc shape joining it to another building is a mystery. It clearly shows the abbey precinct wall along the riverfront as well as the abbey wall to the left of the city wall running down to the Multangular Tower. The abbey walls here soon disappeared with the rebuilding of the King's Manor. St Mary's Tower and Lendal Tower can be seen on the north bank of the Ouse.*

worked it up into a watercolour. John Sell Cotman, visiting with Paul Sandby Munn in 1803, made use of the site to pursue his own ideas on composition and light, removing or adding background, as in his painting of the north transept arch (Illustration 53), or leaving his etching of the King's Manor doorway printed in reverse (Fig.113). Perhaps he preferred it that way; it seems churlish to complain! Thomas Rowlandson's view of the abbey gateway, however, was carefully worked up from a sketchbook wash drawing (Illustration 197; Fig.61), and he has skilfully combined relative accuracy with an indication of the run-down, bucolic nature of the site.

In 1829 Charles Wellbeloved's excavation of the abbey site for the Yorkshire Philosophical Society made new advances, as one of the first excavations in the country to move beyond the church to include the whole claustral complex, and to publish a full report. The illustrations, mainly by Frederick Nash, are particularly revealing, some as clear depictions of sculptural detail, others more unusually showing the archaeological excavations actually in progress. Excavations in the late 19th and early 20th centuries, though on a smaller scale, produced valuable

plans and now had the advantage of photography (but be warned – even the photographer can lie; see Illustration 28 and Figs.1 and 22). Gradually interest extended to include the outer precinct and the precinct walls. Ridsdale Tate was able to use this increasing knowledge, along with surviving masonry, to create his stimulating 'reconstructions' (Illustration 117; Figs.18, 27, 41, 65).

Meanwhile, artists continued to be intrigued and fascinated by the King's Manor, where a complex mixture of additions and alterations had achieved a pleasingly picturesque and harmonious whole. For the most part they were drawn to the elaborate doorways, but there are useful sketches of areas now largely hidden by later buildings, and several views showing the spatial relationship between abbey and Manor. Storey's Bird's-eye View of the Gardens, c.1860 (based on his lithograph of Whittock's view of York), puts everything into context, and contains enough detail to keep the local historian happy for hours (Figs.2, 64).

The 20th century saw further excavations, at first mainly by museum curators, later by York Archaeological Trust, small in scale and answering specific problems. There were also developments in documentary research, including the editing and publication of the Chronicle of St Mary's Abbey, the Anonimalle and the *Ordinal and Customary* (see Bibliography). There are, however, gaps in the documentation as in the structural remains, in both the early history of the abbey and that of the King's Manor during the residency of the Council in the North.

The aim of the present volume is to provide the student with a further research tool in the form of a guide to existing pictorial evidence, including drawings, paintings, prints, maps and plans. After brief introductory essays, the main section is an annotated catalogue of illustrations, giving date, title, artist, medium, location and reference number, with explanatory notes. There are also a select index of artists and a list of the principal sources.

Note: The Abbey church is actually oriented north-east to south-west, but here liturgical orientation has been used. For the sake of consistency and ease of reference, the same compass points have been used in describing the King's Manor.

Fig. 5 South-east view of the remains of St Mary's Abbey, F. Nash (from Wellbeloved 1829, pl.55). *This lithograph shows excavations in progress: the east walk of the cloister with chapter house vestibule foundations uncovered. Piles of stones are everywhere and there are people watching the excavation. An interesting and useful general view, showing the claustral buildings in relation to the church. The foundations of the three aisles of the warming house/common hall can be seen towards the left, running down towards the hospitium in the background. The foundations of the chapter house remained open until 1912–13, when the Tempest Anderson Hall was built.*

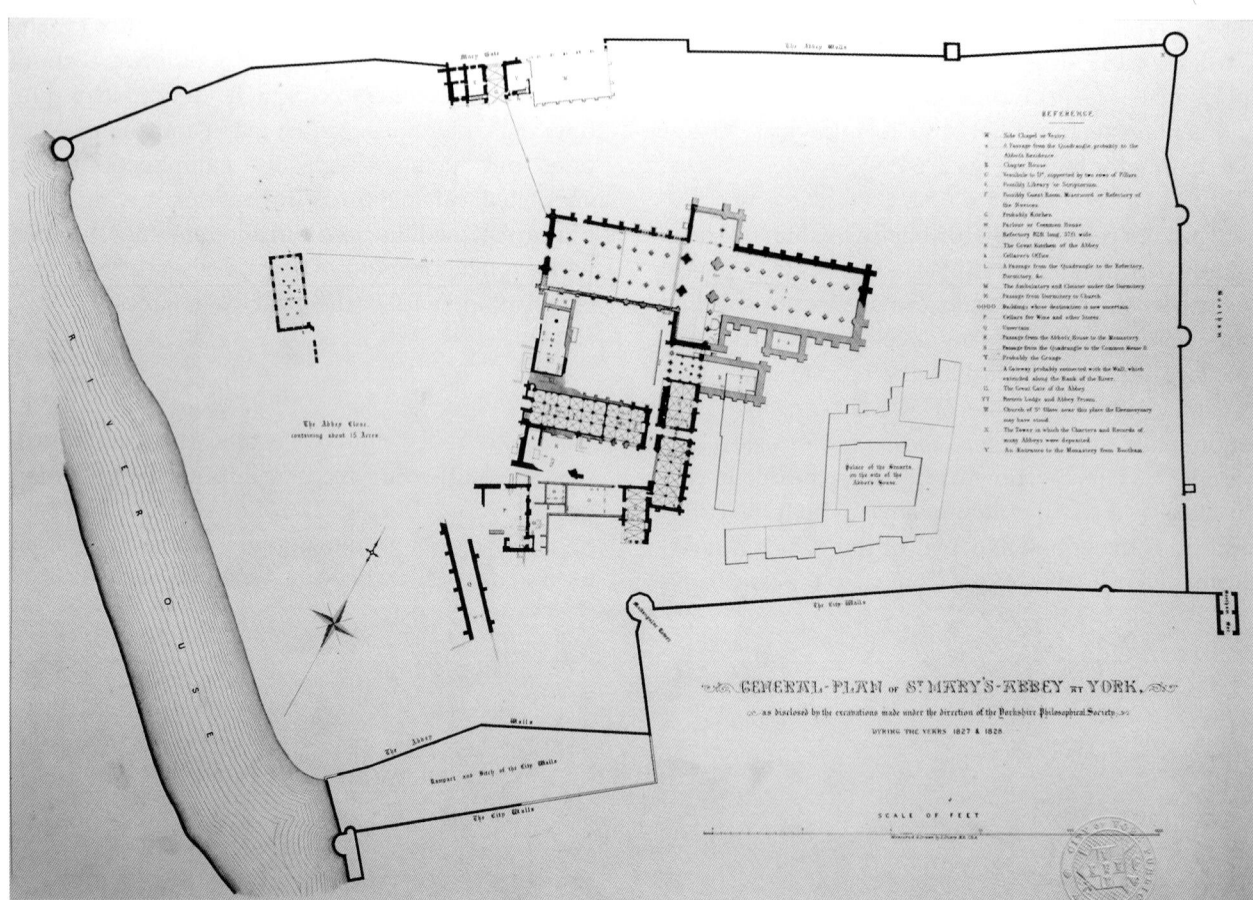

Fig. 6 Scale plan of the abbey, Richardson, 1843: 'General plan of St Mary's Abbey at York as disclosed by the excavations made under the direction of the Yorkshire Philosophical Society during the years 1827 and 1828'. This is useful because it shows all the abbey buildings and precincts ('The Abbey Close containing about 15 Acres') as well as the King's Manor ('Palace of the Stuarts on the site of the Abbot's House').

A brief history of monasticism and the Benedictine Order in England

At the end of the 6th century, a papal mission headed by Augustine introduced the Rule of St Benedict into England. Composed by Benedict of Nursia (c.480–547) earlier in that century, the Rule detailed the laws by which a community of monks or nuns should live, including its organisation, daily routine, ownership of property and provision for the sick. Roman monasticism was slow to gain ground in England, the 'Celtic' model of monastic life, introduced by Irish missionaries, being more familiar and therefore more acceptable. In time, though, Benedictine customs supplanted those of the Irish ascetics, and the observance of the Rule became widespread. By the middle of the 8th century, England was home to a number of substantial religious houses, including both all-male and mixed-sex monasteries, and Benedictine monasticism thrived.

There was a decline in monastic life in the 9th century. Viking raids and Danish invasions played an important part in this, particularly in eastern and north-eastern England, in terms of loss of books and other treasures, sites abandoned, at least temporarily, and impoverished communities unable to resume full religious life. There were other factors at play, however, including exploitation by some Anglo-Saxon kings, lords and patrons, a gradual underlying trend towards secularisation, and competition from newer institutions. The amount of destruction has been overstressed by 10th-century monastic chroniclers who 'portrayed an obliterated religious landscape awaiting reclamation' (Blair 2005, 295). The situation in the North in the 9th century was not a total disaster so much as a decline from the heights of the 'golden age' of Northumbria. Overall, enough of monastic life remained to allow for the reconstruction of ecclesiastical sites by reformers in the 10th century; wayward houses were brought back into line and new communities were established.

The Norman Conquest of 1066 brought further upheaval. The new masters of England were determined to transform the country's monastic culture by imbuing it with Norman traditions. In addition to founding a number of new male Benedictine monasteries, the Normans altered the character of the pre-Conquest communities by placing them under the leadership of influential French houses. These endeavoured to supplant English customs with continental conventions. Given the shift from an Anglo-Saxon to a Norman ruling class following 1066, this was a natural process, since the nobility formed the pool from which nearly all religious were drawn during this period. Simultaneously, the Normans began to replace the old conventual churches and claustral complexes with structures built on a scale more magnificent than had previously been common in England. Ultimately, assimilation was successful: by the early 12th century, the pre-Conquest houses were little different from their Norman counterparts.

St Benedict's model for the monastic life was the family, with the abbot as father and all the monks as brothers. Internally, Benedictine houses organised themselves along standard monastic lines, with an abbot (superior), a prior (the abbot's deputy), a cellarer (who managed the collection and storage of foodstuffs), a precentor (who directed choral liturgical celebrations, and oversaw the library and scriptorium), a master of novices and an infirmarian who cared for sick and old monks.

Most Benedictine communities did not include lay brethren or sisters. Instead, laypeople were employed as servants. These were merely hired workers and had no power or status within the communal hierarchy. In the typical Benedictine monastery, servants outnumbered the monks they served, occasionally by two or even three to one. In general, only impoverished houses that could not afford to maintain enough workers would expect their members to perform menial tasks.

The Benedictine Order was unique in that individual houses often had little oversight imposed upon them from outside the cloister. With the exception of visitations (when an external ecclesiastical authority, sometimes the local bishop, sometimes a papal legate, inspected the community to ensure that it was functioning properly), they were generally responsible for disciplining themselves as they saw fit with regard to observance of ritual and the Rule.

The Benedictines were known as the 'black monks' and 'black nuns' because of the predominantly dark colours of their garments. Their communities varied widely in size and stature. A very large male community might number over 100 monks, though most were much smaller, with some having fewer than the minimum apostolic ideal of twelve brethren or sisters and one head. A male Benedictine community was termed a priory if it was subordinate to another house, and an abbey if it was independent. St Bees Priory in Cumbria, for example, was set up c.1130 as a cell or small subordinate house of St Mary's Abbey, which served as the motherhouse to several small cells (see p.9).

Benedictine monasteries were not usually built in places of solitude. The black monks and nuns normally lived near or within towns, which gave them access to traders and craftsmen, and the hospitaller provided lodgings for pilgrims and guests. Indeed, sometimes the abbey itself might be the stimulus that encouraged the town to grow up, as was the case with the medieval town of St Albans.

The physical layout and structure of an early Benedictine enclosure generally followed a standard pattern, with the church forming the northern side of the cloister if possible (as it did at St Mary's; see Figs. 6 and 124). The church frequently featured a tower at its crossing, or between the nave and chancel if it lacked transepts. Its chancel often had an apsidal east end. Semicircular projections containing altars might also extend from the east wall of the transepts in a male house, where some of the monks were ordained from the 13th century onwards and might celebrate private masses.

The other three ranges of a Benedictine monastery held the dormitory, chapter house, parlour (where the monks could talk), refectory and storage cellars. The refectory was often aligned east–west (as it was at St Mary's), with the kitchen and calefactory (warming room) located either to one side of it, or below the dormitory, or in a detached building to the south of the refectory. The latter arrangement reduced the risk of a fire spreading through the complex.

St Benedict's Rule organised the monastic day into regular periods of communal and private prayer, sleep, spiritual reading and manual labour – *ut in omnibus glorificetur Deus*, 'that in all things God may be glorified' (Rule chapter 57.9). In subsequent centuries, intellectual work and teaching took the place of agriculture, crafts or other forms of manual labour for many Benedictines.

Traditionally, the daily life of the Benedictine revolved around the eight canonical hours. The monastic timetable or *horarium* would begin at midnight with the service, or 'office', of *Matins*, followed by the morning office of *Lauds* at 3am. This office was said in the dark or with minimal lighting, and monks were expected to memorise everything. These services could be very long, but usually consisted of a chant, three antiphons, three psalms and three lessons, along with celebrations of any local saints' days. Afterwards the monks would retire for a few hours of sleep and then rise at 6am to wash and attend the office of *Prime*. They then gathered in Chapter to receive instructions for the day and to attend to any judicial business. Then came private Mass or spiritual reading or work until 9am when the office of *Terce* was said, and then High Mass. At noon came the office of *Sext* and the midday meal. After a brief period of communal recreation, the monks could retire to rest until the office of *None* at 3pm. This was followed by copying books or craft work until after twilight, the evening prayer of Vespers at 6pm, then the night prayer of *Compline* at 9pm, and off to blessed bed before beginning the cycle again. There were slight changes to the *horarium* three times a year, resulting in a winter schedule, a Lenten schedule and a summer schedule.

Benedictines were not permitted to converse except during certain times of the day, generally work periods. Even when talking was permitted, it was expected to concern administrative or practical matters, not frivolity. On feast days, when no work was done, such discussion was not allowed. At any time when conversation was forbidden, but was deemed absolutely necessary, it should either be conducted using hand signals, or else transacted in the parlour.

The Benedictine diet was not known for its severity. Though the Rule of St Benedict proscribed the eating of meat, fish was eaten at all Benedictine houses, and some inmates partook of lard and the flesh of birds as well. Child novices might be allowed the full range of meat dishes, and the head of a house might well have the flesh of pigs, deer or other animals at his or her table. Quantities were often generous, and pittances (extra dishes of fish or eggs) were common additions to the daily meals. Feast days featured elaborate banquets, with ten or more courses served in the refectories of the wealthiest houses on important holidays. Ale was the usual beverage, or wine if the community could afford it. The customary drink in the refectory in the afternoon during the summer and in the evening during winter was sometimes accompanied by light bread or cakes. Not surprisingly, reformist clergy often held up Benedictine diets as evidence that the Order had strayed from the path of true monasticism into sinful corruption.

At the time of the dissolution there were nearly 300 Benedictine houses in England. The grave charges brought against the monks by Henry VIII's 'visitors', though long accepted, are not now credited by serious historians. Throughout the period of suppression the monks were the champions of the old faith, and when turned out of their homes very few conformed to the new religion. Some sought refuge abroad, others accepted pensions and lingered on in England hoping for a restoration of the former state of things, whilst not a few preferred to suffer lifelong imprisonment rather than surrender their Catholic beliefs.

Richardson's drawing of a seal of St Mary's Abbey. This 11th-century seal is a vesica, c.69mm by 61mm, with a design of Our Lady crowned and seated, holding the Child and a book. Above the Child is the sun and on the left side is a lily. Only a few words – SIGILLVM SANCTE MARIE – remain of the broken legend. This seal continued to be used throughout the life of the abbey.

St Mary's Abbey

Foundation

To a large extent St Mary's Abbey rose out of William the Conqueror's 'Harrying of the North' in the 1070s. Accompanying the Conqueror's army on its trail of destruction was a Norman knight, Reinfrid, whose travels took him to Whitby; there he was deeply moved by the remains of the once-great abbey of St Hilda. Monasticism had declined in the 8th century, partly as a result of Viking raids and Danish invasions, especially in the North. On his return south, Reinfrid became a monk at Evesham.

There was already a growing desire to revive the holy places of Northumbria (Bede's *History of the English Church and People* was read by Saxon and Norman alike), and within a few years he was travelling north again with two companions, Alfwig, also a monk at Evesham, and Aldwin, prior of Winchcombe. They may not have intended to re-found monasteries as such, but they soon attracted enthusiastic followers and the result was the re-establishment of communities at Jarrow, Lindisfarne and Whitby, and a Benedictine priory at Durham which replaced the earlier secular community.

Fig. 7 *Stephen and the abbey church, 13th century (MS Bodley 39, fo.92). Having led the breakaway group of monks who left Whitby Abbey and founded what was to become St Mary's Abbey, Stephen became the first abbot in c.1086. He is shown here seated and holding a crozier. On the left are eight monks, some kneeling, and on the right a representation of the abbey church. Artistically inaccurate this may be, but at least it shows the abbey with some real monks in it.*

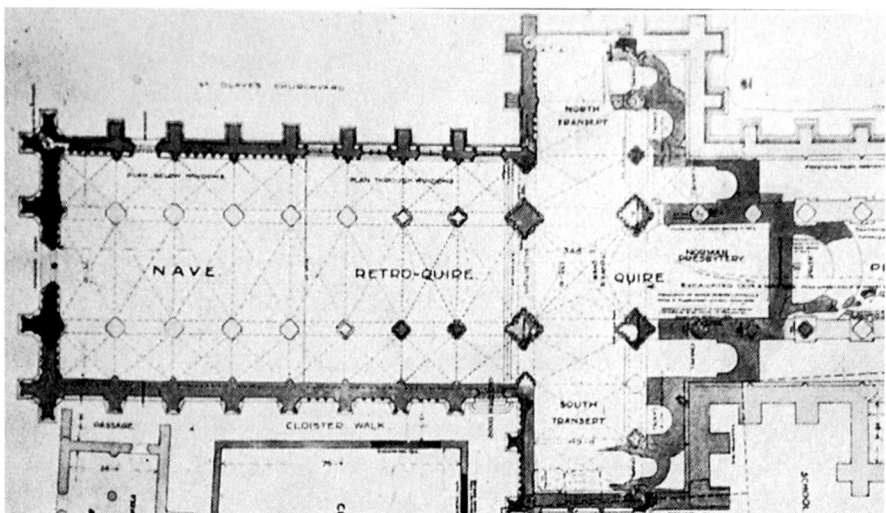

Fig. 8 Plan of the Norman church from The Charm of St Mary's Abbey *by Edwin Ridsdale Tate, 1929, showing the inner apsidal east ends but with the north and south aisles squared off externally.*

Reinfrid himself settled at Whitby, where he was joined, among others, by Stephen, a man of ability who was soon elected abbot. Plagued by pirates, robbers and the hostility of the local landowner, William de Percy, and possibly also by ideological differences, the community split, however. Reinfrid remained at Whitby while Stephen and his followers moved to Lastingham in around 1080. Stephen apparently already knew the Norman landowner Alan of Brittany, who had been granted vast estates in Yorkshire by William I, and before long Alan offered the monks 4 acres of land north-west of the city of York, together with the Church of St Olaf in Marygate, which had been founded by Siward, Earl of Northumbria, in 1030–55. Permission was granted by the king, and a reference in *Domesday Book* shows that by 1086 the community was established in York.

Early in 1088, William II, visiting York and seeing that the monastic site and its church were too small and constricted, granted the monks a larger area of adjoining land. According to Stephen's account, the king himself cut the first turf for the foundations of the new church. Count Alan added further land, probably in Bootham, and formally handed over patronage to the king. Thus the new abbey, re-dedicated to St Mary, became a royal foundation (Fig.7), though the monks continued to remember Alan and his successors as founders and benefactors in their prayers. St Olaf's Church (now St Olave's) was retained as a chapel serving local residents.

The story of the abbey's foundation comes from a 12th-century manuscript which claims, probably with justice, to be Abbot Stephen's own account (BL, MS Add 38816; Dugdale *et al.* 1817–30, 3, 545–6; *AY* **1**, 25, 201–2). Although its authenticity has been queried, it accords with attitudes and events of the time. Monasticism had been seriously damaged in the 8th and 9th centuries, but there was already a movement towards its rehabilitation in the 10th century and this continued after the Conquest. The Normans could be brutal but also deeply religious, and in the founding of churches and abbeys by kings and barons there may have been an element of atonement for the destruction and loss of life. Stephen says that the abbey was founded 'so that the light of holy religion should shine eternally in that city where evil had abounded, and where more blood had been shed than in other English cities'. In granting land to Stephen's abbey Count Alan would gain both prestige in this world and the prayers of the monks for his soul in the next. For the Norman kings there was an added political dimension: together with the new castle and the new Minster, the splendid new Romanesque abbey would represent a significant Norman presence in the city, and its site on the former residence of the earls of Northumbria, together with the loss of its dedication to St Olaf, signified a break with York's links with Scandinavia.

Unlike the later Cistercians, the Benedictines did not deliberately seek rural seclusion, and York provided Stephen's monks with the relative safety of a fortified city. The devastation caused by William is now considered to have been less complete than the more lurid chroniclers would have us suppose (Palliser 1990, 18–19) and Alan had assured Stephen that the citizens were well disposed towards his monks. The hope of gifts and endowments from a busy trading and ecclesiastical centre must have been an important consideration, and that hope was well founded: St Mary's Abbey was to become the richest and most influential abbey in the North of England.

The Romanesque church

William II's grant of 4 acres of land, followed by other endowments, gave the monks the space and, one may assume, the financial resources to embark on an ambitious building project. Virtually nothing remains visible today of the new Romanesque church begun in 1088 and completed c.1120–35, but its site was excavated by the Yorkshire Philosophical Society in 1827–29 and again in 1902 and 1912. These excavations revealed the foundations, which are now marked out in stone. The church was aligned towards the north-east rather than the usual due east, probably to make the best use of the higher ground, away from the low-lying area near the river which was subject to flooding. The building was cruciform, with an aisled nave much the same in area as its Gothic successor, a central tower and north and south transepts. The presbytery, which had an apsidal east end, was flanked by shorter and lower aisles, also apsidal but squared off externally, and two apsidal chapels projected from each transept; the general effect was thus of seven apses set in echelon (see Figs.8 and 9).

The only piece of Romanesque masonry still visible *in situ*, part of a shallow extension buttress, reveals that the church was built of gritstone, almost certainly including re-used Roman material. The excavation of 1912 also uncovered cement bedding for floor tiles, and a few red tiles were found partly embedded in the walls some two feet below the 13th-century transept (YPSAR 1912, 16).

The statement that the church was seriously damaged by a great fire in 1137 is given a little credence by the existence of mid- to late 12th-century architectural fragments now in the Yorkshire Museum, suggesting necessary rebuilding (John of Worcester, c.1150, Trinity College Dublin, MS E 6 4 (503), 130; Stow 1631, 144; Harvey 1965, 365). The extent of the fire was clearly exaggerated, and Pro-

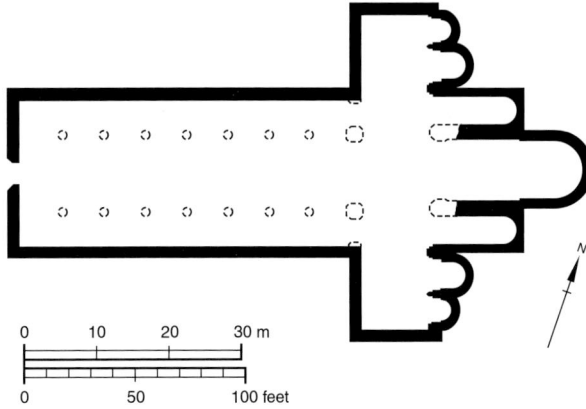

Fig. 9 Outline plan of the Norman church (based on fig.7 on p.xl of RCHMY **4**)

fessor Christopher Norton has argued that it never actually occurred, its alleged existence arising from a misreading of *consecrata* as *conflagrata* (Norton 1998). Fire was, of course, a constant hazard in candle-lit medieval churches, and some such occurrence might well have necessitated repair work in the course of the 12th century. A few fragments of masonry from the Romanesque church are in the Yorkshire Museum: these include two walling blocks, still with their original plaster and paint indicating the church's internal decoration; part of a late 11th-century capital with a face and foliage simply carved, in contrast to four, more elaborate, 12th-century arch stones; and part of a statue of the Virgin and Child similar in style to French sculpture of c.1160. Though only a fragment, the quality of the carving and the roughly finished back suggest that it may have come from the west front of the abbey church (RCHMY **4**, xlv, 22b, pls.27a, 41b; Wilson and Burton 1988, 15).

Excavation by York Archaeological Trust (YAT) in 1986 just outside the sculpture gallery which forms the basement of the Tempest Anderson Hall (YAT site code 1986.19) confirmed that the Hall (built in 1912) had been placed directly on top of the southern wall of the south transept of the abbey church which was constructed late in the 13th century. This wall had been uncovered during excavations in the 1820s and remained exposed until its reburial in 1912. In 1986 it was decided that this wall should be left visible to the public beneath the Tempest Anderson Hall.

Excavation in the 1820s had exposed most of the interior of the south transept, and examination of Wellbeloved's plan showed that YAT had rediscovered part of the foundation of the south transept of the first, Romanesque, church built after William II's grant in 1088. The east end of this transept had a series of apses, and the eastern wall of the later church was positioned slightly further to the east when it was built in the years following 1270. YAT first removed soil that had been replaced over the remains after their discovery in the 1820s. In 1912 drains had been placed in trenches which cut through the foundations of both the 11th- and 13th-century churches. In 1986 it was decided to investigate the depth of the late 13th-century foundations by partially removing the material used to fill the gap between the foundations of the two churches. The foundations were found to consist of carefully finished pieces of ashlar, presumably re-used after the demolition of the earlier church. At a depth of 1.7m below modern ground level, the courses of stone rested on a raft of cobbles set in mortar. The material removed from the gap between the foundations of the two churches contained a lot of disarticulated human bones, probably from early burials disturbed during the 13th-century building work (*Interim* **12**/1, 8–13). The excavation also uncovered a piece of painted wall plaster (see p.21).

Historical development 1088–c.1500

The century following 1088 was a period of outstanding success for the abbey. Norman barons were quick to emulate the kings of England in making grants of manors, townships, churches, fairs and markets, and before long it had acquired estates from all the major landowners in Yorkshire. Most of the abbey's property was therefore within the county, but some was further afield, mainly in Cumberland and Lincolnshire. The abbey held a large amount of property in the city of York, some donated by great magnates such as the earls of Richmond, some bequeathed by the townspeople themselves, and though St Mary's Abbey was less popular than other religious houses (and much less so than the parish churches), possibly because its royal connections made it stand somewhat apart, over the years it acquired a considerable portfolio of holdings. Most were in the neighbouring streets – Marygate, Bootham and Gillygate – but some were held in Ousegate, Fossgate, Spurriergate, Hungate and Micklegate among others, mostly rented out for amounts varying from 6d to 16s per annum (Burton 1988, 62–73; Palliser 1971, 17).

Landed estates could be leased out to tenants for rents in cash or produce, or managed directly by the community's own officers to supply both the monastery's needs and a surplus which could be sold for cash. In the 12th and 13th centuries the country's population increased, new markets developed and prices rose, and direct management came to be seen as the more profitable option. In general the granges (estates) nearest to the abbey produced food, fuel and other necessities for the monks, while those further away produced goods for market. Much of the economy of the granges, however, would depend on the nature of the soil and of the original grants. Some of these were specific: watermills and windmills; orchards and gardens; woodland, providing fuel, charcoal and, importantly in a period of church building, standing timber. Hunting rights provided hare, partridge and pheasant for the abbot's table as well as sport at his country retreats; warrens provided rabbits, highly prized for meat and fur; fisheries provided stock from which the abbey could replenish its fishponds in what is now Almery Garth (Drake 1736, 574). A grant of fourteen salmon a year went from Cockermouth to the cell at St Bees. At the other end of the scale, land near Ousefleet at the confluence of the Aire and the Ouse was developed by the abbey into the town and river port of Airmyn (YASRS 81, 1931, 55–69). Gifts of churches brought tithes and other payments as well as influence; they included churches in Lincoln and Boston as well as in the city of York: St Olave (from Alan, Earl of Richmond), St Saviour and St Michael Spurriergate (William I), St Wilfrid (Richard, son of Fin) and St Crux (Nigel Fossard), incidentally all in relatively wealthy communities.

As well as lands, the abbey garnered many privileges from William II and his successors. The abbey lands were free from certain royal exactions, and the monks were free from payment of tolls such as market dues and from service in the county courts. Anyone wishing to bring a case against the abbey was obliged to take it to the abbot's own court by the abbey gate. In addition, the abbot had the right to collect fines for certain offences, and he had his own gaol beside the abbey gate, and his own gallows at Gallows Closes, Burton Stone Lane (*VCHY* 1961,

497). From Henry I the abbot also held the custody of all the royal forests in Yorkshire. He was a mitred abbot, entitled to full episcopal regalia and the title Lord Abbot, an honour he shared in the north only with the abbot of Selby. By the 14th century, with a seat in the House of Lords, he was much involved in the affairs of government, and he had a London residence as well as country retreats.

An abbey of such standing, with a secure economic base, had no difficulty in attracting recruits. Figures are available only intermittently, but the number of religious seems to have remained fairly steady, more or less at 50 (Barnwell *et al* 2005, 20). Evidence from the mortuary roll of Matilda of Caen shows that from an early period the abbey had monks drawn from both Anglo-Saxon and Norman families (Burton 1988, 7). There was a setback in 1132, when simmering discontent with the growing worldliness and ill discipline in the York community came to a head. Six monks, with the support of the prior, demanded a return to the simplicity and austerity of the past. This was strongly opposed by the abbot, and the matter dragged on until Archbishop Thurstan arranged a Visitation on 6 October 1132 in the hope of effecting a settlement (Coppack 1993, 17; Walbran 1863). Feelings were running high, however, and he and his entourage were forcibly prevented from entering the abbey's chapter house. He therefore took the dissident monks under his protection. By now there were thirteen, enough to found a new community. The archbishop granted them land beside the River Skell near Ripon, and here they founded the abbey that was to become the great Cistercian house of Fountains. The fact that several of these monks later became abbots or noted men of learning indicates the quality of St Mary's recruits. Despite this loss, St Mary's Abbey continued to flourish and to attract sufficient new recruits to found a cell of at least six monks and a prior at St Bees, Cumbria, followed by five other cells of up to ten men at Wetherhall (Cumbria), St Martin's Richmond (N. Yorkshire), Romburh (Cambridgeshire), Sandtoft and Henes (Lincolnshire) and St Mary Magdalene near Lincoln.

It was natural that an institution of such wealth and power should be involved in disputes. Lawsuits were part of daily life for landowners, and the abbot was no exception. There were disputes with neighbouring landowners over boundaries or property rights; with tenants over rents and dues or the right to cut down timber; and with parishioners over tithes, payments (eg for burial) or over relative responsibility for church upkeep (YASRS **81,** vol.2, 1931, 55–69). Abbots were at times portrayed by laymen as grasping, avaricious landowners, and indeed some were. Most, however, were well aware that the estates which supported the abbey community were given so that the monks in turn might, through their prayers, ensure the salvation of the patron and his family. Efficient maintenance was thus a duty.

In particular, the two powerful institutions of abbey and city corporation faced up to each other over areas of jurisdiction, and occasionally these disagreements flared up into violence. Drake suggested that disputes were mainly over fairs and markets, but Richardson argues that there is no evidence for this: the main problem was the ownership of property and the rights that went with it (Drake 1736, 581; Richardson 1961, 7–11). In 1218 a case over the abbot's claim of juridical rights in Bootham led to a decision that the street was within the suburbs of the city, and therefore came under the jurisdiction of the mayor and corporation. The question of rights in Bootham was not solved, however, and in 1262 it was reported that citizens of York had attacked the abbey, killing some abbey servants in the ensuing affray, and had burnt several houses built by the abbey in Bootham. As a result, the abbot, Simon of Warwick, promised £100 to the city council in compensation for their loss of revenue, and made a down payment of 40 marks. In fear of further violent outbreaks, he also judged it prudent to absent himself from the monastery for more than a year. Some partial reconciliation was achieved in May 1266 when each side renounced its 'claims and quarrels'. Only a month later, however, Abbot Simon began building a stone wall round the precinct. This is the stretch lying between the main gateway in Marygate and St Mary's Tower and then along Bootham; much repaired, it still stands today (see Fig.56). Fear of Scottish invasion is given as one reason for the erection of this wall, and the Scots certainly presented a real threat; both the castle and the city walls were already being replaced in stone. But mutual suspicion between town and abbey remained a potent factor. In 1314 a renewed threat of Scottish invasion led the abbot to strengthen the precinct defences by digging a ditch round them; as this was on city land the citizens filled it in again, and in 1316 five men died in an attempt by York citizens to pull down an earthen wall.

Fig. 10 St Mary's Abbey, Joseph Halfpenny, 1807. Engraving of the view from the south-east showing the inner sides of the north and west walls of the nave, with very clear detail. Workmen and a lean-to shed can be seen – the land was in agricultural use at the time – but Halfpenny has removed other unsightly sheds and so on that block the view (compare Fig.95).

Confrontations, occasionally violent, continued intermittently until the dissolution of the abbey in 1539, and even beyond (see pp.11–12). For the religious, however, there were developments in the 1260s that were more important and much more interesting; work began on the rebuilding of the church choir and Abbot Simon laid the foundation stone on 24 April 1270. Then, when cracks appeared in the church tower in 1278 the community launched into a full-scale rebuilding of the church, and Abbot Simon was still there to witness its completion in 1294. Not surprisingly, the Archbishop's Visitation of 1318 found the abbey to be seriously in debt. The monks were told to get their finances in order and appoint a bursar, leaving the cellarer responsible only for domestic expenses. The sturdily independent monks complied eventually, but they took their time: a year later nothing had been done. Anyway, by now they had already started work on replacing the claustral buildings.

Thus the monastic community was committed to years, decades even, of noise and inconvenience, the silence of the cloister broken by sawing, hammering and chiselling, the creak of over-laden wagon wheels and of hoists and pulleys, and the quickly muffled comments of the workmen. Hours of work had to conform to the hours of service, however, and building took place only between Easter (or February) and Michaelmas (the end of September), so quiet came in the winter, as half-built walls were covered with straw as protection from frost. The community also shared the sense of excitement, the joy and a little excusable pride at the splendour and elegance of the new building.

In general, the monastic developments of the previous centuries could not be maintained, and in the 14th century the numbers of new recruits and of new donations began to decrease. This was partly because there were new openings for young men

Fig. 11 St Mary's Abbey, W. Richardson, 1843. This lithograph, based on an original watercolour, is one of a series published in The Monastic Ruins of Yorkshire. *It shows the north wall and west end of the nave, with the north-west pier of the crossing on the right. In the foreground can be seen part of the chapter house vestibule, uncovered during excavations in 1827–29.*

– the stricter Carthusian order for the ascetic, the universities for the academic – but also because some religious houses could no longer afford to recruit, as a downturn in agricultural prices reduced the profits and rents upon which they relied. Some northern monasteries suffered further losses resulting from Scottish raids on their estates following Robert Bruce's victory at Bannockburn in 1314; Bolton Priory in Wharfedale, for example, had to close for a time when its estates were plundered. The effects were variable, however; some smaller houses experienced severe financial difficulties, while the larger monasteries were able to adapt and survive.

The Scottish wars affected St Mary's Abbey in several ways. The precinct walls were extended and improved in 1315–18, with towers added in 1324, all costly and causing further friction with the city authorities. Between 1296 and 1337 the kings Edward I, II and III were frequently resident in the city, together with their armies, state officials and courtiers, as well as occasionally summoning parliaments, and they made full use of monastic resources. In 1316–21 the Chancellor and his entourage were housed in St Mary's Abbey, and they were men accustomed to 'five-star' accommodation. It was during one of these visits that the view of York showing the abbey church in c.1320 was made, probably by a royal clerk (Fig.1). On the other hand, armies, officials and courtiers needed food, clothing and weapons (and in Edward II's case, luxury goods; VCHY, 87–8; Childs and Taylor 1991). Traders and craftsmen were thus attracted to the city and while England's population as a whole was in decline, that of York increased, and with it the demand for housing. City property held by St Mary's Abbey at least cushioned the effects of agricultural losses. Even the plague attacks of 1348–49 and later, appalling as they were, affected the city only temporarily, as craftsmen and workmen flocked in from the country to fill the vacancies, and it was only in the 15th century that York's prosperity began to decline.

Fig. 12 Compartment of the north aisle of the nave from Wellbeloved 1829 (pl.54), based on a measured drawing by R.H. Sharp. This shows the inner face of the north wall of the nave aisle, with the section at window level. This feature can still be seen today.

Differences with York citizens over property rights continued. In 1275 St Mary's had been declared a free borough, that is, the monks were excused from paying tolls and murage, and the abbot exercised the right to the assize of measurements (enforcing standards) within his area of jurisdiction. In the 14th century, however, the corporation attempted to assert its rights in Bootham by collecting tolls and administering the assize. By 1350 the disputes over jurisdiction had become so serious that they came to the attention of the king. On hearing that 'some of the city are uttering grievous threats of firing the abbey and killing the abbot and convent and their men and household servants, and at other times of crucifying them', Edward III ordered the mayor to issue a proclamation forbidding illicit assemblies or attempts to hinder the monks from entering or leaving the abbey, moving goods, or buying and selling in the city, on pain of death. A commission was appointed to investigate the matter. In 1354 it was agreed that all of Bootham should be within the mayor's jurisdiction except for Marygate from the 'new round tower' to the river, Almery Garth and other specified properties. The abbot kept his jurisdiction over the Liberty (a large district in and around York, based on Bootham, was known as 'the Liberty of St Mary'), but the actual area was reduced (Drake 1736, 595–7).

Tempers flared again in 1377 when the mayor received a complaint that although the citizens had rights of passage in Marygate, the abbey's bursar, John Staynegrave, had caused a ditch to be dug across that street, making it impossible to unload a boat at the staith there (see Fig.56). Further, he had *ex malicia* removed the ship's rudder so now it could not unload anywhere else. The mayor sent a deputation to have a few words with the bursar, who replied that if the mayor would care to apply for a licence one would be issued without delay. The mayor did not care to apply for what he considered his by right, and eventually the bursar filled the ditch in again (*YMB* **1**, 26–8). Thereafter, squabbles arose again on occasion – a wordy dispute over property in Bootham in March 1500 lasted for three years before ending wearily and inconclusively in March 1503 (*YCR* **2**, 147–81 *passim*), but at least the abbot was prepared to compromise, and while the mayor and corporation remained unmoved, they did also resist an offer from the citizens to settle the matter by force (*YCR* **2**, 162–3). In general St Mary's suffered none of the terrible events recorded elsewhere, notably where fairs or whole boroughs were controlled by the local monastery. In 1327 St Alban's Abbey was comprehensively looted, in 1381 the Prior of Bury St Edmunds was murdered and his head paraded on a lance, and there were riots in many other towns. News spread quickly in the monastic world and tales of violence elsewhere may have encouraged moderation between St Mary's abbots and the city fathers. Moreover, relations between city and convent were normally more harmonious than the documentation suggests, and on occasion the abbot would be asked to settle disputes between the corporation and other bodies.

Despite economic problems, building and rebuilding continued. Some of it arose from force of circumstance, including fear of Scottish raids and concern about local hostility. In 1377 the steeple of

Fig. 13 North-west view of the nave by F. Nash from Wellbeloved 1829 (pl.53). A rare view of the exterior of the nave north wall, clearly showing the solid standing buttresses. View from St Olave's churchyard, with artist included (few people have seen it from this angle, even today!). To the left is the exterior west wall of the north transept.

the abbey church was struck by lightning, and in its fall the timber spire set fire to the roofs of the nave, south transept and cloisters. The new tower was rebuilt with a parapet and pinnacles in place of the spire. There were also improvements. The east range of the cloister beyond the chapter house was built or rebuilt in the early 1300s and new work was added in the south and west ranges later in the century. Alterations and additions to the infirmary and to service buildings in the outer precincts were made in the 14th and 15th centuries. Work on extensions to the abbot's house, which may have begun under Abbot Booth c.1483, continued under Abbot Sever (1485–1502), and, not to be outdone, Sever's successor Abbot Wanhope rebuilt his country residence at Overton.

There were also developments within the monastery. In 1390 a commission was appointed to draw up the *Ordinal*, setting out instructions for the celebration of Divine Office throughout the year. A manuscript copy from the abbot's chapel survives in St John's College, Cambridge (MS D27). As well as giving an insight into the conduct of the liturgy, it gives a useful indication of the arrangement of the church interior and information regarding the various uses of the claustral buildings.

Gradually, however, the Benedictine monastic rule was relaxed, partly the result of a decline in religious fervour, and partly of the increased pressure of work involved in running a complex institution with extensive property; it has been estimated that at least half the monks in a community would be obedientiaries, expending much of their time and energy on administrative duties. Moreover, as their founder had not wished to be too prescriptive, the Benedictine Order was open to change. Rules about the eating of meat were already changing to allow for a more varied and interesting diet. The practice of giving monks a money allowance for the purchase of clothing became a regular wage, eventually sanctioned officially in 1421 (the corollary being that they could now be fined for offences). Regular annual holidays became common: by the end of the 15th century virtually every Benedictine house had turned a nearby manor into a holiday retreat and some monks were allowed to visit friends and relations. It also became increasingly common for them to exchange the dormitory for private quarters. For some time the abbot had been living apart, and in York, as elsewhere, the abbot's lodging became increasingly grand. Lack of documentary evidence makes it difficult to estimate how far St Mary's Abbey was affected by these developments, but the trend at least left the community open to charges of laxity and moral decline. In Henry VIII's reign government propaganda would make much of this. But it was not the abbey's shortcomings that caught the eye of Thomas Cromwell and others; it was the abbey's wealth.

Fig. 14 William Lodge, St Mary's Abbey. The ruins of St Mary's Abbey church from the south, c.1678, looking through the arches of the six bays of the nave to the ruins of the north wall. Two sets of pillars of the nave are still standing (the south arcade at the front, the north arcade behind), but the outer south wall has gone by this date. Today only the north wall and part of the west wall survive. Above the south arcade arches are the first-floor clerestory windows; nothing survives to this height today. Much of this stonework disappeared during the course of the 18th century. On the right can be seen part of the precinct wall, and the early gatehouse and the tower of St Olave's Church are in the background on the left.

The Gothic church

The success of the abbey in attracting recruits and benefactors encouraged and facilitated rebuilding of the abbey church during the 13th century. The foundation stone was laid by Abbot Simon of Warwick on 24 April 1270 and building commenced with the walls of the choir outside the existing Romanesque structure, the intention being to keep this standing as long as possible. However, digging the foundations, recorded as having been up to 26 feet (8m) deep, weakened the walls, which had to be demolished (Craster and Thornton 1933, 15; RCHMY **4**, 3b; Hutchinson and Palliser 1980, 143). The original intention, to retain the rest of the 11th-century church, was abandoned in 1278 when cracks developed in the central tower and it had to be demolished. The foundation stone for a new tower was laid in 1279, and the dedication of six new altars in 1283 suggests that the choir, crossing and transepts were ready for them. The whole church was completed in 1294. The original architect was Simon of Pabenham (d.1280), related to the architect of the same name who was responsible for the Angel Choir at Lincoln Cathedral, and detail in the abbey shows Lincoln's influence. There are also similarities with those parts of York Minster and Southwell Minster which were being built in the same period.

Very little but the north wall of the nave, a crossing pier and part of the west front remain visible today, but the standing remains, documentary evidence, and excavation of masonry fragments, together with early drawings, make it possible to attempt some reconstruction of the original appearance of the church. It consisted of an aisled nave and a choir, each of eight bays, north and south transepts each of three bays, and a central tower surmounted by a spire. The church was built of pale magnesian

Fig. 15 *Ruins of St Mary's Abbey, J. Haynes, 1735. View of the abbey church from the south-west. By this date the abbey has lost much stone to the debtors' prison (1705). Still standing is the north wall of the nave, with windows blocked in and square inserts, and the remains of the north arcade with triforium above, much reduced since Lodge's picture of c.1678. The south arcade has gone in the 50 or so years since Lodge's engraving. St Olave's Church is to the left, much rebuilt in 1722 in 15th-century style, and part of the abbey gatehouse on the far left. Inset is the Multangular Tower with Minster behind.*

Fig. 16 *View of the Abbey Church, W. Lodge, c.1680. The church from the south-west, before the removal of large amounts of masonry during the course of the 18th century (to the debtors' prison, Ouse Bridge or Beverley Minster). Because of the angle of view the picture is not easy to disentangle; it should be considered alongside other views of the west end, including Ridsdale Tate's reconstruction. It shows the west window of the north aisle, blocked in and with a square window inserted, and, on the right, the west doorway leading to the main body of the nave. Both north and south aisle arcades are still standing, each surmounted by its triforium. The outer wall on the south side has gone completely, making the west door appear off-centre. The detail of the triforium arches and the lower arches is exceptionally clear. The square crenellated wall at the back is not part of the abbey church.*

Fig. 17 *Western front of church, F. Nash, from Wellbeloved, 1829 (pl.52). View of the west front from further back than most, enlivened by children playing with a hoop in the foreground. This picture contains useful detail and gives a good impression of the rise in the ground at the west end and the building's relationship with the King's Manor (far right). It makes the west front look wider and less tall than some other pictures of the same feature.*

Fig. 18 West front, St Mary's Abbey, E. Ridsdale Tate, published 1929. A reconstruction drawing of the west front before the dissolution, based on standing remains and architectural fragments. This was drawn before the discovery of the central part of the carved Coronation of the Virgin in 1952, now in the Yorkshire Museum. This was probably placed in the gable over the main west window (see RCHMY **4**, 24 and pl.40) and was significant, given the abbey's dedication to the Virgin Mary. On the right can be seen part of the western claustral buildings (the cellarer's stores with either guest rooms or a hall above). The door immediately to the right of the church is the Gate of Tobias, the only entrance to the cloisters from outside the abbey.

Fig. 19 At York, St Mary's Abbey, S. Prout, 1821. Detail, probably of the inner side of the north-west corner of the church. The haystack shows the agricultural use made of the abbey ruins at this time. This soft ground etching clearly shows the unusual square window within the gothic pointed window.

limestone, apart from some re-use of earlier millstone grit. The large nave windows were alternately of three and two lights, with simple blank arcading beneath, broken by one north doorway (Figs.10–12). More ornate detail is shown in the capitals, mainly of stiff-leaf design, though more naturalistic towards the west end. Solid standing buttresses on the outer side can be seen from St Olave's churchyard and in Nash's engraving of 1829 (Fig.13). On the south wall, limited by the adjoining cloister, the buttresses were smaller. Drawings by Lodge and Place in the late 17th century, before the removal of further stone for building work at Beverley Minster, show that the nave had slim, elegant pillars surmounted by a triforium with semi-circular arches, each enclosing four openings with tracery of three quatrefoils (Figs.14–15). All that remain now of the south aisle are a few courses of the wall, partly rebuilt in 1912.

The west front of the church, containing the main entrance for visiting dignitaries and laymen, was more richly carved (Figs.16–17). Today only the window of the north aisle remains relatively complete, the doorway and the window which surmounted it having gone apart from the base of the north jamb. The decoration that remains is similar to that of the south transept of the Minster. The gable over the tall central window probably contained a large sculpture showing the Coronation of the Virgin, fragments of which are now in the Yorkshire Museum (RCHMY **4**, 24 and pl.40). The carving and

17

Fig. 20 St Mary's Abbey, York, Francis Bedford, 1843. This is a semi-coloured lithographic view of the church from the south-west, showing clearly the west front, part of the north nave wall and crossing pier. By this time the abbey was surrounded by the Yorkshire Philosophical Society's gardens which were open to the public.

posture of the figures were designed to minimise the foreshortening effects of figures placed at considerable height, and the subject was appropriate to a monastery dedicated to the Virgin Mary. Edwin Ridsdale Tate's essay in reconstruction of the west front pre-dates the discovery of the central part of this sculpture, but gives a good general impression of the majesty of the medieval facade (Fig.18). Even in its ruined state the west front was a popular subject with both local and visiting artists, on its own or as part of a larger composition, and examples are numerous (Figs.19–21).

East of the nave the crossing and central tower were flanked by north and south transepts, each with three bays and an aisle on the east side. The tower was surmounted by a spire until 1377, when the church was struck by lightning; the tower and transepts were damaged and the ensuing fire spread to the south aisle of the choir, the nave and the cloister, though the rest of the church was saved. The spire was not rebuilt, but it can be seen in a rare medieval view of York (Fig.22; see also Fig.1), drawn in c.1320 as an illustration in a copy of Geoffrey of Monmouth's *History of the Kings of Britain*. The view is from the west, with the Minster (partly erased) in the centre and St Mary's Abbey church on the left. This has two slender towers with spires and a central tower, also with a spire. A photograph of this drawing appears in Caesar Caine's 1897 edition of Widdrington's *Analecta Eboracensia*, p.7, but here the abbey's central tower is shown as it appeared after 1377, with crocketed finials but no spire. It is possible that the photograph was 'enhanced' (inaccurately) by the photographer or the printer in 1897.

Of the central tower and crossing, the only substantial remains – and they are substantial – are

Fig. 21 St Mary's Abbey, west end, W. Richardson, c.1843. This view of the west front has useful detail and includes masonry fragments still lying on the ground (other artists seem to have cleared them away!).

those of the north-western pier. This provided a dramatic subject for artists, and it appears in numerous prints, notably J.S. Prout's clear and detailed view of 1840 (Fig.23). Visiting artists also found it attractive: in 1807 Paul Sandby Munn and John Sell Cotman sketched it from several angles (incidentally including each other in the view; Fig.24), and Cotman's watercolour of c.1807–08, while inaccurate in detail, is an interesting example of an artist's ability to use line and light to create what is essentially a work of pure art (Illustration 53).

Of the church choir, a few parts of the foundations remain and the rest has been marked out in stone. It was excavated and photographed in 1912 and 1913 (Figs.25–26). The nine-bay choir was built in the same style as the nave and crossings, and had the whole building survived 'St Mary's would no doubt be famous as the only major 13th-century English church besides Salisbury Cathedral to have been completed in accordance with a design laid down at the start of the work' (Wilson and Burton 1988, 8). At 360 feet in length, it would also bear comparison with the Minster's internal dimension (when completed) of 486 feet (see Fig.27).

Virtually nothing remains of the church fittings and furnishings, which can only be reconstructed from documentary evidence such as details of the order of services given in the *Ordinal*. The east end of the chancel where the monks celebrated their morning mass held three altars, the most important being that of the Holy Trinity. Four bays to the west was the high altar, with panels depicting the life of the Virgin, and backed by a screen over which hung a large crucifix. To the west, the next four bays and the crossing comprised the monks' choir, though openwork screens allowed the laity standing in

Fig. 22 Ebrauc, c.1320 (© British Library Board. All Rights Reserved. MS Royal, 13.A.III fo.16v). Detail from an ink drawing in the margin of the manuscript copy of Geoffrey of Monmouth's History of the Kings of Britain. *St Mary's Abbey is shown with west towers and a central spire (see also Fig.27). The spire was destroyed by lightning in 1377, and replaced by a tower with crocketed finials.*

the aisles to follow the services. The actual choir stalls were placed under the crossing where the tall windows of the tower provided the best natural light. They were set parallel to the screens on the north and south sides, the rows of choir monks thus facing each other. The screens and carved canopies helped to reduce the draughts, and the hinged seats, with misericords, eased the strain of long standing on cold stone. Even so, a warm choir habit was often provided (and needed) for the winter services. In the centre of the choir stood a large lectern, probably two- or four-sided, to hold the large music books used by the cantors. Rules were laid down in the custumals or customaries about the singing of the services, and also about behaviour in the choir: there were to be no muttered conversations, no paring of nails, no lolling with legs apart or feet extended, no noisy raising or lowering of seats, for the choir was the centre for worship, and therefore the focal point of the monk's vocation.

Beneath the western arch of the crossing a stone pulpitum occupied the full width of the church. In the easternmost bay of the nave was the retrochoir for old and infirm monks, and west of this was the third major altar, again dedicated to the Virgin Mary and surmounted by a cross. Daily masses were sung here, requiring the voices of the boys from the almonry as well as outside assistance. Benefactors were also remembered here, the main altar of the nave, where lay folk could gather. Four other altars, dedicated to Saints Nicholas, Thomas Becket, Mary Magdalene and Benedict, stood against the east walls of the transepts, and in the course of time other altars to popular saints were added in the nave and its aisles.

Little remains of the glass of the abbey, apart from a few poorly preserved and incomplete fragments including one depicting an angel, which can be seen at the Yorkshire Museum (YORYM : 2006.2990; Fig.28). There is, however, a list of the subjects in 28 of the windows, made by a monk of Bury St Edmunds in the 14th century, in which they are described in Latin verse (College of Heralds: MS Arundel XXX). This was translated by M. R. James for the Yorkshire Philosophical Society, and both original and translation are in Benson 1915. The windows depict 29 saints and martyrs, including some of particular interest to the York abbey: St Helen finding the True Cross, St Benedict with kneeling monks of St Mary's Abbey, St Olaf, and St William and the fall of Ouse Bridge among them. This seems scant evidence for monastic glass in a centre of the craft like York, where it is probable that the monks' glass vied with that of the Minster for quality. In the Yorkshire Museum's collection is a round ventilator grille with a pattern of intricate heart shapes used in a window in the abbey to provide fresh air in the buildings (YORYM : 1947.633; Fig.29).

Decorative floor tiles were valuable and usually sold or stolen after the dissolution, and only a few of St Mary's remain. Those on view in the Yorkshire Museum (eg YORYM : HB9, HB42, HB56, HB74.1) were produced near Nottingham in the 14th century, but are of a type widely available in north and central eastern England (Fig.30). The tiles were handmade, moulded to give a design, and glazed. The tiles were very thick, as they were used on floors rather than as wall tiles (RCHMY **4**, iv and 28b; Wilson and Burton 1988, 16; Stopford 2005).

Fig. 23 St Mary's Abbey, York, east end of nave, J.S. Prout. This semi-coloured lithograph shows the north-west pier of the crossing from the north-east, the only one that stands to the springing of the crossing arches. Prout has successfully combined clear detail of the stonework with an overall impression of majesty.

Fig. 24 St Mary's Abbey, York, John Sell Cotman. This etching is dated 8 October 1810, but is probably taken from a sketch of 1803, when Cotman and Paul Sandby Munn visited York, sketching the same views (and occasionally each other). Both artists subsequently worked their sketches up into paintings (see Illustrations 53 and 56). This view shows the north-west pier of the crossing from west-south-west, with clear detail of the stonework. The window at left is part of the inner side of the north wall.

No signs of plaster or paint remain on the standing walls of the church. Fragments of masonry from statues have colour, suggesting that at least parts of the interior were probably very colourful, and some screens have survived from other monasteries (see Fig.31).

In 1986 the Yorkshire Museum, which had been suffering from damp penetrating the wall of the gallery of medieval sculpture and damaging the remains of the abbey chapter house, decided to remove the soil piled against the outer wall of the gallery; in December YAT was called in to observe this operation (YAT site code 1986.19). These works uncovered a piece of painted wall plaster measuring c.200 x 200mm on two of the stones forming the foundations of the east wall of the south transept of the Romanesque church. The plaster was white and incised with one vertical and one horizontal line, each filled with red paint. It would have formed part of a decorative scheme representing imitation stonework (false masonry), common from the 12th to 14th centuries. It was thought likely that the two stones bearing the plaster had formerly been part of the fabric of the Norman abbey church and were then re-used in the foundations of its 13th-century successor. 'If so, this provides us with an interesting (albeit small) indication of the interior decoration of a long-vanished major Norman abbey church' (*Interim* **12/1**, 13).

Fig. 25 Photograph of the foundations of the church choir uncovered in excavations of October 1912 (from Ridsdale Tate 1929). The view is looking east, with the King's Manor, Art Gallery and part of the abbey walls in the background.

Fig. 26 South arcade pillars (from Ridsdale Tate 1929). This photograph shows the south arcade pillars rebuilt in February 1913 with fragments of stone found during excavation. The tall pillar at far right was part of the north-west pier of the tower crossing.

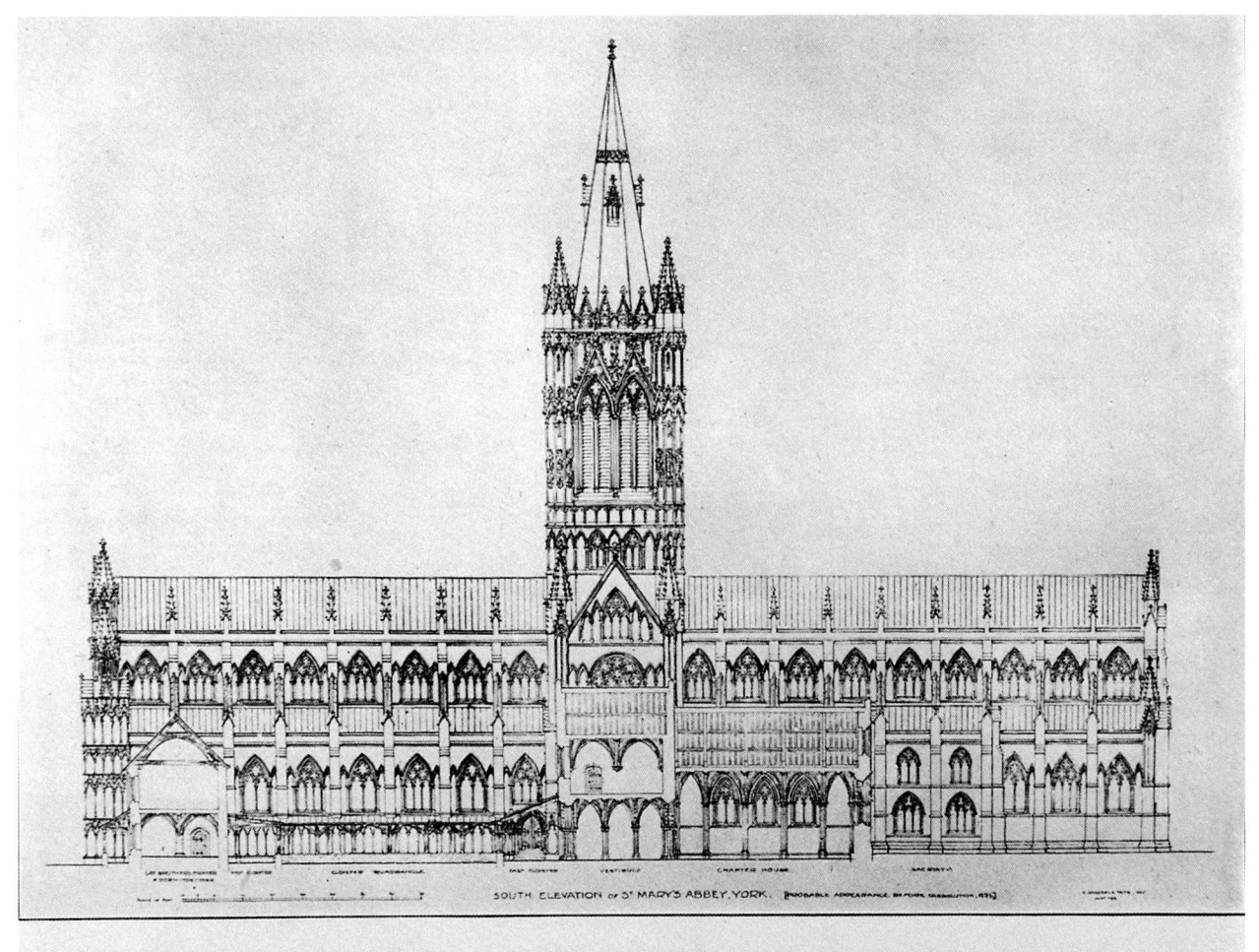

SOUTH ELEVATION OF THE ABBEY CHURCH OF ST. MARY, YORK. (By E. Ridsdale Tate)

Fig. 27 Probable appearance of the south elevation of St Mary's Abbey before the dissolution in 1539 (from Ridsdale Tate 1929). Edwin Ridsdale Tate's reconstruction of the entire south side of the church before 1377 (that is, before it lost its spire) gives a good impression of the full length of the church which, had it survived, would have been the only example of a major 13th-century church built according to one original plan. This is well demonstrated here. The nave is to the left of the spire and the choir to the right, with the end of the south transept and chapter house vestibule in the centre in front of the spire. The vestibule is obscuring part of the rose window in the south transept and the chapter house is in front of the choir, nearest the south transept. All the features are flattened, making them difficult to pick out.

Monastic churches were divided into compartments by screens. The principal ones were the stone pulpitum, which at St Mary's was beneath the western piers of the crossing and ran the full width of the church, thus enclosing the west end of the monks' choir, and the rood screen at the west end of the retrochoir (see Fig.124). Such screens were usually decorated with carved or painted figures of saints, apostles or learned doctors of the church. Lesser screens between the pillars closed off the choir from the aisles; these were of wood, probably painted, and delicately carved with openwork, allowing lay visitors to follow the mass. One such screen (dated to c.1500), the great rood screen which once stood between chancel and nave in Jervaulx Abbey, survives in Aysgarth Church, North Yorkshire, where it has been repainted (Fig.31).

The rich colours of stained glass and painted screens formed the background for much ceremony, especially on great festivals such as Christmas, Easter and saints' days. In contrast to the monks' usual black habits, the celebrants' vestments of silk and cloth of gold were richly embroidered with religious motifs and biblical scenes. Production was labour-intensive and demanded professional

Fig. 28 Fragment of painted glass showing an angel playing a gittern (a small quill-plucked stringed instrument originating in the 13th century). YORYM : 2006.2990, ©York Museums Trust (Yorkshire Museum)

Fig. 29 Round ventilator grille with intricate heart-shaped pattern used in a window in the abbey to provide fresh air. YORYM : 1947.633, ©York Museums Trust (Yorkshire Museum)

Fig. 30 Two tiles from St Mary's Abbey. (a) A large fragment with a grotesque or hybrid, half-man, half-beast (YORYM : HB56). He is wearing a liripipe (a long-tailed hood fashionable in the late 13th and early 14th century; in a religious context this figure could perhaps be seen as a mockery of worldly vanity, as some hood tails were so long that they had to be hooked over the arm). (b) A large fragment with Aries the Ram and an inscription SOL IN ARIETE (YORYM : HB74.1). ©York Museums Trust (Yorkshire Museum)

skills (for which the English embroiderers were famous), so they were expensive and highly prized. Needless to say, most of them disappeared, along with the silver chalices and candlesticks, at the dissolution. A few fine examples remain, such as the early 14th-century Syon cope (Victoria and Albert Museum, London) or the late 14th-century Cistercian vestments from Whalley Abbey (Towneley Hall Museum, Burnley, Lancashire).

All services were sung, and the Benedictines were particularly associated with the development of plainsong; in addition, two-part hymns appear in the MS *Ordinal* of St Mary's Abbey, and there is

24

Fig. 31 Wooden rood screen originally from Jervaulx Abbey. In front are the vicars' stalls. The screen has been dated to c.1506, the work of the Ripon school of carvers, and was removed from the abbey to Aysgarth Church in 1536 to save it from destruction at the time of the dissolution of the monasteries. It is said that the screen was carried from Jervaulx in one piece on the shoulders of twenty men. The screen was originally somewhat wider, having four bays on either side of the central doors, and was used to separate the nave of the abbey from the chancel. During a 19th-century restoration, however, the size of the screen was reduced so that it could fit in its present position. The screen has been repainted, giving a good idea of the colour and splendour of English abbeys.

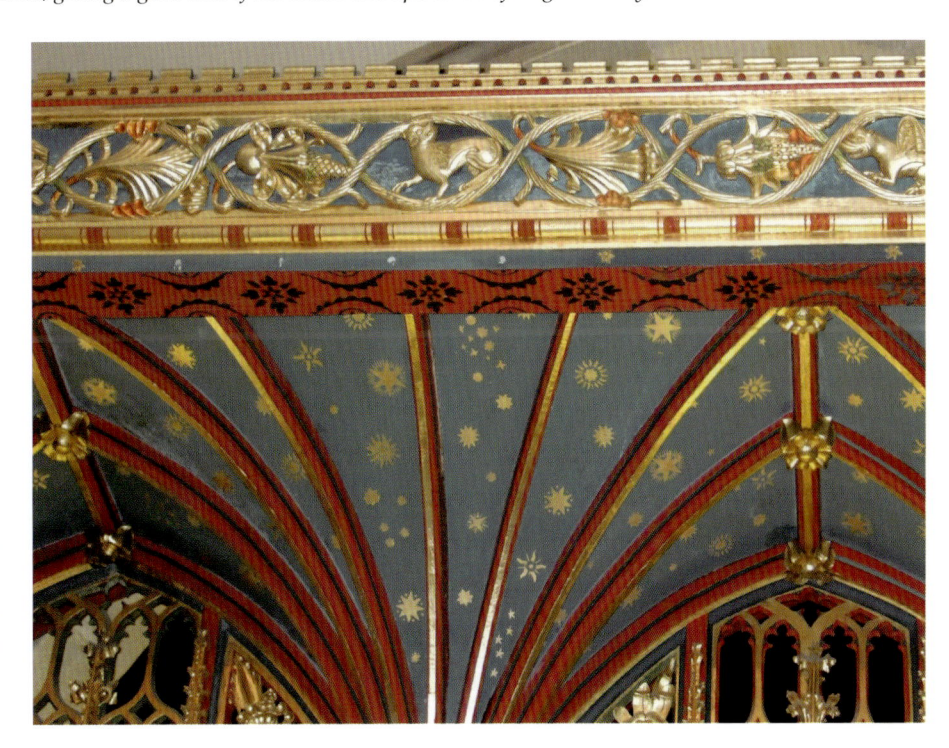

Detail of the top of the intricately carved and richly gilded Jervaulx Abbey rood screen; the animals in the frieze all represent various sins.

25

evidence that boys from the almonry assisted in the polyphonic music of the masses for the Virgin. Most monasteries had at least one organ, and St Mary's may (like Durham) have had four or five. If a church had at least two organs, one would have been placed in the choir for daily services, and the other near the lady chapel altar for services to honour the Blessed Virgin Mary. Early organs were clumsy affairs which had to be thumped with the fist (Bottomley 1995, 261), but they soon became more elaborate, some needing several men to assist on the bellows. The obedientiary in charge was the precentor: he led the singing, arranged the music for the services, took choir practices and checked the condition of the choir books.

Many pre-Reformation bells have survived, though sadly none from St Mary's. The oldest dated bell in England is one hanging in Lisset Church near Bridlington, East Yorkshire, bearing the date MCCLIIII (1254) (Downman 1898). Jervaulx Abbey at one time had five bells, one of which has survived and is now in St Gregory's Church, Bedale. St Mary's bells would have met the same fate as the vast majority, being melted down for their valuable metal.

The numerous daily offices meant that timekeeping was of utmost importance. During daylight hours mass dials or sundials could be used, but night posed more of a problem. It is no surprise, then, to find that religious communities were among the first to develop mechanical clocks which would strike a bell to waken the monks for the night office, 'thus inventing the alarm clock' (Bottomley 1995, 76). Dials were added later, and by the late 13th century mathematician-monks were producing complex machines; the first record of a minute hand on a clock is 1475. There is evidence that St Mary's had a clock, though there are no details. The discovery in York of a seal matrix relating to 'Robert the clockmaker' is thus of interest. The style of the seal indicates that it probably dates from c.1300. If Robert worked for York Minster, as is likely, he

Fig. 32 View of the remains of St Mary's Abbey from the west, F. Nash (from Wellbeloved 1829, pl.56). Excavation of the foundations of the chapter house vestibule, looking east with the King's Manor and the Minster in the background. The wall with the small pilasters is the south wall of the south transept and in front of this is the passageway between the south transept and the vestibule which comprised three aisles. There is clear detail of columns, grave slabs and architectural fragments.

might well have done work also on the abbey clock (*Yorkshire Archaeology Today*, **12**, 20).

The claustral buildings

Nothing remains of the cloister and claustral buildings except fragments and foundations, some of which are preserved in the Yorkshire Museum. Most of our information comes from excavations or can be deduced from the *Ordinal*, or from the fact that Benedictine monasteries generally conformed to a similar layout (see Fig.124).

The area was excavated in 1827–29 when the site was prepared for the Yorkshire Philosophical Society's museum (now the Yorkshire Museum), and much of the east side is now covered by the museum. The *north walk* was excavated again in 1912 for the building of the Tempest Anderson Hall, and the back wall was partly rebuilt. As this was also the south wall of the church, it had buttresses, though they were shallower than those of the church's north wall, presumably to allow unobstructed passage. The wall was decorated with gabled arches like those on the west wall of the church, and the inner, or garden, wall had smaller similar arches; two doorways gave access to the church. The style suggested that most of this was 12th century, while the rest of the cloister was largely late 13th-century reconstruction.

The north walk received the most light and sun, and was therefore used for reading and study. It may have been divided into separate carrels, or study-cubicles, each with its own desk for reading, writing and storage of materials; these were usually of wooden construction, however, and no trace remains. The floor would have been covered with hay, straw or matting for warmth and noise reduction; the windows, if not glazed, would have had shutters or leather curtains, and oil lamps were provided at night (but see below, warming room).

The *east walk* gave access to the private parlour, the chapter house and what was probably the novices' schoolroom, with the dormitory on the upper floor. The foundations of these were uncovered in the excavations of 1827–29 and are described and illustrated in Wellbeloved's report. Subsequently most of the area was covered by the Yorkshire Philosophical Society's museum, where a substantial amount of the stonework is displayed. Immediately south of the church transept was a narrow room with doorways to east and west; this

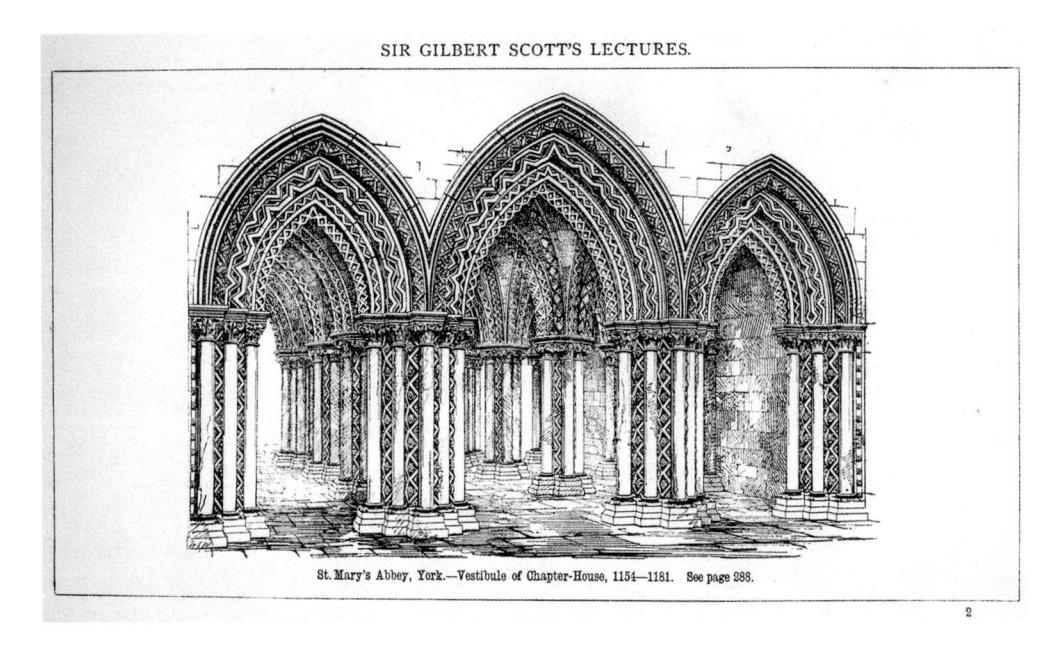

Fig. 33 St Mary's Abbey, York: Vestibule of the Chapter House, 1154–81. *This illustration from a lecture by Sir George Gilbert Scott shows a reconstruction of the probable appearance of the vestibule entrance to the chapter house, based on architectural fragments. Scott (1811–78) was an architect, chiefly associated with the design, building and renovation of churches and cathedrals in the Gothic Revival style. He delivered a series of lectures on the rise and development of medieval architecture at the Royal Academy. The print, in York Art Gallery, is unprovenanced and undated.*

Fig. 34 St Mary's Abbey, York, ruins of the Chapter House, J.S. Prout, 1840, semi-coloured lithograph. View from the south-east showing the remains of the chapter house some ten years after excavations, with the abbey church in the background. A number of stone fragments, including a stone coffin with part of its lid and the decorated pillar (see Fig.35), are clearly visible.

Fig. 35 Photograph of a ruined arch, by Good. Sepia print (n.d.). Very clear detail of the pillar shown in Fig.34 and elsewhere, now, partly reconstructed, in the Yorkshire Museum. It was part of a pier at the entrance to the chapter house.

was the passage to the monks' cemetery (Fig.32). South of this was the *chapter house vestibule*, or galilee (Figs.32 and 33), which was probably the original chapter house until the end of the 12th century, when a larger one was added east of the cloister where its height would not be limited by the dormitory above.

After the church, the *chapter house* was the most important part of the monastery. Here the monks met every day following the morning mass, presided over by the abbot. After the reading of a chapter from the Rule and a lesson and sermon by the abbot, the monks discussed monastic business. First, they had the opportunity to confess (or be accused of) any breaches of discipline, and be assigned a penance. Then they would hear reports from obedientiaries, discuss further plans or witness the signing of tenancy agreements. The meeting has been described as like 'both a board meeting and a managerial briefing' (Wilkinson 2006, 105). Decisions here affected the life of the whole community, and the splendour of the building reflected its importance. The room was rectangular, measuring 61ft x 26ft (18.6m x 7.9m), and of five bays. Some carved masonry survives, notably seven late 12th-century voussoirs, six of them reassembled into a pointed arch in 1987–88, part of a group of three windows in the east wall originally with between 40 and 60 scenes from the life of Christ (Wilson and Burton 1988, 22). The entrance to the chapter house from the vestibule has also been partly reconstructed. It combined the round arches and chevron ornament of the Romanesque with the pointed arches and foliate capitals of the Gothic (Figs.34 and 35; see reconstruction in Wilson and Burton 1988, 19). The same authors suggest that the work was started by Abbot Clement (1161–84), whose new policy of granting leases to abbey property allowed him a more effective cash flow, and who may have been influenced by a visit to the exceptionally fine chapter house at St Albans Abbey. The Royal Commission on Historical Monuments, however, assigns the work to the abbacy of Robert Longchamp, after 1198, on the grounds that Clement was described as a 'ravening wolf' (*lupus rapax*) (RCHMY **4**, xlii, 4).

Fig. 36 Statues discovered in excavating a part of the south aisle of the nave of the church, from Wellbeloved 1829 (pl.60). The figures have been identified as (from left to right) Moses, horned, with a rod and tablets; three apostles, one headless. All were carved c.1200 and were originally coloured. Probably from the chapter house vestibule.

The most imposing carvings are the standing figures representing prophets and apostles now in the Yorkshire Museum. They are also the most contentious. Seven were found buried under the south aisle of the abbey church (in 1834 according to RCHMY 4, xlii, but four are illustrated in Wellbeloved 1829 and dated to that year; Fig.36). Two more came from St Lawrence's Church (Lawrence Street), lying on the churchyard wall in 1736, where they were illustrated by Drake (Fig.37), but having been moved to stand on either side of the church doorway by 1843; they are shown here in Bedford's lithograph of that date (Wilson and Mee 1998, fig.71) and in Pumphrey's photograph of 1853. One came from Clifton Bridge. Two were found near Cawood Church, but despite their similarity to the abbey group it is possible that they actually came from the Archbishop's palace there. The origins of a fragment of torso and a very worn head are unknown. The figures are a little over life size, and were clearly designed to be attached to a wall or pillar. Six are almost complete, though the two from

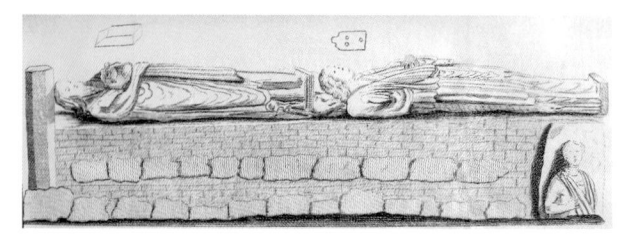

Fig. 37 Engraving from Drake's Eboracum (1736) of two figures on the churchyard wall of St Lawrence, York. At that time they were generally thought to be a 'Roman senator' and his wife, though Drake had doubts, and they were later recognised as from the sequence of prophets and apostles in St Mary's chapter house (SS James and John). By c.1843 they had been moved to stand on either side of St Lawrence's church door (see Wilson and Mee 1998, 93–7) and were transferred to the Yorkshire Philosophical Society's Museum in 1860.

St Lawrence are badly weathered, the rest being headless. The figure of Moses, horned and holding the stone tablets and brazen serpent, is easily identifiable, and the beardless young man is probably

Fig. 38 Fragments of St Mary's Abbey in the Yorkshire Museum, J.S. Prout, 1840. The material includes carved figures of some apostles. The museum opened in 1830.

St John the Evangelist; the two from St Lawrence have been identified as John the Baptist and possibly St James. These six clearly belonged to the same group, though not all by the same hand; they were created about the end of the 12th century. Traces of colour on those from the abbey church indicate that Moses had a pink face, very red lips, gold hair and a cloak of expensive lapis lazuli blue, picked out in white and black, while St John's cloak was rose red.

The complete assemblage probably represented twelve prophets and twelve apostles, and must have made an imposing display. But where were they from? The authors of RCHMY 4 suggest that the apostles come from the twelve springing points of the five-bay chapter house, with the prophets in the vestibule. The whole would therefore form a logical sequence leading to the figure of Christ in Majesty at the east end (RCHMY 4, 12b). Christopher Wilson argues that the supports of the chapter house vault held all 24 figures in two tiers, the apostles above the prophets (Wilson 1983, 65–78; Wilson and Burton 1988, 19–21). The proximity of their burial site to the chapter house gives credence to either theory, but Christopher Norton upholds earlier views that the whole sequence came from the west front of the abbey church (Norton 1994, 277–8). Nor is it clear when or why some were buried. The 16th-century mortar covering them suggests a date shortly after the dissolution, though it is likely that the statues were taken down when the chapter house vestibule was extensively altered late in the 14th century. There is, however, general agreement that the statues comprise 'the most important late 12th-century sculpture to have survived in England' (Wilson and Burton 1988, 20).

There appears to have been no scriptorium, implying that the copying of manuscripts was done in the cloister. There is no information on the library at St Mary's and the abbey's collection of books seems to have been of modest size (Childs and Taylor 1991, 5). The *Victoria County History* volume for York shows 'Scriptorium and Library' on a plan of the east cloister range, where most writers have the novices' schoolroom with dormitory above. This is almost certainly just a surmise.

South of the vestibule was the **inner parlour**, a vaulted room of three bays. Here the general rule of silence was relaxed at certain times to allow discussion of essential business such as matters to be raised in Chapter. Unlike the outer parlour (see p.35), access was limited to members of the community. Such parlours as survive are formal and uninviting; the stone seats along the walls would have offered no temptation to linger in idle chat.

A passage beyond the parlour led to the abbot's lodging and south of this the ground floor, or undercroft, was occupied by the **novices' schoolroom**, six bays long and extending beyond the south range of the cloister. The *Chronicle* refers to the *scola infantum* in the 14th century (Craster and Thornton 1934, 85–6), though the practice whereby children as young as seven could be dedicated to the monastery by their parents as oblates ended in the late 12th century. However, new entrants (postulates) normally spent a year as novices under the guidance of a novice-master, who ensured that they could understand the services, the scriptures and the Rule, as well as the minutiae of everyday behaviour – how to stand, how to sit, in the church, the refectory, the dorter, even the reredorter – which developed personal restraint and probably helped to smooth relationships in a life lived entirely communally. In addition, many novices would study more academic subjects and, once the Benedictines had overcome their initial suspicion of the universities, a few would proceed to Oxford or Cambridge.

In November 1988 work started on an extension to the south side of the Yorkshire Museum. Excavation (YAT site code 1988–89.18) revealed part of a standing structure and a series of limestone blocks. Examination of Wellbeloved's plans showed that these were the remains of the c.1310 schoolroom and dormitory, consisting of the west wall, complete with entrance, and the foundations for one of the central vaulting pillars. The wall was constructed of limestone ashlar and stood to a height of c.1.5m. Its most striking feature was a half-octagonal pillar attached to support the ceiling vaulting. A stone threshold marked the position of an entrance. The floor of the entrance was made of re-used roof tiles, set in sand, and rounded limestone blocks, some of which were also re-used. The pillar foundations would have supported one of the central piers from which the roof arch would have spanned to the pillar on the west wall (*Interim* **13**/4, 23–8).

A portion of wall was uncovered directly underneath the west wall; this had well-faced sides on the north and south, and extended 1.5m beyond the

Fig. 39 St Mary's Abbey drain uncovered during excavation in 1984 to the south-east of the Yorkshire Museum. Buildings used by the prior would once have stood in this area. This substantial drain was constructed of well-cut, coursed blocks of magnesian limestone, mortared together, and has a roof of corbelled blocks. It stood about 1m high.

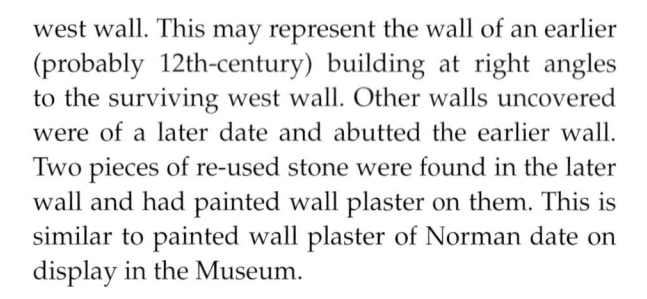

Fig. 40 Another drain in the same area incorporated re-used architectural fragments in its arched roof; these have been dated to the mid-13th century and presumably came from the abbey buildings.

west wall. This may represent the wall of an earlier (probably 12th-century) building at right angles to the surviving west wall. Other walls uncovered were of a later date and abutted the earlier wall. Two pieces of re-used stone were found in the later wall and had painted wall plaster on them. This is similar to painted wall plaster of Norman date on display in the Museum.

Above the east range was the *dorter,* or dormitory, of which nothing remains visible today. The beds were arranged with their heads against the long walls, each with a straw pallet, a woollen covering and a pillow with a woollen cloth under it. As they had to rise for the night services, the monks slept in their habits, apart from the outer cloak: too hot in summer and too cold in winter, when the straw spread on the floor can have done little to diminish the chill. From a doorway in the north wall the night stairs led into the church. An oil lamp gave a little light, and two monks were on duty each night to waken any sleepers for the night office;

rules of behaviour were strict, to ensure as much quiet and privacy as such communal living could allow. Eventually, the abbot moved out into his own separate accommodation, and it became normal for the dorter to be subdivided into separate cubicles.

A door in the south wall allowed access from the cloister by means of a staircase built into the thickness of the wall, and in the opposite wall a door led to the *reredorter*. This was immediately behind the dorter and had a row of cubicles with wooden seats and partitions. The tendency of weary monks to fall asleep here was notorious, and the two monks on 'night duty' were required to make regular checks. Beneath the reredorter was a drain, probably with flowing water.

Monastic water engineering was the most advanced of its time, so it would be reasonable to expect an elaborate system in an abbey of the size of St Mary's. Although much of it was probably lost in the building of the Yorkshire Museum, some has come to light during excavations in the Museum Gardens. In 1984 three exploratory trenches were opened by contractors in the area to the south-east of where the Yorkshire Museum now stands (YAT site code 1984.6). Wellbeloved suggested that this area would have been largely covered by buildings used by the prior. In each trench remains of the abbey's drainage system were found (Figs.39–40). In one trench the remains of the corner of a building were uncovered, comprising walls 1.30m high, although foundation levels were not reached. The abbey's stone drain (into which a smaller Victorian brick sewer had been inserted) respected the corner of this building. The abbey's drain was traced running in a north-westerly direction for 65m, and was seen again in the other two trenches. It was constructed of well-cut blocks of magnesian limestone, well mortared together in courses. It stood 1.05m high and was 0.55m wide with an arched roof, some of which was formed of re-used architectural fragments. In places, probably where the drain passed below abbey buildings, a flat roof replaced the arch and the roof level fell to 0.90m. Entering the main drain from the north-east was another small, square stone-lined drain, 0.40 x 0.25m, which served the King's Manor, originally the abbot's lodging to the east of the abbey. The re-used architectural fragments in the arched roof (Fig.40) were dated to the mid-13th century and presumably came from abbey buildings. The roof of the drain could not therefore have been constructed before that date, although it is quite possible that the original feature was open and may have been constructed much earlier. The square drain from the King's Manor may date to as late as the Tudor period when that range of buildings was being modified (*Interim* **10**/1, 13–18).

Again in 1988–89, during excavation in connection with a small extension on the south side of the Yorkshire Museum, a series of large capping stones was uncovered just 0.2m south-east of what was believed to be the foundation for one of the central vaulting pillars in the schoolhouse/dormitory. This was a well-made ashlar drain, with a flagstone floor and large capping stone cover. The drain was c.0.6m wide and 1.07m high internally, and had been robbed out in the area east of the pillar foundation (*Interim* **13**/4, 23–8). This drain ran beneath the building to join the drainage system recorded in 1984.

The *south range* was rebuilt in the 14th century. A buttress and a short length of panelled walling excavated in 1829 (Wellbeloved 1829, pl.58) has been rebuilt in the Yorkshire Museum (RCHMY **4**, pl.13; it is no longer in the hospitium, as stated in the caption), and in 1913 Ridsdale Tate was able to attempt a reconstruction of the east end of the south cloister walk 'based on fragments discovered in rockeries' (Fig.41). West of a vaulted passage two buildings occupied this range, the warming house and the common hall, with the refectory over. Apart from the kitchen and the infirmary, the *warming house* was the only room with a fire, a welcome haven for frozen-fingered monks working in the north cloister in winter. Medieval monasteries were based on Mediterranean models, and York's climate is not Mediterranean. (Guides at Fontenay say the fire was to keep the ink from freezing, not the monks.) Informal conversation was also permit-

Fig. 41 East end of the south cloister walk by Ridsdale Tate. This reconstruction drawing was based on old prints, excavation reports and existing fragments 'discovered in rockeries'. Note the decorative stonework of the blind arcading, the tiled floor and the wooden pentice roof. The building beyond the wall at the right would have been the warming house.

Fig. 42 *Detail from Wellbeloved 1829 (pl.57) showing the fireplace from the warming house and a carved head from the fireplace.*

Fig. 43 *Detail from Wellbeloved 1829 (pl.57) showing a roof boss with the Virgin Mary and vine-branches from the warming house; and a roof boss with a musician (monk playing a viol according to RCHMY **4**, 22b) from the warming house. Both are now in the Yorkshire Museum.*

Fig. 44 *Detail from Wellbeloved 1829 (pl.59) showing a roof boss from the warming house depicting two monsters or sea creatures intertwined and biting each other.*

Fig. 45 *Detail from Wellbeloved 1829 (pl.58) of the centre knot from the warming house showing the Lamb of God, with a staple and ring for a hanging lamp.*

ted here. Later, as individual rooms and more fires became the norm, the room was used for meetings and for celebratory parties on festive occasions. The fireplace still stands in the basement of the Museum, and it is illustrated in Wellbeloved 1829, pl.57, I, i (Fig.42). Carved roof bosses found here are probably from the warming house vault; they are late 13th- to early 14th-century naturalistic leaf carving, some with figures including a musician, the Virgin Mary, and two intertwined biting monsters; a further boss, with the Lamb of God, still has an iron ring for suspending a lamp (Figs.43–5).

A door in the west wall led to the ***common hall***, a vaulted room of six bays and divided by two rows of columns into three aisles, probably the room built in 1313 for recreation and used by monks not eating in the refectory (see p.35). As it was also used for the entertainment of the abbot's guests, it would be more sumptuously and impressively decorated than usual, so some of the carved masonry found in the warming house may have come from here. Its main doorway was at the west end, leading directly from the outer courtyard, and on the northern side of the door was a lobby with a circular stair leading to the upper floor.

On the upper floor of the south range was the frater, or *refectory*, entered from the south-west corner of the cloister by a flight of stairs, of which the foundations were uncovered in 1827–29. The room would be large and airy, the walls plain except for a pulpit in the south wall and a figure of Christ in Majesty behind the raised dais and high table at the east end. The monks' tables, provided with spoons, dishes and well-laundered tablecloths, lined the longer walls, and the well-swept floor was strewn with rushes, herbs and sweet-smelling flowers from the cloister garden. The similarity to a church is no accident. Meals were regarded as sacramental and symbolic of community. Rules for their conduct were precise and strict. After ritual washing of hands at the *lavatorium* in the south-west corner of the cloister, the monks processed into the refectory, took their places in order and said grace. Thereafter the meal was eaten in silence broken only by a devotional reading from the pulpit.

The monks ate dinner every day, but supper only between Easter and 13 September. The Benedictine Rule encouraged simplicity of diet, but no undue abstinence. Meat was forbidden in the refectory, but available in the infirmary and the misericord, where monks could eat on a rota system; it was also provided for guests at the abbot's table. Evidence from contemporary accounts reveals that the choir monks' diet was comparable to that of the gentry or urban elite, and that of the abbot and senior monks to that of the aristocracy of the time – indeed, in quantity it exceeded the amount needed by an average adult male today.

The *west walk* was almost entirely taken up by the *cellarium*, or storehouse, a long vaulted room with entrances from the cloister and from the outer parlour (see below). The main doorway, however, was on the outer, or south-west side, and was usually large enough to admit bulky goods brought in by way of the abbey's main gateway. A small projecting building may have been the cellarer's chequer, or office. Medieval artists liked to portray the cellarer furtively sampling the wine in his cellar; in fact, next to the abbot, he had the most responsible and demanding office in the monastery, in charge of the provision, storage and transport of food, drink and fuel. He spent much of his time travelling, to the abbey granges, to fairs and markets, and to outlying mills; back at home he supervised the brewhouse and bakehouse, interviewed salesmen and kept the accounts. He worked closely with the chamberlain, the guestmaster and the fraterer, and he managed his own staff – in 1322 the cellarer of Canterbury had a staff of 36 (listed in McAleavy 1996, 40). He had psalms and special prayers sung for him by the choir monks and at times he must have felt that he needed them.

Above the store was a guest hall, or perhaps a series of rooms. It is uncertain whether the 'Hall of the Wlays' (strangers) mentioned in the *Chronicle* refers to this or to the common hall in the south range.

North of the store was the *outer parlour*, where monks could meet to discuss business matters with visiting laymen. It also formed a passage between the cloister and the outer precincts. The gateway was the 'Gate of Tobias' where alms and food were distributed daily to the poor (see Fig.18).

The outer precincts

Immediately south of the refectory was the *monastic kitchen*, described in the 1545 survey as 40½ feet (12.34 metres) square, and having two 'rainges'. The foundations uncovered in 1829 revealed fireplaces on the east and south sides, and showed that the kitchen was linked to the refectory by a servery. Conventual kitchens were a good deal less grand than the more famous surviving examples, such as Fontrevault (Loire) or the abbot's kitchen at Glastonbury, would suggest, but some reconstruction is possible from documentary sources. The monks' main diet consisted of rye or wheaten bread, eggs, cheese and milk, fish and vegetables (onions, leeks, peas, cabbage), flavoured with herbs from the cloister garden. The monks had their own fishpond at the bottom of Marygate. The kitchen may have had a central hearth; it would certainly have been equipped with cauldrons for washing vegetables and utensils, knives, sharpeners, jars of herbs and seasoning, strainers, towels and protective clothing such as sleeves and gloves. According to the Rule, monks should do the kitchen work themselves, but this rarely amounted to more than 'shelling the new beans or rooting out weeds … in the garden' (Lawrence 1984, 100); in practice the kitchener was assisted by professional cooks, often with specialist skills. The kitchen was a centre of intense, sometimes frantic, activity. Nearby, according to the 1545 survey, were the meat larder and 'pastrie' as well as the abbot's kitchen, which Norton suggests may also have been the conventual meat kitchen.

In the Yorkshire Museum's collections are some artefacts which would probably have been used in the abbey kitchen or at table. These include an exquisite medieval green-glazed lobed drinking bowl with an animal in the centre (YORYM : 1992.140; Fig.46) and a small green-glazed cooking vessel with a long handle.

To the south again were the *prior's chamber*, a vaulted room containing a fireplace, where he entertained visitors and senior monks, and a long room running east–west, probably the *prior's hall*.

The survey also records the *infirmary*, without giving its location. RCHMY **4** places it south of the kitchen, but Norton points out that Wellbeloved had doubts about the purpose of these buildings and that a more usual situation for an infirmary was east of the claustral buildings. He suggests therefore that its foundations may lie under the second courtyard of the King's Manor, an area as yet unexcavated (Norton 1994, 268). The monastic infirmary usually consisted of a hall, with beds arranged along the walls, sometimes divided into single cubicles, perhaps a central fire, a chapel ('newly built' in 1455 at St Mary's), its own kitchen and refectory, and accommodation for the infirmarian. There was a strong tradition of medical knowledge in some monasteries, many ideas having been brought from the Middle East by travelling monks, but the infirmarian was not necessarily a medical specialist, being chosen largely for his personal qualities. He would, however, have some knowledge of herbs and access to books of herbals in the monastery library (he was often the librarian), and for more serious cases he could call on the expertise of a lay physician from the town.

The infirmary catered for three types of inpatients: the old and infirm, who were permanent residents; the sick; and the monks who came for those regular sessions of blood-letting, performed by a lay barber-surgeon, that were regarded as so conducive to health. Each 'seynie' or bleeding was followed by three days' rest in the infirmary where the number of offices was reduced, the food included meat and was more appetising, the rule of silence was relaxed, and the brethren were allowed to take walks outside the normal confines of the monastery. As breaks from routine they were very popular, eagerly anticipated and just occasionally abused.

The sole surviving relic of the infirmary is the bronze two-handled mortar, now in the Yorkshire Museum. It is finely decorated with twisted handles and the body has quatrefoils containing animal figures; it is inscribed *Mortaria sci Johis Evangeli de Infirmaria be Maria Ebor, Fr Wills de Towthorp me fecit AD MCCCVIII* (RCHMY **4**, pl 44). Benson claims that this mortar 'was cast in 1308 by William of Towthorpe, one of the monks' (Benson and Haslehust 1911, 61). It would have been used by the infirmarian to grind the herbs with which he treated the monks or his other patients.

Fig. 46 Medieval green-glazed lobed drinking bowl with an animal in the centre. This was found near the Multangular Tower. YORYM : 1992.140, ©York Museums Trust (Yorkshire Museum)

Burials and the cemetery

In theory the death of a monk was not a momentous event, as he had already renounced the world on entering the monastery; in practice, it was an occasion for muted ceremony, as the community gathered round to support their brother. In York, as elsewhere, the monks' cemetery lay south and east of the church choir, approached from the cloister by a narrow passageway, or slype. The monk would be buried in his habit, usually without a coffin and with or without a headstone. He remained a member of the community in that the cemetery was not entirely set apart: in York there is evidence that, at least on occasion, the novices were sent to play there (Wilson and Burton 1988, 22).

With a few exceptions, abbots were interred in the chapter house, with a stone coffin or grave-slab. One such, a slab carved with a foliate cross, is shown in Nash's view of the 1829 excavations (Fig.32) and others appear in J.S. Prout's 'Ruins of the Chapter House' (Fig.34). Three abbots are known to have been buried in the church: Simon de Warwick (1258–96) and John Gilling (1303–13) before the high altar, and Benedict de Malton (1299–1303, resigned) before the altar of St Benedict. All were particularly connected with the building of the Gothic church. The grave slab of Thomas de Spofford, or Spofforth (1405–21), was found in 1912 on the site of the chancel. A notable scholar and administrator, he went on to become Bishop of Hereford; he retired to St Mary's in 1448 and died there in 1456. His grave slab showing him in bishop's vestments, flanked by two university doctor's caps, is now in the Yorkshire Museum (drawings in RCHMY 4, fig.26, 23; Wilson and Burton 1988, 18). Other fragments of grave slabs, some with scraps of inscription (listed in RCHMY 4, 22–3) probably relate to benefactors and their families. Patrons and benefactors had endowed monasteries for the good of their own and their families' souls, so while monastic communities were usually reluctant to see their church turned into a mausoleum, they had to allow burial within the church. What evidence there is suggests that St Mary's may have resisted more successfully than most, though it is far from conclusive. Grave slabs were useful for building and particularly for paving stones, so they have often been moved (probably after the dissolution) from their original location. The 13th-century grave slab of Emma de Beningfield (Fig.47) was apparently

Fig. 47 Memorial cross slab, drawn from a rubbing by D.A. Walter in 1874. This broken cross slab has a 13th-century floriated cross and part of an inscription. It was probably that of Emma de Benefield, widow of Adam de Ben[ing]field of Morton in Cleveland, and a benefactress of the abbey. According to Walter it was 'found under the Hospitium'. It may have been re-used because while monks were usually buried without headstone in the cemetery east of the church, and abbots under a memorial stone in the chapter house, founders and benefactors were often buried and commemorated in the abbey church itself. The slab is now in the Yorkshire Museum.

found under the hospitium, but as a benefactress of the monastery she is much more likely to have been buried in the church.

Excavation of monastic cemeteries was not a priority of early archaeologists, who tended to concentrate their interests on the church. Where such work has been done, it has proved informative, especially when it can be collated with monastic records relating to such matters as life expectancy, morbidity, diet and general welfare, and comparison made with conditions among the contemporary laity (see Harvey 1989). In general it would appear that monks had a standard of living similar to that of the gentry, with the senior brethren approaching the standard of the aristocracy. Glyn Coppack has pointed out, however, the tendency of monks to suffer from diffuse idiopathic skeletal hyperostosis, the result of over-indulgence and lack of exercise (Coppack 2006, 80).

On the south-west side of the precinct lay a group of *storage and service buildings*, just within, and mainly aligned with, the abbey's river wall (Fig.48). These are listed in the survey of c.1545, some with measurements given. From north to south they were: four stables under one roof; a barn, 78ft x 39ft, resting on eight posts; a garner, of timber

Fig. 48 Restored view of St Mary's Abbey by R.H. Sharp, c.1836 (Ridsdale Tate 1929, pl.3). This is an imaginative reconstruction of all the buildings in the abbey precincts. To the left is Marygate, St Olave's Church and the lodge. In the foreground are the river and a conjectural range of buildings behind the riverfront abbey walls (guesthouses and stables are mentioned in this area in historical documents). The surprisingly small cloisters are to the right of the abbey church, with the chapter house and dormitory above, the warming house and refectory (common hall) to the right and the cellarer's stores in front. There is nothing that looks like the hospitium.

Fig. 49 The Abbey Grounds, York, by J.S. Prout, 1840. This is a view directly across the river from the opposite bank, showing the hospitium, with the west end of the abbey behind, and, on the left, the abbey gateway and St Olave's Church. Though the Marygate Landing is off the picture, the barge is a reminder of the former importance of control of the riverbank for transport; this resulted in many heated arguments between the city and the abbey.

and stone, 150ft x 38ft; a brewhouse (with millhouse attached on the west side), bakehouse and cooperhouse (coopers made casks and barrels); the 'great garner', of stone and brick, 150ft x 54ft, lying east to west; and a 'litill garner' of freestone, 118ft x 26ft (see Norton 1994, 278–9 and fig.7; Wilson and Burton 1988, 11 and reconstruction on p.4). There are references in other documents, too: the *Chronicle* records the inundation of buildings in the flood of 1315, specifying the bakery, brewery, tailor's workshop, stable and almonry (Craster and Thornton 1933, 67–8; the almonry, however, was probably nearer the main gateway). The buildings may well have undergone changes of use over the years.

This group of structures appears on Archer's plan of York c.1675 and therefore on Jacob Richards' plan of the Manor grounds c.1695 (see Fig.74, C), most of them disappearing during the course of the 18th century. The only building still standing is the barn, stubbornly keeping its name of *hospitium*, 'an appellation for which there is not the slightest medieval evidence' (Norton 1994, 269–70), though a hospitium, or guesthouse is named, without location. The building is of two storeys: the lower is 14th-century and of stone; and the upper is 14th- or 15th-century and timber-framed, its floor carried on two rows of octagonal stone columns (Figs.49–52). Before 1840 part of the east end was missing, but there have been many changes: the steps are late 19th-century and in 1930–31 the roof was reconstructed with a steeper pitch (Fig.53). Adjoining the hospitium is a length of wall of ashlar with brick on the inner side, with a gateway, a smaller doorway and a window, of c.1500, known as the 'water gate' (Fig.54). A print of 1735 (Fig.55) shows that it stood on the line of a path from the main abbey complex towards the river, probably reached by way of a postern doorway in the precinct wall, now gone (*Interim* **11**/1, 1986, 1–13).

Fig. 50 Granary, St Mary's Abbey, 'after' Twopenny, 1832. The building is generally known as the hospitium, or guesthouse, but documentary evidence suggests that it could have been a barn or a workshop, had a dual purpose or had different roles at different times. It was probably put to use as a granary or a hayloft after the dissolution. This view shows the north-east and north-west elevations before the steps to the upper floor were added in the mid- or late 19th century (though a door is shown at the left on the upper floor) and the roof was replaced by one of steeper pitch in 1930.

Fig. 51 Columns supporting the Granary floor, St Mary's Abbey, W.T., 1832. Interior of the ground floor of the hospitium, showing the construction details clearly: lath and plaster, two of the columns and a small arched doorway. This illustration is probably by William Twopenny.

Fig. 52 *St Mary's Abbey, Old Hospitium, 1886, by W. Moore, Jr. View of the south-east end wall, showing clearly the method of construction: ground-floor ashlar, upper-floor timber and plaster. This pencil drawing also shows the window designs and columns supporting the upper floor.*

Fig. 53 Hospitium steps and water gate, by W.J. Boddy, 1897. This postcard reproduction of an original watercolour shows the view from the inner (eastern) side. It is not as detailed as Harper's view (Fig.54) but more well proportioned. By 1897 the hospitium had acquired the permanent wooden staircase, leaving the entrance to the lower hall visible. The red-roofed part is a ground-floor extension built on to the original hospitium but the upper hall was not extended until 1930.

Fig. 54 Part of St Mary's Abbey, E. Harper, lithograph by Monkhouse. This undated view shows the archway adjoining the hospitium, from the inner (eastern) side. Sometimes known as the water gate, it gave access to the riverbank from the abbey by a pathway, now gone. It is part of a linked group of buildings, as the ruined window shows. The gateway is dated c.1500. The building seen through the arch has now gone. This view dates from before 1860 when the esplanade was created.

Fig. 55 West view of the abbey by W.H. Toms, reproduced in Eboracum *(published 1736). This is a general view from the south-west across the River Ouse, showing the river frontage of the abbey, the hospitium and water gate, St Olave's Church and the ruins of the abbey. Behind the wall alongside the hospitium is the roof of the lodge and the entrance way, here shown roofed and not crenellated (see Fig.60).*

The precinct walls

Though now incomplete, the precinct wall of St Mary's Abbey is the finest surviving example in the country. It stands virtually complete, if much restored, on the north-west side of the abbey precinct, facing Marygate; the north-eastern section, facing Bootham, stretches as far as the tower opposite Bootham Bar. Most of the south-eastern part has gone, though it can be traced along that side of the King's Manor, but nothing is now visible of the wall formerly along the river bank (see Fig.56). The building of a stone wall was under consideration in 1260, when a commission of enquiry decided that a wall below the abbey as far as St Leonard's hospital (in effect, towards the city wall) would 'strengthen and improve rather than damage the city of York' (RCHMY **2**, 160). Clearly one incentive was the fear of Scottish attack that had led Henry III to rebuild York Castle in stone and the city council to start rebuilding the town defences. Disputes between town and abbey also produced a real and in the event well-founded fear of assault by riotous citizens (see p.9). Theft, vandalism and petty pilfering were of course a constant problem. It has been noted that the wall begun in 1266 would not have withstood a military attack (RCHMY **2**, 160); it would, however, give an angry mob pause for thought and deter thieves by funnelling all entries and exits through the imposing main gateway under the watchful eyes of the porter (and probably his dog).

Building began in 1266, though alterations and additions continued until 1497. The walls were of magnesian limestone, in general 2ft 6in (0.9m) thick and some 11ft (3.35m) high. In 1318, again a time of Scottish threat and of disputes with the city, this time regarding ditches, the abbot was granted licence to crenellate – except for the wall between the abbey and the city, which must not be above 16 feet (4.88m) high. Crenellation was added along Marygate and Bootham, in effect adding some 5–6 feet (1.52–1.83m), the embrasures being enclosed with wooden shutters to protect the defenders. Two towers, St Mary's Tower and Marygate Tower, together with interval towers, were built in the early 14th century and the walls were extended as far as the river bank on both the north-west and south-west sides. The wall along the river side was completed in 1354. The total length of the enceinte

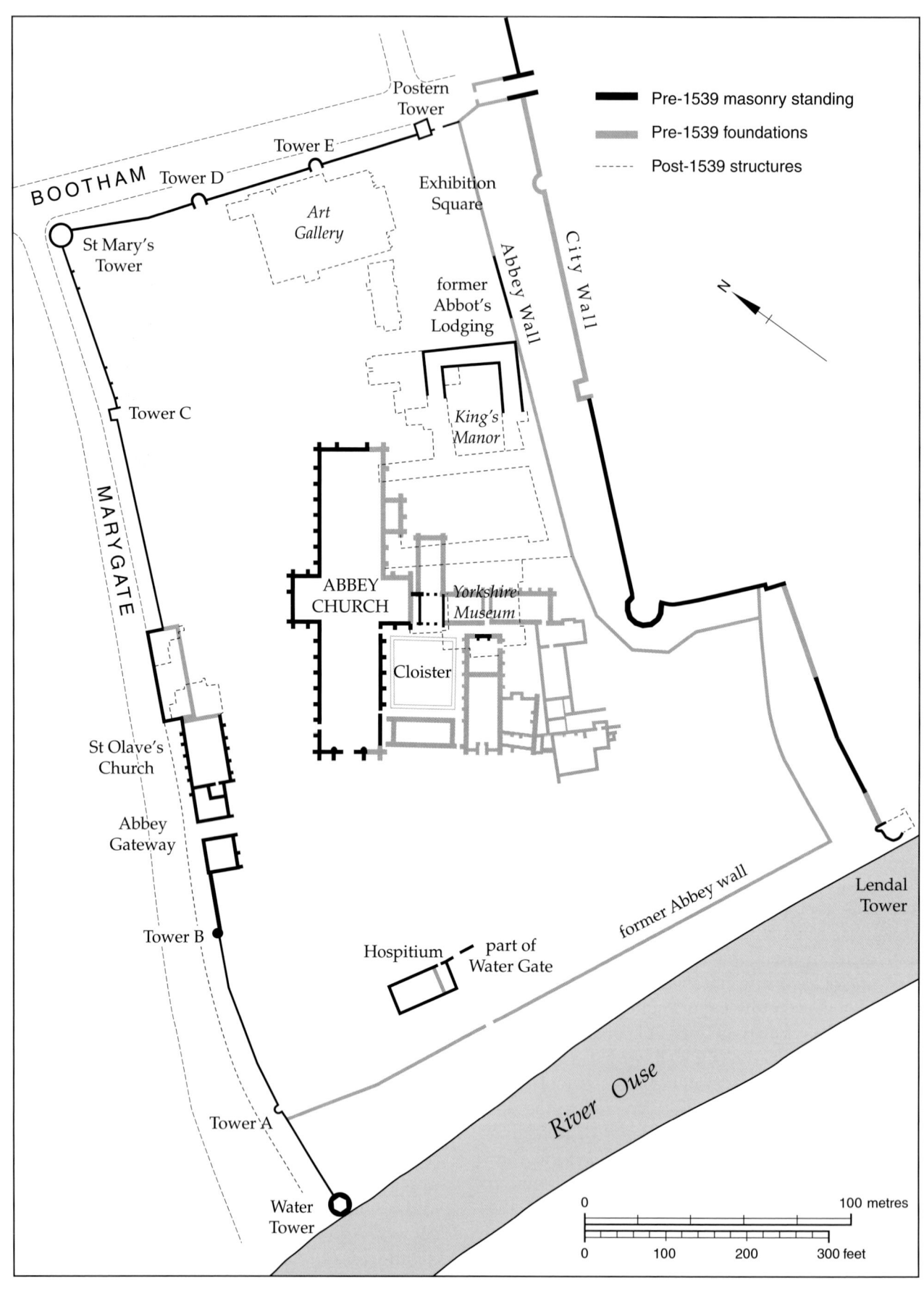

Fig. 56   Outline plan of the abbey precincts and walls

was, according to Drake, some three-quarters of a mile (1200m). In the 15th century, probably about 1470, additions were made to the gatehouse, and in 1497 a postern gate (Queen Margaret's Arch) was opened near Bootham Bar.

After the dissolution of the abbey in 1539 most of the wall on the south-east side of the precinct was removed, to make way for extensions to the King's Manor or to become part of its fabric (see pp.51–2), and gradually the whole of the riverside wall was also lost. The walls along Marygate and Bootham remained, however. They had been gathering an accretion of houses from at least 1500 (predictably leading to dispute between city and abbey over ownership of the ground; YCR **2**, 147–73), and by 1800 much of the wall was hidden. After its acquisition by the Yorkshire Philosophical Society in 1877 a process of removal was begun. It was continued when the city council took over responsibility for the walls in 1896 (see Fig.57). In 1922 the abbey wall became a Scheduled Ancient Monument and more houses in Marygate were demolished in 1937–40 (Fig.58). Today only a row of shops in Bootham and one house (no.29) in Marygate remain.

Until the mid-19th century antiquaries and archaeologists showed less interest in the abbey precinct than in the church, and study of the walls was somewhat cursory. This has been rectified by the Royal Commission on Historical Monuments, with authoritative and well-illustrated studies (RCHMY **2**, 160–73; **4**, 15–22). The following description follows the same order as the plan in RCHMY **4**, p.5, clockwise from Marygate Tower on the river bank at the west corner of the precinct, and uses the same nomenclature (see Fig.56).

Marygate Tower, also known as the water tower, stands on the river bank at the west corner of the precinct. It was built c.1324, after the abbey was given licence to crenellate; the upper wall has now gone, but drawings by Place c.1705 show the crenellation (Illustrations 183 and 184). The tower would give early warning of a river-borne enemy and it guarded the abbey staith, important for the landing of supplies to the abbey or the departure of the abbot by barge to his country retreat at Overton near Beningbrough. The tower is circular outside but hexagonal inside, and has six arrow-slit openings. There was originally an upper floor and Cave's print of 1813 (Fig.59) shows a door leading to a wall-walk, with another door above which can have been accessible only by ladder. Originally there was a roof, with room for a narrow walkway round the top of the tower (RCHMY **2**, 164, and pls.28 and 53). The wall between the tower and the abbey gateway is early 14th century, but it has lost some of its crenellation and is now much restored. It contains two projecting semi-circular interval towers, the first (A) mainly original, the second (B) rebuilt in the late 19th century. Between Tower B and the gateway the wall stands to its original height of 13ft (4m), and has its crenellations, the embrasures with slots for wooden shutters.

The gatehouse stands on the line of a putative Roman road which ran between the river and the south-west frontage of the fortress; it may also have been the site of the main entrance to the residence of the earls of Northumbria. Today only the outer arch and part of the side walls remain of the conventual gateway, begun in 1197–99 and thus pre-dating the stone walls. The side walls are decorated with blind arcading, and there are two doorways on the west side and one on the east, all now blocked. Early 18th-century drawings by Place, Lodge and Poole (Illustrations 1, 2, 193–4, 196 and Fig.60) show that it had inner and outer arches and there was an intermediate arch which held doors. The crenellated tower had upper rooms, used for guests. It was decorated with niches for statues of saints, and there was probably provision for heraldic devices displaying the coats of arms of patrons and benefactors. Monastic gatehouses, marking the threshold between secular and religious power, were (like town gateways) 'statements of authority and influence' (Steane 2001, 81), designed to impress the visitor.

On the west side of the gateway is *the lodge*, built c.1470. It contained the abbot's courthouse and prison, and replaced a timber courthouse built in the late 12th century. It continued to function as a courthouse until 1722, when it became the Bay Horse Inn. This was probably when it acquired the steeper hipped tiled roof shown in early 19th-century drawings (Illustrations 197–214; Figs.61–2). In 1840, when it became the house of John Philips, the curator of the newly built Yorkshire Philosophical Society's Museum, a stone parapet was added, restoration work was done on the windows and the interior was modernised. Otherwise it is still largely a 15th-century building.

46

Fig. 57 (facing, top)   Photograph of abbey walls exterior after removal of houses in Marygate. The abbey walls were largely obscured by houses until they became the property of the Yorkshire Philosophical Society in 1877, after which most of those in Marygate were cleared away. This section of wall has been much restored but parts of the 1266 foundations and of the 1318 alterations have survived, built into the houses that remain. This photograph was taken by the city engineers in c.1900. Other houses in Marygate were demolished during the 1930s and properties in Bootham were cleared in the late 19th century and in 1914–15, allowing the abbey walls to be seen. (Imagine York Y9_MAR_3673_A, © City of York Council www.imagineyork.co.uk historic images from York's libraries and archives)

Fig. 58 (facing, bottom)   Photograph of inner side of abbey walls with terraced houses outside. This photograph was taken from the Museum Gardens c.1933. It shows the rear of nos. 7–23 Mary-gate, a row of terraced houses built on to the front of the abbey precinct wall. These houses were demolished in 1937–40. St Mary's Tower can be seen at the right of the picture and the rear of an open-backed turreted tower at left. The bowling green in the foreground was created in 1912. (Imagine York 157_A1C_264, © City of York Council www.imagineyork.co.uk historic images from York's libraries and archives)

Fig. 59   Marygate water tower, incorrectly called St Mary's Tower by Cave in 1813, was built in c.1324 on the west corner of the precinct, guarding the all-important landing on the river bank at the bottom of Marygate. Drawings by Lodge and Place some 100 years earlier than Cave's show the tower still with its original crenellations, but these have gone by 1813. A doorway gives access by a stair to the ruined wall parapet; originally the tower was roofed, leaving room for a wall-walk round the top. This view is looking down Marygate towards the river.

Between the east side of the gatehouse and the Church of St Olave stood the **Chapel of St Mary**, built between c.1314 and 1320. It had two storeys, as shown in views by Place and Poole, c.1705, but the upper storey had gone by 1800 (Fig.61). The chapel, on the upper floor, had a statue of the Virgin Mary and a fine stone screen, part of which is now in the Yorkshire Museum. A *capella ante portam*, or chapel at or outside the gate, was a usual feature in a monastery, and was used by visitors and their servants, women or others not permitted inside the cloister.

The north wall of **St Olave's Church** forms a continuous frontage with the gatehouse and the chapel. The church was rebuilt in the 15th century. The five bays nearest the gateway were built by the monks, and they were also responsible for the upkeep of the chancel. The nave was used as the local parish church, leading to disputes over respective responsibilities – a common feature of medieval life. The church was largely rebuilt in 15th-century style and re-using the old stone, in 1720–22 (see Wilson and Mee 1998, 141–4).

Beyond the church, the line of the precinct wall is interrupted by the remains of a building 22.5m long and 6.4m wide, now built over by a late 18th-century house, no.29 Marygate. The Royal Commission identifies this as the almonry (RCHMY **2**, 167b; RCHMY **4**, 17, 84b). The giving of alms was a duty of all monks, and the St Mary's almoner was required to collect the remnants of each meal taken in the refectory and one loaf in ten from the bakery for distribution to the poor. In winter he must keep a large fire burning to provide them with warmth. The almonry also housed a school for poor boys. In addition, the abbey maintained a boarding house for 50 boys at the minster school, and this is described as also being by the outer gate of the monastery.

Fig. 60 *St Mary's Abbey, gatehouse and lodge, F. Place, c.1700. The gatehouse was begun 1197–99 but the gate was added in the 15th century. Monastic gatehouses often survived the dissolution as they became private houses. Here the lodge continued to house a courtroom on the upper floor and a prison below until 1722. This view from the inner side shows an arched entrance with a crenellated tower that had rooms for guests. There are niches for statues and possibly spaces for coats of arms. Monastic gatehouses were largely for show, and it was common for them to display the arms of founders and benefactors. The building on the right with the smoking chimney has now gone.*

Fig. 61 *St Mary's Abbey Gateway, T. Rowlandson, 1801. In this watercolour painting the gateway has lost all but the outer archway and its flanking walls. The chapel to the right (the chapel of St Mary-at-the-gate) has also gone, but the lodge survives. The land was being used for livestock, as the distinctly bucolic cows show, and farm workers can be seen at bottom left. York Art Gallery also has the original sketch on which this was based, but it is less detailed and less attractive.*

Fig. 62 Entrance to St Mary's Abbey, J. Halfpenny, 1807, showing the gateway and lodge from the outer side. One ruined arch is all that remained of the entranceway into the abbey precincts by the early 19th century, but the lodge still stood, having become the Bay Horse Inn (this has now moved to the other side of Marygate). It has a hipped tile roof, to be changed in 1840 when the lodge became the home of the curator of the Yorkshire Museum.

Fig. 63 St Mary's Tower, incorrectly titled Marygate Tower by H. Cave, 1813. The tower stands at the north corner of the precincts and, as a very distinctive feature of the Bootham approach to the city, was popular with artists. It was built c.1324 but severely damaged by a parliamentarian mine during the Siege of York in 1644. It was subsequently rebuilt with thinner walls, giving an irregular curve. The upper windows are early 17th century, originally parts of a bay window in the King's Manor, and the 17th-century doorway probably also came from the Manor; the ground-floor window contains 15th-century work, presumably from elsewhere in the abbey. The unfortunate join with the abbey walls on the Bootham side was hidden by a house until 1896.

Fig. 64 Detail from 'The Gardens of the Yorkshire Philosophical Society', J. Storey, c.1860. This view across the abbey precinct shows the north-eastern wall running along Bootham (across the top of the picture). Much of the outer side of the precinct wall is still obscured by houses but it shows the archway known as Queen Margaret's Arch (top right) and the lane running between the King's Manor (on the line of the former south-eastern precinct wall of the abbey) and the city wall.

From here to the interval tower (Tower C) the wall has been much restored. Tower C is rectangular and open at the back. It had an upper floor and stood higher than the wall, but it has since been reduced. Between Tower C and St Mary's Tower is one of the best-preserved lengths of wall, still with its 1318 parapet. The wooden shutters are a modern restoration.

St Mary's Tower is a prominent feature on the corner of Marygate and Bootham. It was built c.1324, with strong walls, and stood over 9m high. Internally it is octagonal, and it had two floors (see RCHMY **2**, 169–71, with plan and cross-section). A doorway on the ground floor led to the inner side of the precinct; two doors on the upper floor gave access to the wall-walk, and there was a cruciform arrow slit in the side facing Bootham. A staircase in the thickness of the wall led to a walkway on the top of the tower. Three windows on the north side were taken from a large bay window in the King's Manor in the early 17th century. The 17th-century doorway (Figs.63 and 109) probably also came from the Manor, as did part of the 15th-century ground-floor window which re-used stone from the abbey; these two features were incorporated into the tower as part of the rebuilding undertaken after the siege of 1644.

On 16 June 1644, during the Civil War, the parliamentarian army besieging York 'put into Execution their Hellish Design and ... did blow up Saint Maries Tower at the North-East corner of the Mannor; and at the same time, they made a Battery, and a breach in the Wall, lower down in St Maries Gate, whereat they endeavoured to enter' (Torr 1719, 107). After fierce fighting in the grounds of the King's Manor they were driven out, suffering heavy losses. The tower was subsequently rebuilt with thinner walls. The clumsy ragged join between original and repair work was hidden behind a house until exposed by the clearances of 1896 (Wenham 1970, 57–74).

From St Mary's Tower the abbey wall continues along Bootham, a distance of c.132m. This is the wall of 1255, heightened and strengthened in 1318, when the two interval towers (D and E) were built. The towers are semi-circular on the outer, projecting, side and open at the back. They are of two storeys, with crenellated parapet walks and doorways leading to a former timbered wall-walk. Along this face of the wall the inner edge of the pavement marks the approximate outer line of the defensive ditch.

Until the 19th century virtually all of the outer face of the abbey wall in Marygate and Bootham was hidden by the houses built against it, as is clearly shown in Storey's 'bird's-eye' view of the Yorkshire Philosophical Society's gardens in 1860 (Fig.64). The society began a programme of clearance after it acquired the walls in 1877. The length of wall between the water tower and the gatehouse was cleared and restored by 1895. After 1896 when

Fig. 65 *The Abbey Walls from Bootham, AD –?, E. Ridsdale Tate, 1915. The precinct walls from St Mary's Tower (right) to Queen Margaret's Arch (left), parallel to Bootham, but with the slight change of alignment greatly exaggerated by the artist. This entire stretch of wall was built in 1266 and heightened in 1318. After clearance of some houses from the Marygate walls, the Yorkshire Philosophical Society began the process of clearing the walls in Bootham, and in 1915 Ridsdale Tate produced this drawing to show how the walls had originally appeared and should look in the future. Ridsdale Tate shows much more than the abbey walls (including also the inner side of the precinct walls running down Marygate): Bootham Bar, the De Grey Rooms, Theatre Royal, St Wilfrid's Church, the King's Manor and St Olave's.*

the city council took over responsibility for wall maintenance the process of demolition continued and by 1940 only no.29 remained in Marygate; clearance of the inner side of the wall continued into the 1930s. Gradually, property owners along the Bootham frontage were persuaded to sell, and the sites were cleared. The process was closely monitored by antiquaries and conservationists, and has been recorded in many photographs and drawings (see Figs.57–8). Of particular interest is E. Ridsdale Tate's panoramic view of Bootham, drawn in 1914, showing the appearance of the walls before the accretion of houses and how they might look again (Fig.65). Today only a short row of shops near Queen Margaret's Arch remains, leaving the wall frontage largely visible.

The ***Postern Tower and Gate***, erroneously known as ***Queen Margaret's Arch***, was created for a proposed visit by Henry VII in 1497, not for the visit of his daughter Margaret in 1503. The visit never materialised, but the archway remained, as it provided the abbot with a much more convenient entrance to his lodging than the main gateway in Marygate. The tower is rectangular, some 8m high, and built of brick with ashlar facing. Extra height comes from the tiled hipped roof, probably added in the 17th century when an extra floor was constructed, turning the two storeys into three. There were also 17th-century alterations to the doors and windows and there has been some restoration since: a plain three-light window now replaces the bay window of Edward Bearpark, seedsman, shown in Bedford's view of c.1843 (Fig.66). Hidden by adjoining buildings but visible from the inner side is a cruciform arrow slit with large oeillets (illustrated in RCHMY **2**, 173a). The postern gate has an arch 3.3m high, surmounted by a crenellated wall. A group of buildings adjoining the arch on the south-west side (the ironmongery business of the late James Ward in Bedford's view, and the Bird in Hand public house) were removed for the construction of Exhibition Square in 1879 (Fig.67; Cooper 1897, 19).

The original abbey wall continued for a short way nearer to Bootham Bar, before turning south-west, continuing alongside the city wall to the river near Lendal Tower. It was the ditch here that had caused so much contention between abbey and city (see p.43), and the licence to crenellate of 1318 made an exception of this section of the wall. It had also been specified that the abbey walls must not overtop the city walls. What remains visible today is a stretch of c.18m on the south-east side of the

Fig. 66 Ancient Gateway to the Yorkshire School for the Blind, F. Bedford, 1843. The archway was built in 1497 for the intended visit of Henry VII, and not for that of Queen Margaret in 1503; thereafter it provided the abbot with easy access to the Minster and city from his residence. The shop shown here on the left was taken down in 1878 for the creation of Exhibition Square. Many views of Bootham Bar show the postern and tower from the inner side (see Wilson and Mee 2005, 99–100). The King's Manor was occupied by the School for the Blind from 1833 to 1958.

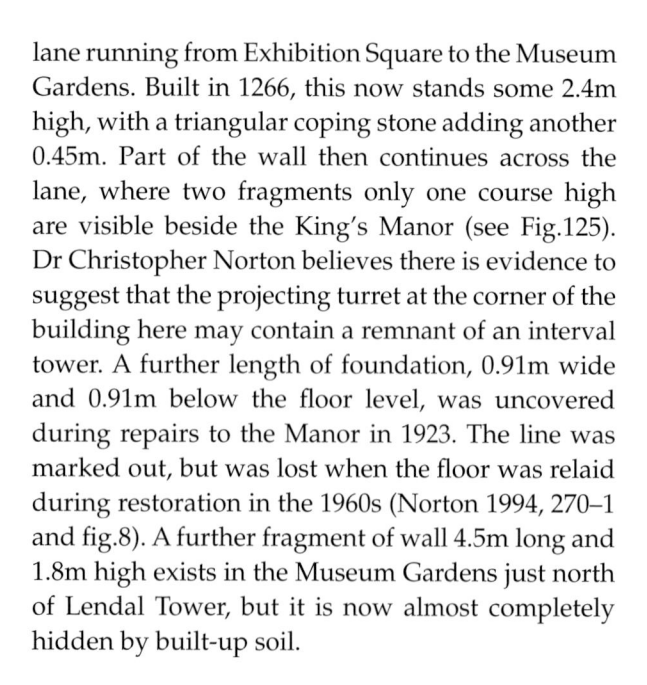

Fig. 67 Men working on the inner side of the abbey precinct wall in Exhibition Square, probably in the 1890s. Just off the picture to the right would be the postern tower and Queen Margaret's Arch. On the other side of the wall is the old White Horse Inn. (Imagine York Y9_11092, © City of York Council www.imagineyork.co.uk historic images from York's libraries and archives)

lane running from Exhibition Square to the Museum Gardens. Built in 1266, this now stands some 2.4m high, with a triangular coping stone adding another 0.45m. Part of the wall then continues across the lane, where two fragments only one course high are visible beside the King's Manor (see Fig.125). Dr Christopher Norton believes there is evidence to suggest that the projecting turret at the corner of the building here may contain a remnant of an interval tower. A further length of foundation, 0.91m wide and 0.91m below the floor level, was uncovered during repairs to the Manor in 1923. The line was marked out, but was lost when the floor was relaid during restoration in the 1960s (Norton 1994, 270–1 and fig.8). A further fragment of wall 4.5m long and 1.8m high exists in the Museum Gardens just north of Lendal Tower, but it is now almost completely hidden by built-up soil.

The wall along the river side of the precinct must have been begun by 24 June 1354, when an agreement declared 'that it shall be lawful for the abbot and convent to make their wall on the said water (of Ouse) in the manner in which it has been commenced' (RCHMY 2, 162). It appears on maps of the city by Speed, who shows it as crenellated (Fig.4), Archer, and therefore Richards (Fig.74), and by Horsley in 1694, but not thereafter. In 1736 Drake commented that 'the foundations of the wall that faces and ran parallel to the river were of late years dug up, which I myself saw run very deep in the ground, and all of Ashlar stone', adding that the material went to repair the staith at Lendal Ferry (Drake 1736, 577). Remains are shown in two early prints, both reproduced in *Eboracum*. An engraving by Place based on a drawing of c.1680 shows a length of somewhat dilapidated wall with an

Fig. 68 Detail from an engraving by William Lodge, showing (from left to right) the still crenellated Marygate water tower, the abbey precinct wall running parallel to the River Ouse, the hospitium with the adjacent water gate behind, and Lendal Tower.

Fig. 69 Detail from west view of the abbey by W.H. Toms, reproduced in Eboracum (published 1736), showing a small part of the southern precinct wall between the hospitium and river bank. Drake comments that the abbey precinct wall along the river had gone by 1736, but part of it was uncovered by archaeologists in the 1980s (see Fig.70).

archway for a path leading down to the river (Fig.68 is a very similar engraving by Lodge). The lithograph by Toms of c.1736 shows a small fragment on the site of the archway (Fig.69). The wall stood back from the river, close to the hospitium and service buildings, but not attached to them. Evidence in the masonry of the Marygate wall suggests that the river wall may have joined it some 4m south-west of Tower A.

Excavation by York Archaeological Trust in 1986 uncovered a stretch of wall foundations, with dressed blocks of limestone on the outer face, a filling of rubble and mortar, and an irregular inner face (Fig.70). Unlike the riverside wall shown on the maps, the real wall did not run in a straight line, so its exact course is uncertain. A further trench uncovered the side wall of the archway shown by Place and Toms (*Interim* **11**/1, 3–13). An excavation undertaken the following year uncovered a paved surface on a bed of mortar over levelling material, part of the sloping paved way which ran from the precinct through the hospitium range and out through the precinct wall to the staith on the Ouse (*Interim* **12**/3, 9–14). The quality of the stonework supported the view that 'to serve the functions of flood defence, security and advertisement of the wealth and prestige of the Abbey to those approaching by river, one would expect a finely-finished face fronting the Ouse'. As the archaeologists added

Fig. 70 Photograph of part of the southern precinct wall (at right) between the hospitium and the river after excavation in the 1980s.

ruefully, however, this also made it attractive to stone-robbers, and nothing remains visible today.

Decline and dissolution

The Dissolution of the Monasteries

The Dissolution of the Monasteries was the formal process between 1536 and 1541 by which Henry VIII disbanded monastic communities in England, Wales and Ireland, and confiscated their property. He was given the authority to do this by the Act of Supremacy of 1534, which made him Supreme Head of the Church in England, and by the Suppression Acts of 1536 and 1539.

In 1534 parliament authorised Thomas Cromwell (and later a commission of laymen) to 'visit' all the monasteries (which included all abbeys, priories and convents), ostensibly to make sure their members were instructed in the new rules for their supervision by the king instead of the pope, but actually to make an inventory of their assets (the *Valor Ecclesiasticus*) and find pretexts for their closure. In the summer of that year, the visitors started their work, and 'preachers' were sent out to deliver sermons from the pulpits of the churches on three themes: the monks and nuns in the monasteries were sinful 'hypocrites' and 'idle drones', who were living lives of luxury and engaging in every kind of sin; they were living off the working people and giving nothing back, representing a serious drain on England's economy; and finally, that if the king received all the property of the monasteries, he would never again need to collect taxes from the people.

Meanwhile, during the autumn of 1535, the visiting commissioners were sending back to Cromwell written reports of all the sexual as well as financial misdemeanours they claimed they had uncovered. A horrified parliament enacted laws in early 1536, allowing the king forcibly to dissolve monasteries with annual incomes of less than £200. The property of the dissolved smaller houses reverted to the Crown, while their monks and nuns were given the option of secularisation or transfer to a continuing larger house of the same order. The majority chose to remain in the religious life. Monastic life had certainly been in decline for some time. By 1536, for example, the thirteen Cistercian houses in Wales housed only 85 monks between them. However, the claims of misbehaviour were greatly exaggerated.

These moves did not raise as much capital as Henry had expected. Government lawyers then established a key legal principle that the head of a religious house was the nominal owner of the monastic property and that if the head were to be convicted of treason, all the property of the abbey would legally revert to the Crown. A further significant development was the voluntary surrender of Lewes priory in 1537, where for the first time the monks were offered life pensions if they co-operated. Abbots and priors came under pressure from communities to offer voluntary surrender, if they could obtain favourable terms for pensions. In 1538 applications for surrender became a flood, and Cromwell appointed local commissioners to encourage rapid compliance with the king's wishes, to supervise the orderly sale of monastic goods and buildings, and to ensure that the monks and nuns were properly provided for with cash and clothing.

In April 1539 Parliament passed a new law legalising acts of voluntary surrender, but by then the vast majority of monasteries had already been dissolved. Some resisted, and that autumn the abbots of Colchester, Glastonbury and Reading were hanged, drawn and quartered for treason. St Benet's Abbey in Norfolk was the only abbey in England which escaped dissolution. Instead Henry VIII exchanged it for lands owned by the Diocese of Norwich. Although it was soon closed and all the buildings except the gatehouse were demolished, the Bishop of Norwich can still claim to be Abbot of St Benet's to this day.

The local commissioners were instructed to ensure that where abbey churches were also used for parish worship this practice should continue. As a result, over 100 monastic churches survive in whole or in part. The most marketable fabric in monastic buildings was the lead from roofs, gutters and plumbing; this, along with building stone and slate roofs, was sold off to the highest bidder. Many monastic outbuildings were turned into granaries, barns and stables.

The Crown became richer to the extent of around £150,000 per year gained from estate rents and profits, and Cromwell had intended that the bulk of this wealth should serve as regular income of government. However, after Cromwell's fall, Henry needed money quickly to fund his military ambitions in France and Scotland, so monastic property was sold off at the market rate of 20 years' income, raising over £1,400,000 by 1547. The purchasers were predominantly leading local magnates and gentry, with no particular bias in terms of Catholic or Protestant opinion.

The decline and dissolution of St Mary's Abbey

The Archbishop of York, Edward Lee, visited St Mary's Abbey on 7 September 1534, and issued his injunctions from Bishopthorpe a year later. He ordered that the Benedictine Rule should be strictly kept, and that offending monks should be duly punished. The abbot was charged with being too familiar with a married woman, Elizabeth Robinson of Overton. He was ordered to abstain from all intercourse with her or any other suspect woman, and to reside always in the monastery. The abbot had tried to refuse entry to the archbishop's men, citing papal exemption from such visitations. Archbishop Lee claimed that the pope no longer had any authority in England, but on appeal to Thomas Cromwell (the king's vicar-general), Abbot Thornton's claim was upheld. The reference in the Archbishop's injunctions of 1535 to Thornton's association with a married woman – which the abbot denied – may have been inspired by personal animosity. Other injunctions stated that the abbot was not to use silk in his hood or sleeves, nor gilt spurs, saddles or bridles. The monks were ordered not to wear worsted or other costly garments, but were to wear habits of cheap material and of the same colour. Wine was not to be sold in the abbey precincts. Once a year the abbot should render an account of the state of the house and his administration of it.

In 1535/36 commissioners were sent to the northern monasteries in the form of Dr Thomas Le[i]gh, conceited, humourless and overbearing, disliked by his associates as much as by his victims, and Dr Richard Layton, a Cumbrian lawyer who held several ecclesiastical livings; he had an overfondness for stories of sexual misconduct, going into Latin for the more salacious bits, and his letters to Cromwell were racy and vivacious. How true they were is open to question. Before his journey he had written to Cromwell: 'There can be no better way to beat the King's authority into the heads of the rude people of the North than to show them that the King intends reformation and correction of religion. They are more superstitious than virtuous, long accustomed to frantic fantasies and ceremonies, which they regard more than either God or their prince, right far inaliate from true religion' (Knowles 1976, 155). The commissioners arrived at St Mary's Abbey on 13 January 1535/36, having already informed Cromwell that 'we suppose to find much evil disposition both in the abbot and the convent'; their report makes no mention of the abbot's conduct, though they found seven homosexual monks whom the Archbishop seems to have missed. In the event, only the lesser religious houses were closed in 1536 and St Mary's was spared, for the time being.

The closure of religious houses was only one of a variety of grievances leading to the rising that became known as the Pilgrimage of Grace, but their restoration was one of the principal aims of its leaders, particularly of Robert Aske who expressed the case with sincerity as well as all the skill of a trained lawyer. The movement quickly gathered support and some 10,000 men entered York, unopposed by the citizens, on 16 October 1536. Here the flamboyant Sir Thomas Percy rode 'gorgeously through the King's Highness' city in complete harness with feathers trimmed as well as he might deck himself at that time', and against the wishes of Robert Aske, he and Oswald Wolsthrope compelled the Abbot of St Mary's to lead the procession carrying his finest cross. Abbot Thornton was himself fairly flamboyant but on this occasion he slipped away at the earliest opportunity, leaving his cross in Pilgrim hands.

Lulled by false promises, the Pilgrimage soon subsided, the rank and file returning home, the leaders rounded up and executed, and by 12 July 1537 Aske's body was hanging in chains from Clifford's Tower. The voluntary surrender of the larger monasteries was soon arranged, aided by the offer of relatively generous pensions to the monks who acceded and by the hanging of a few abbots considered obdurate. Abbot Thornton did not hesitate and St Mary's Abbey came to an end on 26 November 1539, at which time there were 50 monks and the abbot resident. Thornton's plea to Cromwell for its survival was ignored: government orders were that all religious houses were to be destroyed unless they could be 'altered' to become cathedrals or collegiate churches. The proximity of St Mary's to the Minster (and the abbot's relations with the archbishop!) made that impossible, and the Crown acquired the abbey site and estates valued at £2,085 1s 5¾d.

The abbot received a pension of 400 marks (£266 13s 4d) and the manor of Overton, the Prior, Guy Kelsaye, a pension of 20 marks (£13 6s 8d), the other monks amounts ranging from £10 to £5 per annum according to seniority, and a gratuity towards their clothing; they were also allowed to share household goods among themselves. A number of monks were given livings: Guy Kelsaye at Wilby (where he was succeeded by another St Mary's monk, Thomas Pearson) and Thomas Marche at Harghem in Norfolk; three monks at city churches – St Saviour, St Mary Castlegate and St Michael le Belfrey; three locally at Great Ouseburn, Foston and Alne; and Anthony Hicke first at Flamborough then at Argam (Barnwell *et al* 2005, 113–14; Palliser 1971, 12–14). Details are not known for all the ex-religious, but those who could keep their pensions and the income from their benefices would be reasonably comfortable, at least until inflation began to eat them away. For some, the loss of communal life and support, at work, at prayer, in the refectory or informally in the evenings, must have been felt more keenly. The effect of the dissolution on lay parishioners is harder to assess, but the infusion of ex-religious into the parish priesthood probably strengthened Catholic resistance to the spread of Protestantism: only towards the end of the century did a strongly Protestant – indeed Puritan – element begin to take hold.

The abbey had provided work for some 200 servants, whose fate can only be guessed. The

Fig. 71 *House incorporating parts of the abbey, by John Browne, n.d. 'Might I not as well as others have some Profit of the Spoil of the Abbey?' (Michael Sherbrook's father, in reply to his son's question as to why he had bought timber taken from Roche Abbey in 1539; see Sherbrook in YASRS 125 (1959). After the dissolution in 1539 considerable parts of the abbey gradually found their way into local buildings and gardens. This cottage has acquired a window, almost certainly from the abbey, though possibly not from the church, and the porch looks suspiciously ecclesiastical too. The location of this cheerful little building is unfortunately not given.*

term 'servant' had wider implications than today, and in an institution like St Mary's would include those involved in building and maintenance, catering and management, some with specialist skills. In 1539 York had been in economic decline for almost a century and alternative occupations would be hard to come by. However, the repairs and alterations to the abbot's house, now known as the King's Manor, first in preparation for the visit of Henry VIII and Catherine Howard in 1541, and later for the permanent establishment there of the Council in the North, went some way towards alleviating the situation (Reid 1921, 188–9; Palliser 1979, 262–3). There was also some loss to learning, as the boarding house 'by the outer gate of the monastery' for 50 poor scholars of the minster school was closed down, and of the monastic library only 30 books are known to remain (Palliser 1971, 16; Ker 1964, 217–18).

Shortly after the dissolution the abbey ruins were used as a quarry (see Fig.71). The bells were taken down in 1541–42 and by the time of a survey made in c.1545 (see p.68) the entire church was roofless, as were some other buildings including the dormitory and refectory (Norton 1994, 273). The roofs would have been deliberately stripped of their valuable lead on the orders of the Court of Augmentations, keen to raise as much money as possible from the sale of materials. In October 1550 the Court of Augmentations ordered that timber, iron, glass, gravestones and brass should also be removed and sold.

Nevertheless, there were substantial remains of the abbey buildings, besides those of the King's Manor, in the time of James I: the church walls and steeple were standing, though the roof had been destroyed; the gatehouse was in a good state although the courthouse needed repair; and the frater, dorter, conventual kitchen, abbot's kitchen, privy dorter, infirmary and other buildings remained, although all were in need of extensive repairs. It was the Earl of Strafford, Lord President of the Council in the North from 1628–41, who was responsible for the removal of most of the original monastic buildings. In 1692 the abbey site was leased to Robert Waller (Lord Mayor of York) for 31 years and, later, to Sir William Robinson.

During the 18th century much stone was removed from the abbey ruins for building elsewhere: in 1701 for the York county gaol; in 1705 for St Olave's Church; between 1717 and 1720 for Beverley Minster; and about 1736 for the landing stage of Lendal Ferry. Most of the site was occupied by pasture and gardens in 1736.

The Yorkshire Philosophical Society

The YPS was formed in 1822 to pursue the study of natural sciences, and to combine the private collections of individual members. In 1828 the Society received a royal grant of the abbey ruins and 3 acres of grounds now known as 'the Museum Gardens' on which to build a museum to house its collections and create a botanic garden. The site was, by the standards of the day, carefully excavated and the Society built the Yorkshire Museum in 1829 to designs by William Wilkins (see Figs.72, 73 and 110). The museum, covering the site of buildings to the south and east of the abbey cloisters, was opened in 1830. In 1836 the society purchased a further 5 acres of the site, together with the abbey wall from the Ouse to the main gateway; it then owned most of the site of the abbey church, together with the gatehouse, hospitium, and river tower. Restoration work was carried out on these buildings in subsequent years. Another 3 acres of the abbey site were leased from the Crown in 1862 and in turn let to other tenants; part of this new acquisition was exchanged for the site of the choir of the abbey church which had been leased by the Crown to the Yorkshire School for the Blind as part of the King's Manor. In 1877 the abbey wall from St Olave's Church to the abbey postern was granted to the society.

The British Association for the Advancement of Science was founded with the help of the Society and had its inaugural meeting at the Yorkshire Museum in 1831. This was quickly followed by the building of an astronomical observatory in the Gardens. The Tempest Anderson Hall was added to the Museum in 1912 as a bequest of the vulcanologist, Dr Tempest Anderson, to provide adequate facilities for scientific lectures. The hall covered the remains of the vestibule to the chapter house which are preserved *in situ* in a basement below.

At various dates the Society bought property adjoining the abbey wall and towers in order to expose and preserve them; in 1896 the corporation assumed responsibility for the upkeep of the entire abbey wall, with the exception of the main gatehouse. Further excavation of the church was carried

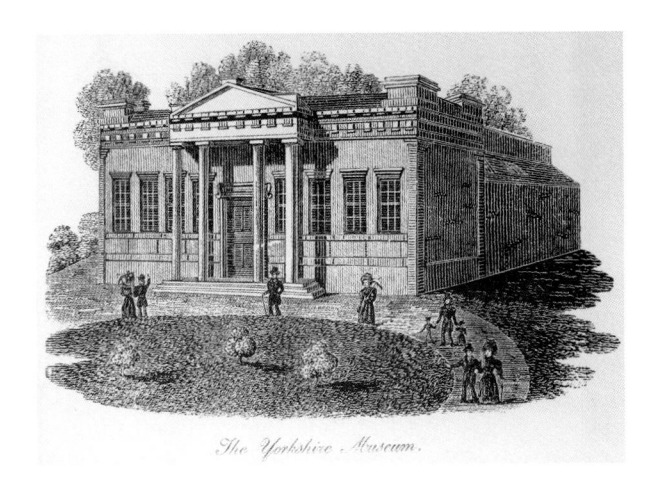

Fig. 72 The Yorkshire Museum, H. and W. Brown, 1836. The museum was built 1827–29 to a design by William Wilkins, who deliberately avoided the fashionable Gothic and chose a Greek Doric design, as York had enough real Gothic to make 'any design in the same style … appear trifling' (Pevsner and Neave 1995). The building cost £6,869. Henry and William Brown's wood engraving gives clear detail of the building.

Fig. 73 Gateway to the Yorkshire Museum, H. and W. Brown, 1836. The gateway with its Doric columns was erected c.1830 and may also have been designed by William Wilkins. It forms a more impressive entrance to the Museum Gardens than its successor of c.1880. The Gothic Lodge was built at the same time as the replacement gateway.

out in 1900–02, 1912–13, 1944 and 1952–56. The church ruins and hospitium were in 1928 and 1929 inspected by the Office of Works, which carried out renovation work in subsequent years. In 1960 the Society handed the Museum and Gardens to the City of York in trust, but continued to take an interest in them, as well as pursuing its objective of keeping members and the general public aware of scientific matters.

Today the ruins of the Gothic abbey church rise above the sloping lawns of the Museum Gardens; these gardens are now managed by York Museums Trust. Other ruins of the abbey are located in the lower-level rooms of the Yorkshire Museum, along with displays about the abbey. On the lower ground near the river a group of buildings including granaries, stables, a bakehouse, a brewhouse, a mill, a fish house and a tailor's workshop once stood. All that remains is part of a 15th-century water gate and a two-storied 13th-century building, now called the hospitium, which has a stone-built lower floor and an upper storey, probably the oldest timber-framed structure in York.

History of the archaeology of St Mary's Abbey

The abbey church was never buried under demolition debris because it remained in royal hands rather than being sold off into private ownership; stone was removed, but more slowly than was the case in other monastic institutions (Norton 1994, 271–5). As a result it was possible for antiquaries to produce ground plans of the church even without excavation. Francis Place, the artist, lived at the King's Manor from 1692 and is recorded as having 'taken pains to trace and measure out the dimensions of the abbey church'. In 1736 Francis Drake published an 'ichnography' or plan of the abbey church in his magisterial history of York, *Eboracum*. There is quite a collection of notes, descriptions, drawings and plans of the abbey from the late 17th century onwards but the first systematic study of the medieval remains did not take place until excavations were carried out by the Yorkshire Philosophical Society on and around the site of their new museum in 1827–29.

These were the first large-scale monastic excavations in the country to be extensively published. Ten illustrations, mostly by F. Nash, were quickly printed in 1829, followed by text by Charles Wellbeloved in 1835 (see Figs.5, 12, 13, 17, 32, 36, 42–5, 102–3). Detailed measured drawings were also made at the time by Eustachius Strickland; these can be seen at the Yorkshire Museum. The early 19th-century excavations uncovered the entire claustral complex and some of the adjacent buildings, but in the church only the transept and easternmost pier of the south nave arcade were excavated and thoroughly recorded. The foundations of the east end were almost at surface level so required little investigation. During the laying out of a path across the nave a set of life-size stone figures was discovered (see Figs.36–8).

In the 20th century there have been other small-scale excavations, mostly within the abbey church (Norton 1994, fig.1). Walter Brierley, the architect, exposed much of the eastern end of the church in 1900–02 (Brierley 1900; 1901; 1902). In 1912–13 Harvey Brook and Ridsdale Tate revealed the rest of the east end apart from its south wall, and re-excavated the north-west corner of the cloister adjacent to the new Tempest Anderson Hall which was built on to the Yorkshire Museum. In 1944 the architect Stuart Syme and the Rev. Angelo Raine, the historian of medieval York, excavated around the foundations of the easternmost pier of the south nave arcade and explored the foundations at the west end (Syme and Raine 1944). From 1952 to 1956 George Willmot, Keeper of the Yorkshire Museum, excavated the western bays of the nave, the adjoining north walk of the cloister and the north end of the west claustral range, although the results were never fully published. In the last quarter of the 20th century building work in various parts of the abbey precincts has revealed small parts of the medieval buildings; these have been recorded and in some cases excavated by York Archaeological Trust (YAT site code 1984.6, *Interim* **10**/1; 1985.6; 1985.10, *Interim* **10**/4 and **11**/1; 1986.19, *Interim* **12**/1; 1988–89.18, *Interim* **13**/4; 1989.2; 1994.0197; 2000.2404). Parts of the medieval drainage system for the abbey (see Figs.39–40), some building foundations, and a section of the riverside precinct wall (see Fig.70) were uncovered during these excavations, as well as a burial, possibly of medieval date, close to the passage between the south transept of the abbey church and the chapter house vestibule.

Abbots of St Mary's Abbey (1082–1539)

Stephen	1082–1112
Richard	occurs 1112
Gotfrid	occurs 1122 and 1128, d.1132
Savaricus/Savarinus	1132–1161
Clement	1161–1184
Robert de Harpham	1184–1189
Robert de Longchamp	1189–1197 (deposed)
Robert	1197–1239 (possibly Longchamp reinstated)
William de Roundell	occurs 1241, d.1244
Thomas de Waterhill	1244–1258
Simon de Warwick	1258–1296
(Three-year interval)	
Benedict de Malton	1299–1303 (resigned)
John Gilling	1303–1313
Alan de Nesse	1313–1331
Thomas de Malton	1331–1359
William Mareys	occurs 1380, d.1382
William Bridford	1382–1389
Thomas Stayngrave	1389–1398
Thomas Pigott	1398–1405
Thomas de Spofforth	1405–1421 (resigned to become Bishop of Hereford 1422; buried in St Mary's Abbey)
William Dalton	1422–1423
William Wells	1423–1436 (resigned to become Bishop of Rochester)
Roger Kirkby	1437–1438
John Cottingham	1438–1464 (former Prior of St Mary's Abbey)
Thomas Booth	1464–1485
William Sever	1485–1502 (became Bishop of Carlisle, then Durham)
Roger Wanhope	1502–1507
Edmund Thornton	1507–1521
Edmund Whalley	1521–1530
William Thornton *alias* **Dent**	1530–1539 (surrendered the abbey)

The King's Manor

History

The vast irregular pile of building distinguished by the name of The King's Manor ... stands within the enceinte of the dissolved Benedictine Abbey of St Mary, near the walls of the city of York. A considerable portion of the edifice occupies the site of the abbatial house of that once celebrated and wealthy monastery – the house in which the princely lord abbot held his state, and dispensed his hospitalities to the many royal and noble personages who at various times were lodged beneath his roof.
(Davies 1883, 3)

The residence of the Abbot of St Mary's was placed to the south-east of the church, close to the chapter house and the parts of the abbey where the abbot's presence was most often needed (Fig.74).

Originally built by Abbot Simon de Warwick in c.1270, it was rebuilt in brick by William Sever, abbot from 1485 to 1502. The main rooms were on the first floor: the abbot's private apartments on the north side, a hall in the central wing, and services in the southern wing.

In 1539 the abbey shared the fate of all religious houses in England, Wales and Ireland, and was suppressed and despoiled. It was the usual practice, however, for the abbot's house to be spared and to be given to whoever was granted the dissolved monastery by the Crown. Before this could happen in York, within a few months of the dissolution of St Mary's, the King's Council in the Northern Parts (the Council in the North), which in 1537 had been permanently constituted by a royal commission, was given permission by the king to take over the abbot's lodgings and to hold its courts and conduct its official busi-

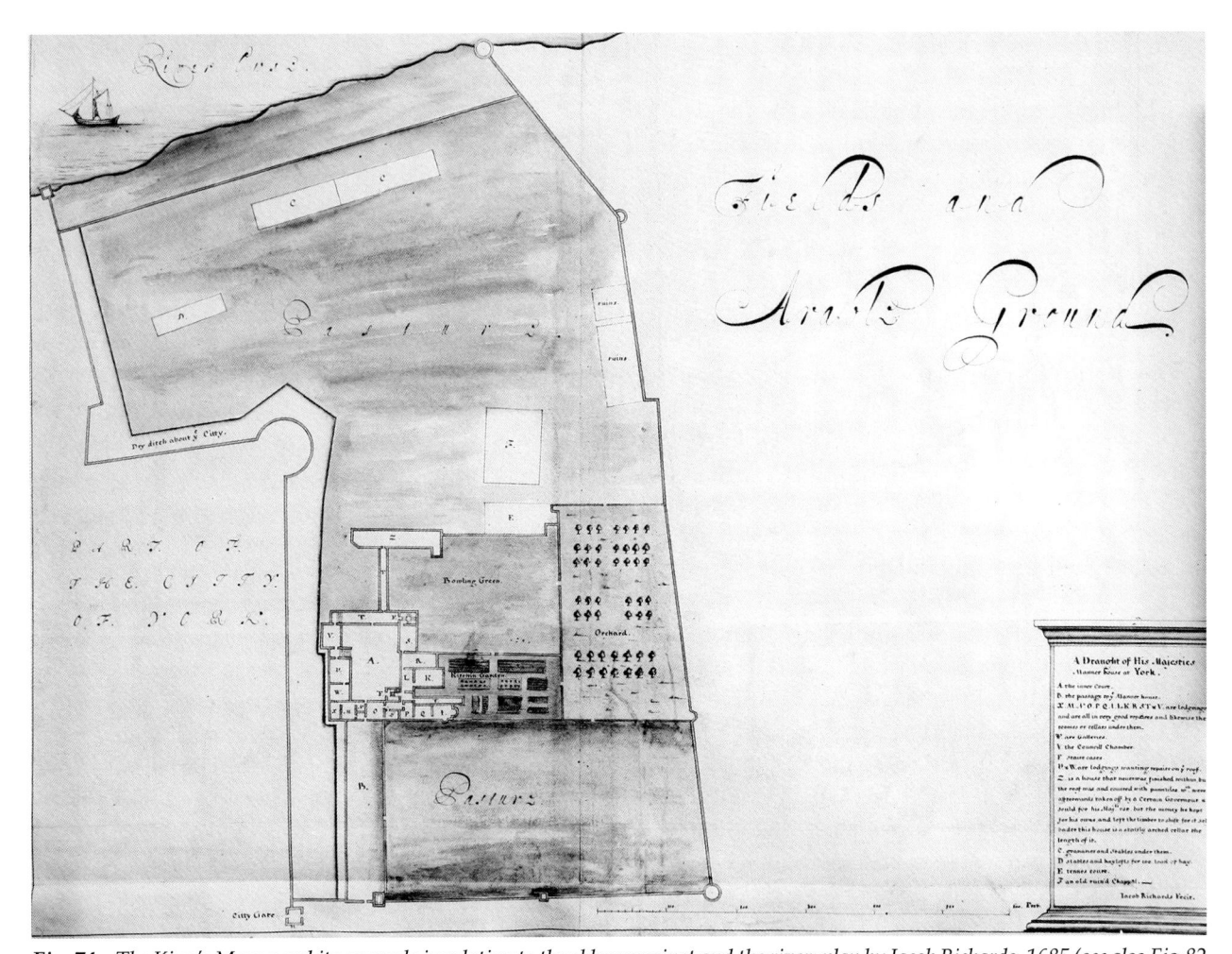

Fig. 74 The King's Manor and its grounds in relation to the abbey precinct and the river: plan by Jacob Richards, 1685 (see also Fig.82 and Fig.123).

ness there. The Lord President was to reside there on occasions, along with members of the council whose duties required them to be on the spot.

Originally set up by Richard III in 1484, the King's Council in the North was re-established by Henry VIII in 1522. The council was a legal body which had three main roles: bringing criminals to justice, hearing cases about debts and other civil offences, and the enforcement of religious observance. It covered an area including Yorkshire, Durham, Northumberland and Cumberland, and had a staff of more than 300. At its busiest the Council dealt with 2,000 cases a year. The Council in the North remained powerful until the end of the 16th century.

In order to emphasise Crown ownership and to erase all memory of its disgraced former occupants, the building was immediately given the name the King's Manor. Successive presidents altered and extended the abbot's house westwards towards the river until the abolition of the Council in 1641.

The first Lord President of the North who, with the executive members of his council, was lodged in the King's Manor was Robert Holgate, Bishop of Llandaff, later Archbishop of York. He was Lord President from 1538 until 1549. Soon after appointing Holgate as Lord President, Henry VIII announced his intention of making a progress to the North, staying for a while in York, and in September 1541 he and Catherine Howard resided at the King's Manor for twelve days. The accounts of Leonard Beckwith, receiver of the revenues of the lands of the dissolved monasteries in Yorkshire, show that over £8 was spent on 'cleansing' the house before the king's arrival, and £400 was spent on 'repairing and beautifying' the building.

During its first 30 years the King's Manor did not undergo any major alteration. In 1561, however, it became the official residence of the President of the Council, and in 1568 Thomas Radcliffe, Earl of Sussex, authorised alterations to the buildings. The repairs and new building work, which eventually cost almost £600, began in November 1568 and took eighteen months to complete. Stone from St Mary's Abbey was re-used in the Manor.

The Earl of Sussex resigned from the presidency in 1572 and was succeeded by Henry Hastings, 3rd Earl of Huntingdon, who retained the post until his death at the King's Manor in December 1595. It was during his presidency that the large and stately brick buildings, standing on the north-west side of the King's Manor, were erected adjacent to the abbot's house. The Earl of Huntingdon and his wife spent several months each year at the King's Manor. The abbot's house was found to be inadequate for the accommodation of the Lord President and his family, and members of the executive council and their officers. The new buildings erected at this time, extending the Manor westwards with residential wings and a service building, were purpose-built to meet the requirements of the Council in the North.

In 1599 Thomas Cecil, Lord Burghley, was appointed president. He lived at the King's Manor and it was there that he received James of Scotland as King James I of England in 1603 after the death of Queen Elizabeth. Soon after this, Burghley ceased to be Lord President and was succeeded in that office by Edmund, Lord Sheffield. During the sixteen years of Sheffield's presidency important additions were made to the buildings of the King's Manor.

In September 1609 Lord Sheffield applied to the Exchequer for a grant of 500 marks a year for repairs to the King's Manor and Sheriff Hutton Castle. The Lord Treasurer demanded an estimate be made of the cost of repairs necessary to restore the King's Manor to the same condition as when the Earl of Huntingdon was Lord President. The estimate was made in December 1609 and constitutes valuable documentary evidence of the extent of the buildings of the King's Manor as they were left by the Earl of Huntingdon. The rooms listed in this document were:

the Greate Chamber, the dyning and Drawing Chamber; Seaven Chambers over the great chamber, dyning and drawing chambers; the north Galleryes with iiij chambers to the east end, and vaults and parlours under them; Galloreys next the Cloister, with iiij chambers at the east end thereof, and five parlours under; the old hall, kitching and paistry etc. 6 roomes; Seaven chambers under the east end of the hall; the larders, with iij chambers over them; the granary, baikhouse, brewhouse, and stables; the new Kitchinge; the parlours, and the chambers at the north end of the Tennys Courte; the parlour and chamber next the garden; the gatehouse and viij parlours and chambers.

All the material required for repairs (*lead, sowlder, tymber, plaster, lyme, lattes, pavinge tyle, casements, doores, tyles, iron* and *glass*) is itemised and costed. The workmen required to undertake the work are listed (*plummer, bricklaer, carpinter* and *plasterer*) and an estimate of the cost is supplied. In addition to the repairs of the above rooms, there is an item listed as 'the building of a new Hall'.

The total cost of materials and labour is given as £758 19s 4d and Henry Busy who signs the document notes, 'I have perused thes particulars and doe fynd both the materials and workmanship, with the rest of the waiges, very reasonable'.

Work did not begin immediately, however, as it was not until June 1611 that the Treasury approved the estimate and another five years were to pass before Lord Sheffield obtained a grant of £1000 towards the expenses he had then incurred. By the time Lord Sheffield sent the Treasury an account of his expenses on the King's Manor in August 1624 they had escalated to £3301 4s. It must be assumed that a large part of this was spent not on the repairs listed in the estimate but on the erection of the large building which now forms the southern side of the western courtyard.

In December 1628 Thomas Viscount Wentworth, later Earl of Strafford, became head of the Council in the North and for much of the first four years of his presidency he and his family lived at the King's Manor. Early in 1633 he was appointed by Charles I as Lord Deputy of Ireland and went to London to prepare for his new duties. During Wentworth's time in London, the king came to York and stayed at the King's Manor. Writing from London in May to the Earl of Carlisle, who was in York with the king, Wentworth says, 'The house you will find much amended since my coming to it, and one thousand pounds more to build a gallery and chapel in that place where you may perceive I intend it, will make it very commodious'. The position of the gallery and chapel built during Lord Wentworth's presidency seems to be indicated by the stone heraldic achievement placed over the doorway on the west side of the eastern courtyard (Fig.81). 'Lord Strafford is charged with unbecoming arrogance in putting up his own arms in one of the king's palaces, and it is popularly but erroneously believed that this was the subject of one of the articles of impeachment against him' (Davies 1883, 10).

Wentworth spent the next three years in Ireland and it was not until the summer of 1636 that he was again able to spend some time at the King's Manor. It may have been at this time that he completed the gallery and chapel. A letter from Wentworth dated August 1639 certainly suggests that by then the chapel was completed and used for worship: 'In the mean time there is a *Gloria Patri* sung at St Mary's Abbey, so as the pillars in that kitchen now may hope to have the honour to become the pillars again of a church, as formerly they were'.

Wentworth spent another three years in Ireland from November 1636 and during his absence the buildings were probably neglected. This may account for the tragic accident that befell the eldest

Fig. 75 *The south, or main doorway on the east front, 1610, etched with great clarity by Joseph Halfpenny, incorporating at its base the initials of James I (IR). It is surmounted by Strafford's addition of the arms of Charles I ('not an improvement' according to Hutchinson and Palliser 1980, 151). The wall and door beyond the archway are somewhat mysterious, though there is also a hint of them in Harper's view (Fig.78).*

son of Sir Edward Osborne, Vice-President of the Council. In October 1638 'the wind blew down with great violence 7 chimneys shafts upon the roof of that chamber in the Mannor House where he was at study, and by the fall of them all the rotten piece of building was beat down, wherein he was found dead and buried in a heap of rubbish' (Davies 1883, 11).

In spring 1639 King Charles I, while on his way north, spent a month in York, staying in the King's Manor. In January 1640 Wentworth was created Earl of Strafford and Lord Lieutenant of Ireland. In August 'the turbulence of the Scots' again brought the Court to York and both the king and Strafford stayed at the Manor for the last time. Both returned to London at the end of October after the English forces had been defeated by the Scots. Parliament was assembled on 3 November and in May 1641 Strafford was executed. Shortly before his execution, the Court of the Great Council in the North was abolished.

In November 1641 the king, accompanied by the Prince of Wales, spent two nights in York on his way north. They were entertained by Sir Arthur Ingram at his house in the Minster Yard, the Manor probably being dismantled and unfit for their reception. During the king's long and last visit to York in the spring and summer of 1642 he again stayed with Ingram rather than at the Manor.

Soon after the abolition of the Council in the North, the King's Manor was committed to the charge of an officer styled with typical verbosity 'the Keeper of the House within the site of the late Monastery of the Blessed Mary near the Walls of the city of York, otherwise called the Pallas, or manor House, or the Mannor Place'. The first keeper was Christopher Stevenson, and he was succeeded in October 1643 by John Stainforth, who was awarded a salary of £6 13s 4d pa.

After the battle of Marston Moor, when the parliamentary army took control of York, Stainforth was removed from his office and the Manor House came into the possession of Colonel Robert Lilburne, one of the king's judges, who during the Protectorate was granted authority over York and later took over command of the army in Yorkshire. For the first few years after the restoration of the monarchy in 1660 there were disputes between rival claimants to the post of keeper of the house but Charles II later appointed a governor over the city and the Manor House became the residence of John, Lord Frescheville, the first Governor. Upon his death in 1682 Sir John Reresby, then MP for York, was appointed his successor. On the accession of James II the King's Manor narrowly avoided being converted into a Roman Catholic college. In December 1687 Father Lawson appeared at the Manor in person and claimed possession of it 'for the honour of God', in spite of Sir John's protestations to the Treasury that the Manor 'was worth £60 a year to him, and that it had cost him above £200 in repairs since he had enjoyed it' (Davies 1883, 15). James II actually leased the Manor to Henry Lawson for 31 years at the annual rent of 10s.

Francis Drake records in *Eboracum* that 'In the unfortunate reign of King James the Second a large room in the Manor [the council chamber according to Torr 1719, 130] was fitted up and made use of as a popish chapel, where one Bishop Smith, as he was called, celebrated mass openly. But it was not long before the enraged populace pulled it to pieces' (Drake 1736, 574). Another York annalist states that in November 1688, a few days after the landing of the Protestant William of Orange, 'The mob of the city pulled down all the new erected popish chapels and fell on plundering several private houses of papists'.

Any hope the Catholics might have had of forming a religious seminary at York was extinguished by the Glorious Revolution. The grant made by James II was annulled and possession of the King's Manor, along with the adjacent ruins of St Mary's Abbey, returned to the Crown. In 1692 a lease for the entire estate was granted by the Treasury to Robert Waller, an alderman and former lord mayor of York, for the term of 31 years at the annual rent of 10s. In 1690 Waller was elected one of the city's MPs and doubtless gained the lease of the Manor property as a reward for his support of the new Protestant government.

Alderman Waller soon converted a large part of the Manor into separate apartments, which he let to 'respectable tenants'. Other parts were let as workshops or warehouses. In 1696 a mint for coining silver money was set up in some of the rooms, and continued in operation for two years. Drake states that the large hall, once consecrated as a place of Roman Catholic worship, was converted into an assembly room for the nobility and gentry attending the races, and was also used as an entertaining room for the high sheriffs at the assizes (Drake 1736, 575).

From 1712 another part was occupied as a boarding school (Mr Lumley's Boarding School for Young Ladies) which continued to function until 1835. Henry Cave was drawing master at this school and produced a fine painting of the King's Manor c.1822 (see Fig.87). In 1813 the Manor National School, a voluntary elementary school for 440 boys, was opened in the King's Manor.

The Yorkshire School for the Blind, located in the King's Manor, was founded in 1833 in memory of William Wilberforce, who had represented Yorkshire as an MP for 28 years and died in 1833 (Fig.76). The school, for the education and training of 80 pupils, male and female, between the ages of ten and twenty, taught all the usual subjects of an elementary education, as well as Braille, handicrafts and music. There was also an outmates department, founded in 1861, to give employment in basket and brush making to fourteen former pupils after they had left the school. The goods produced were sold from a shop at the school, and by the 1870s sales stood at over £800.

Davies, writing at the end of the 19th century, concludes, 'I need not dwell upon the modern history of The King's Manor. We may rejoice that this interesting edifice, dignified as it is by so many stirring associations, has suffered but little injury in its external aspect from the many changes it has experienced, and that it still exists to adorn our venerable city' (Davies 1883, 17).

From the 1870s the Manor was gradually restored and enlarged by the architects J.B. and W. Atkinson and Walter Brierley. In the 1890s they built a gymnasium and a cloister to create the second (western) courtyard. The principal's house, now home to York University's Centre for Medieval Studies, was built in 1900. On the departure of the School for the

Fig. 76 *Entrance to Huntingdon Room by A. Buckle, 1883. A first-floor inner doorway of the north-east wing, leading to the Huntingdon Room from an ante room. In 1883 it was part of the School for the Blind, hence the benches and desks.*

Blind in 1958 to purpose-built premises on Tadcaster Road, the Manor was acquired by York City Council, which leased it to the University in 1963. The University used it to house the Institute for Advanced Architectural Studies. A major restoration by Feilden & Mawson swept away many service buildings and replaced the 1880s schoolroom with a modern tutorial block, now occupied by the University's Department of Archaeology. The 17th-century council chamber is now the Refectory.

Architectural development and layout

The abbot's house stood east of the St Mary's Abbey cloisters. The surviving parts are now incorporated within the King's Manor, which is built around two courtyards. The various parts of the building are identified by the letters A to K on Fig.125 (based on the plans in the back pocket of RCHMY 4). For clarity and ease of description, the buildings are described as though they lay on an east–west axis corresponding to the liturgical east–west of the abbey.

Late 13th century

The first house on the site was almost certainly built c.1270 for Abbot Simon de Warwick. Late 13th-century plinth mouldings, similar to those of the abbey church, still exist and suggest that the house consisted of three wings (making it U-shaped) and occupied the same footprint as the later medieval rebuilding (Fig.77, c.1290). The surviving 13th-century work is of white magnesian limestone and is confined to the ground floor. It probably represents a stone-built lower storey which had timber-framing above, similar to the abbey's hospitium. These were the buildings occupied by the Lord Chancellor from 1316 until 1337.

Late 15th century

As it now exists, this oldest part of the King's Manor is mostly a rebuilding of the late 15th century (Fig.77, c.1500). In September 1483 Abbot Thomas Booth was given a Crown licence to retain Richard Cheryholme, a bricklayer, and his four servants 'as long as it should please him' (RCHMY 4, 30). The building work was continued by Abbot William Sever (1485–1502). The new walls were all of brick above a stone plinth. The windows were framed in terracotta under brick labels and relieving arches, possibly the earliest use of terracotta in England. The late 15th-century house faced inwards towards a courtyard enclosed on three sides but open to the west. Floors and roofs of this period remain in the side ranges (B and C; RCHMY 4, pl.63). Abbot Sever placed an external gallery at first-floor level on all three sides of the eastern courtyard; corbels for its pentice roof survive on the east and south.

Mid-16th century

Immediately after the dissolution, when the abbot's lodging became home to the Council in the North, little work needed to be done other than minor repairs. More expense was required in 1541 when Henry VIII and Catherine Howard visited York and stayed at the King's Manor for twelve days (Drake 1736, 128); two windows set in re-used ashlar may be of this date.

Davies states that the king stayed in a hastily erected palace between the abbot's house and the river, which was ruined a few years later (Davies 1883, 4–5). Foundations that could belong to this building (Fig.125, K) have been uncovered by excavation (Wellbeloved 1829, 9, 11, 14) but its architectural features suggest that it actually dates to c.1600–20.

A survey made just before Henry VIII's death in 1547 shows that many of the abbey buildings still remained. The abbot's house is not specifically mentioned but it may be represented by a block of habitable rooms listed as 'the hall, the chapell, the great chamber, the chamber over the great chamber, two litill chambers, a privie kitchen, two chambers over it, all under one roof covered with leade' and measuring 34 yards (31m) long and 14 yards (12.8m) wide (PRO, E 101/510/17; Norton 1994, 279). This seems likely since the main late 15th-century east range (Fig.125, A) is 31.4m long inside. The outer, eastern, face of this range is the façade of the Manor which can be seen today from Exhibition Square.

Later 16th century

In 1562 it was suggested that a meeting between Queen Elizabeth and Mary Queen of Scots might be held at the King's Manor. The Lord President at that time, the Earl of Rutland, told William Cecil that the palace was not fit for the purpose 'as it has been so defaced that only one large chamber remains'. New building had begun, Rutland receiving £380 for the work between 1561 and 1563. The new building (Fig.125, E) continued the main east range of the medieval house to the north (Fig.77, c.1600). In September 1570 Thomas Radcliffe, 3rd Earl of Sussex (President 1568–72), was granted more money to complete the building, which had not yet been

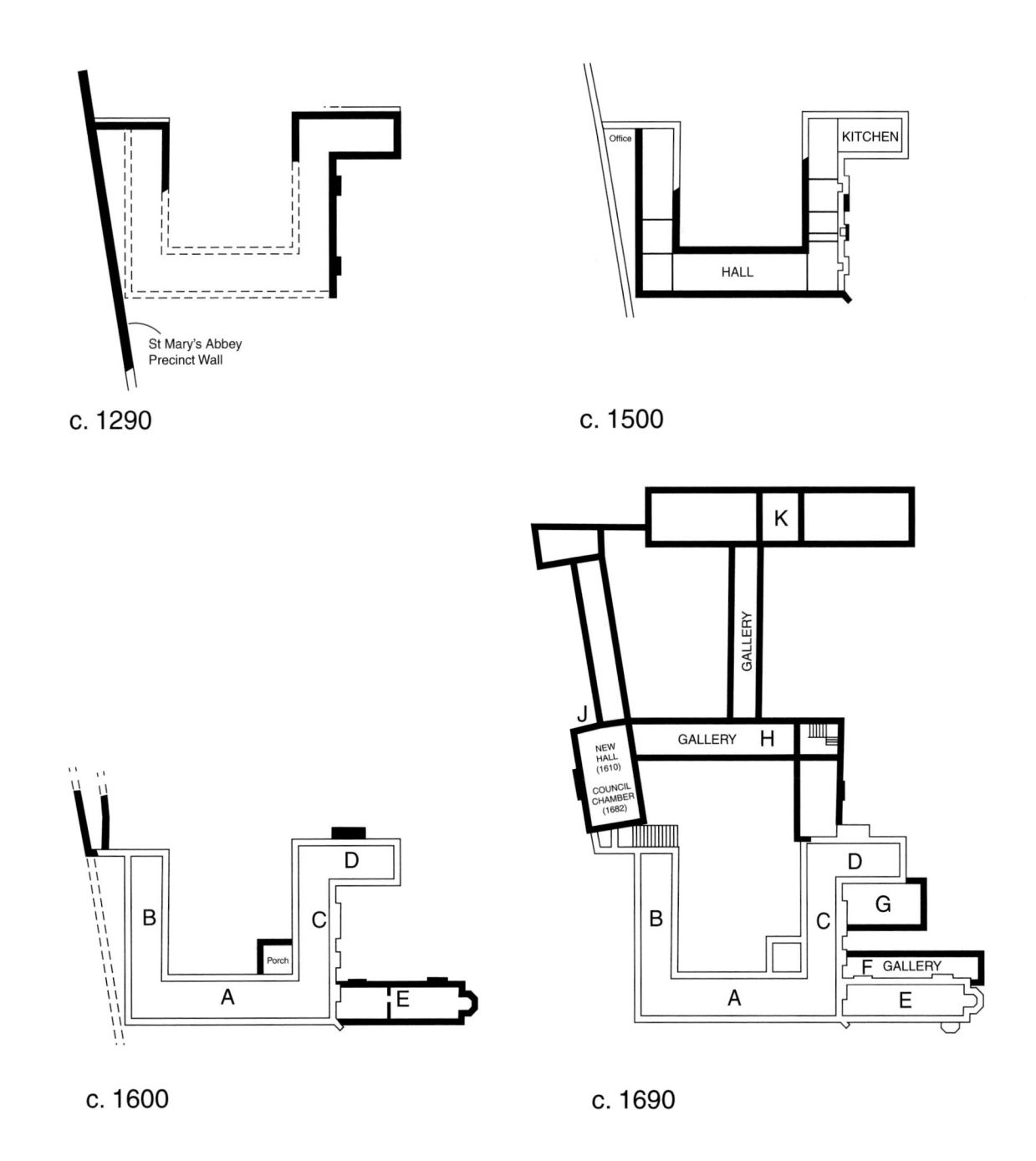

Fig. 77 Plans showing the development of the King's Manor over time (solid black shows new work of a particular period)

roofed and was 'in danger of falling, as the rain has already begun to pierce it'. In all, Radcliffe spent over £400 on the house and was authorised to take 100 oaks from the Forest of Galtres. In addition to the new building, many of the medieval windows were replaced at this time with brick plastered to simulate stone. At the same time a porch was built in the north-east corner of the courtyard, re-using sections of a 13th-century plinth (Fig.77, c.1600; RCHMY 4, pl.57).

The next Lord President, Henry Hastings, Earl of Huntingdon (President 1572–95) created a council chamber on the first floor (RCHMY 4, pl.64), partly in the west end of the north range of the medieval building (Fig.125, C) and partly over the adjoining medieval kitchen (Fig.125, D). A frieze in this council chamber (now known as the Huntingdon Room; Figs.76 and 88) contains Huntingdon's own crest (RCHMY 4, pl.65). The bay window of this room is probably of the same period. In addition,

Fig. 78 Harper's watercolour of 1840 shows the main (south) entrance on the east front with the initials of James I and the arms of Charles I.

Huntingdon erected a building along the south precinct wall of the abbey; evidence of this work can be seen in the undercroft of the south range (Fig.77, c.1600; Fig.125, J).

Early 17th century

In September 1609 Edmund, Lord Sheffield (President 1603–19), applied to the Exchequer for 500 marks a year to repair the King's Manor and Sheriff Hutton Castle. He was asked to produce an estimate, which was supplied in December 1609 and gives details of the buildings already existing. It recommended that work should be done to the great chamber, the dining chamber, the drawing chamber, and the seven chambers above them. It is interesting to learn that the main rooms were on the ground floor. These were probably on the east and south sides of the medieval house (Fig.125, A and B). Work was also needed on the north galleries, with four chambers at the east end and vaults and parlours beneath them (probably the north range of 1570; Fig.125, E); the galleries next to the cloister, with four chambers at the east end and five parlours beneath them (probably the north medieval range; Fig.125, C); the old hall kitchen (the west end of the north medieval range; Fig.125, C); the larders with three chambers over them, the granary, bakehouse, brewhouse and stables (probably removed). A new kitchen and hall were also proposed (the south range; Fig.125, J; Fig.77, c.1690).

The estimate totalled £758 19s 4d and in June 1610 it was approved by the Surveyor of the King's Works, though Sheffield did not receive any money to pay for the work until July 1616. In 1616/17 Sheffield received £3000 for work done (the cost of building work escalated even in the early 17th century!). Buildings erected for Lord Sheffield (Fig.77, c.1690) included the inner north range (Fig.125, F), which almost doubled the width of the 1570 range; the central north block (Fig.125, G); and the outer west range (Fig.125, K). The building of a new hall was a major undertaking, probably a remodelling of Lord Huntingdon's south range. Sheffield was also responsible for linking this new hall to the original north range by a single-storey gallery which now forms the lower storey of the central range (Fig.125, H; Fig.77, c.1690) (RCHMY 4, pl.69). He also created

Fig. 79 Palace of the Stuart Kings by Piper, 1895. A view from the present Exhibition Square which is unusual in showing the two doorways in the east frontage.

Fig. 80 *Rodwell's engraving shows some of the south side of the western courtyard, with part of the former hall (later assembly rooms, then refectory) and kitchen below. The entrance surmounted by the arms of Charles I ('gorgeous if somewhat wild' – Norton in Pevsner and Neave 1995, 189) is shown here approached by a 19th-century external stairway; this was replaced in the 1920s.*

the two elaborate carved stone doorways with the initials IR on the pedestals (see Figs.75, 78 and 79), both on the east elevation, as well as various ornamented fireplaces (RCHMY 4, pl.66, top right). Finally, Sheffield remodelled the medieval house, altering floor levels and improving the outer façade for the visit of James I in 1617.

The final major phase of building took place during the presidency of Thomas Wentworth, Earl of Strafford (1628–41). In 1634 £1712 19s 7d was granted 'circa nova edificia de le Manner House'.

Fig. 81 *Halfpenny's engraving of an inner doorway, 1807. This is the entrance to the cross-wing with the coat of arms of Thomas Wentworth, Earl of Strafford, President of the Council of the North 1628–41.*

Charles I stayed in the King's Manor in 1633 and again in 1639. A letter from Wentworth in August 1639 suggests that he intended to alter Sheffield's hall to create a first-floor chapel over the kitchen. At the east end he added an external staircase and a doorway with the arms of Charles I over it (Fig.80). He also added a second storey to Sheffield's gallery (Fig.125, H), linking the north and south ranges at the upper level. He inserted a new doorway, surmounted with his own coat of arms, from the eastern courtyard into the centre of Sheffield's gallery (Fig.81).

The Civil War and later 17th century

The Council in the North was abolished in 1641, after which no major additions were made to the King's Manor until the 19th century. At least one range of the building (the outer, western range; Fig.125, K) was partially demolished. The Manor was surrendered to the Parliamentarians on 16 July 1644. In October 1653 the Council of State ordered Colonel Beckwith to take care of the damaged King's Manor. In June 1656 it ordered that Colonel Robert Lilburne should receive £400 for repairs to be specified by the Lord Mayor. The King's Manor was in this way kept in a habitable state during the Interregnum.

In 1666, after the restoration of the monarchy, Henry Darcy who was keeper of the Manor at that time was granted £400 for repairs to 'the Presence Chamber, the Withdrawing Room, the Belcony Chamber, the King's Chamber, the Matted Chamber, the Wainscot Chamber and the Councell Chamber'. It is not now possible to identify all these rooms.

In 1667 the Manor became the official residence of John, Lord Frescheville, Governor of the City of York (Drake 1736, 574). In 1675 the Treasury granted Frescheville £150 for repairs, suggesting the re-use of old materials. A valuable drawing by Jacob Richards (Fig.82) gives the plan of the Manor in some detail. It shows that the hall built for Lord Sheffield in the south range extended no further than the south-west corner of the western courtyard where it met the gallery. Wentworth had proposed to make it into a chapel but on Richards' plan it is called 'the Councill Chamber' (Fig.82, V). The earlier council chamber (the Huntingdon Room) had been divided into two smaller rooms (Fig.82, K and L). The outer west range is shown joined to the central range by a gallery running west to east across the western courtyard. This has since been removed, leaving scars on the central range (RCHMY 4, pl.70). A plan

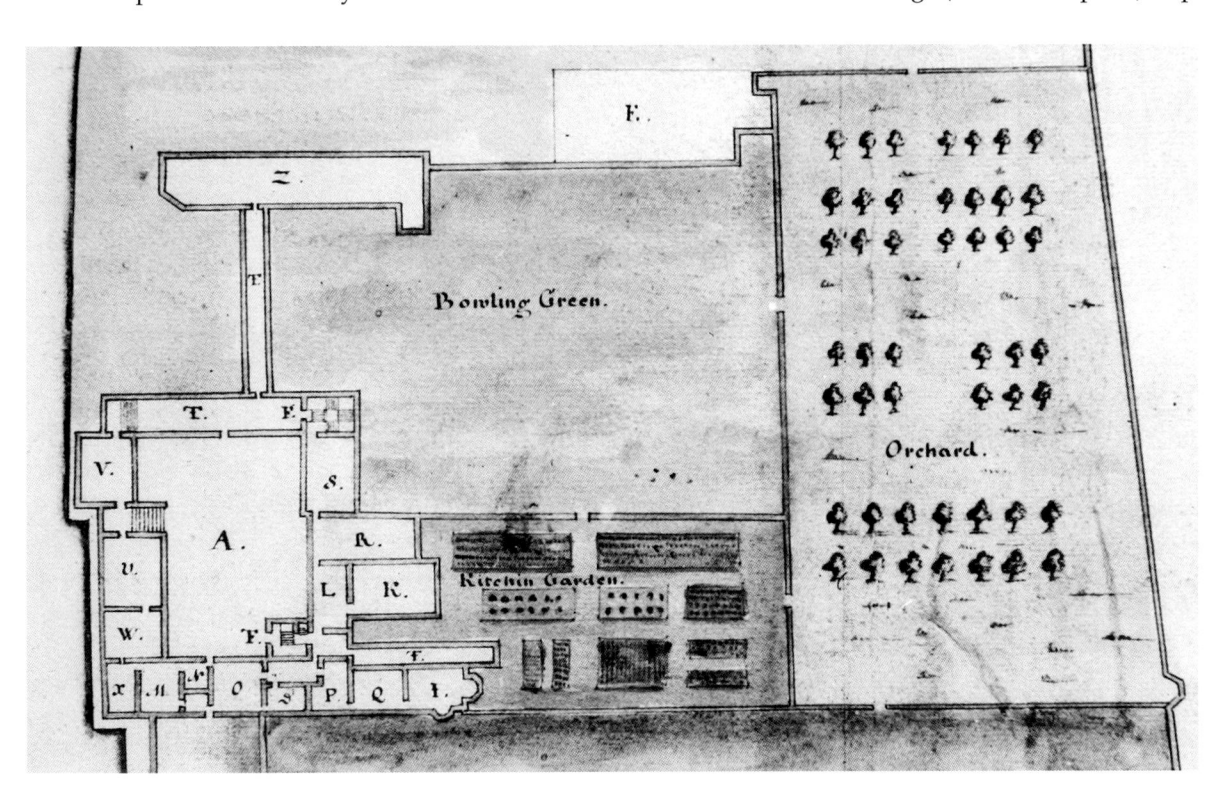

Fig. 82 *Detail of Richards' plan. The basic design of the Manor is already recognisable. The grounds include orchards, kitchen gardens and a bowling green. Richards' plan is a fair copy of that made for a survey of royal defences in York in 1682. The Manor was then the residence of the Governor (military commander of the garrison). Sir John Reresby moved in during 1682 and found it needed improvement. The original key reads as follows:* "A Draught of His Majesties Manner house at York; A, the Inner Court; B, passage to the Manor house; X, M, N, O, P, Q, I, L, K, R, S, T & V are lodgeings in very good repair and likewise the rooms or cellars under them; Ŧ, Galleries; V, the Council Chamber; F, staircases; U & W, lodgings wanting repaire on ye roof; Z is a house that never was finished within but the roof was, and couvered with panntiles which were afterwards taken off by a Certaine Governour and sould for his Majesties Use but the money he kept for his owne, and left the timber to shift for it self. Under this house is a stately arched cellar the length of it; C, granaries and stables; D, stables and haylofts for 100 load of hay; E, tennes court; F an old ruin'd Chappal. Jacob Richards fecit."

Fig. 83 Francis Place lived in the King's Manor and produced several sketches of the building, including this one dated 1718. It shows a ruined wall with the archway of a gate. It has been suggested that it was part of the warming house or kitchen of the monastery, much of which was overlain by the west range of the Manor. This view is given some credence by the chimney on the left and the medieval Decorated period windows.

of the same period by Archer shows a second building connecting the central and western ranges, continuing the council chamber block along the south side of the western courtyard. Richards states that the outer western range (Fig.125, K) was never completed inside, though it was roofed, and that a 'stately arched cellar' ran below the entire length of the building; these cellars cross the abbey chapter house.

In the late 17th century the central block on the north side (Fig.125, G) was heightened, probably in 1682 when Governor Sir John Reresby spent about £200 on work on the Manor (RCHMY 4, pl.53). In November 1687, during the reign of the Catholic James II, the Treasury leased the King's Manor, along with outhouses and 13 acres of land, to Francis Lawson, one of the king's chaplains, for 31 years. Lawson converted the Manor into a 'Popish School' and used the hall as a chapel. He fled the country, however, when James II was overthrown in 1688 and in 1690 the lease was granted to Ralph

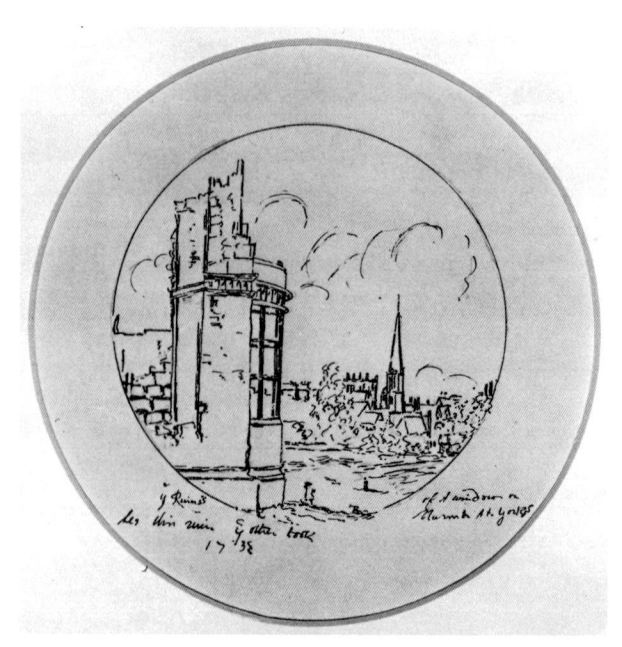

Fig. 84 Another sketch by Place, showing the view towards the river with part of a bay window and detail of a frieze; this feature is no longer standing. The church in the background is All Saints North Street.

Rymer but the house was 'ruinous'. At the very end of the 17th century the roof of the outer west range (K) seems to have been removed.

18th century

By this time the Manor was divided into apartments. A drawing dated June 1726 shows that Sir Tancred Robinson occupied the north range and its annexe (Fig.125, E and F). The artist Francis Place (Figs.83 and 84) lived in the northern part of the front range (A), Mr Lumley and his boarding school occupied the north medieval wing (C and D), and the remainder was tenanted by Mr Owram and Mr Barker. Sir Tancred modernised the north range (E) with hung-sash windows, panelling and fireplaces, and created the staircase there. He was also probably responsible for creating the connecting passage between ranges F and G. The hall which had served as Lawson's chapel in the late 17th century was converted into 'an Assembly Room'. The drawing of 1726 shows the hall enlarged to its present size. A plan of June 1770 shows most buildings as they are today, though the majority of those in the back courtyard were in ruins.

19th century

In March 1812 the York Diocesan Society and National School took over the south-western part of the Manor. The school was opened in January 1813 and buildings on the south side of the western courtyard were partly reconstructed. The school expanded its numbers and in the late 19th century red brick school buildings were erected above the vaulted cellars of the outer west range (K). In 1922 the school moved to Marygate.

In 1833 the Yorkshire School for the Blind was founded in memory of William Wilberforce and acquired the lease of the King's Manor with the

Fig. 85 *The Yorkshire School for the Blind by Monkhouse, c.1840. The School was founded by William Wilberforce in 1833 and occupied the part of the Manor round the eastern courtyard until 1958. The ground floor and some of the upper floor windows were replaced during the 1830s. The plaque above the doorway on the right proclaims 'Wilberforce School for the Blind'.*

exception of the part occupied by the National School (Fig.85). In 1922 it occupied the buildings vacated by the National School too. In 1900 a new headmaster's house was built, standing to the east between the old King's Manor and the City Art Gallery. This was built in Jacobean style, to the designs of Walter Brierley. On the departure of the School for the Blind in 1958 the complex was acquired by the City Council and then leased to the University of York from 1963.

Selected architectural features

Exterior of the medieval house

The eastern elevation of the medieval house (comprising the east side of the hall block A and the ends of two cross-wings, B and C) is of c.1480, though much altered (RCHMY 4, frontispiece and pl.54). This was the rear of the original abbot's house. Above a stone plinth the walling is of brick with remains of a diaper pattern. It finishes at the north end with a diagonal buttress. The positions of the original late 15th-century windows are indicated by surviving brick relieving arches (one shown to the left of the doorway in Fig.86). Alterations to windows in the late 16th century can be identified by surviving fragments of the plaster applied to the brickwork to simulate stone dressings. The five-light stone upper window on the south side of this elevation may be as early as 1540.

The south doorway of the eastern elevation, created in the 17th century, has an elaborate stone surround bearing the initials IR for James I and, above this, a large heraldic panel with the initials CR for Charles I (Figs.75, 78, 86). The north doorway (see Fig.79, right) is an original opening of c.1480 but has a stone surround of c.1610 brought from the west elevation and reset in the 19th century (Fig.87).

The south elevation of the southern cross-wing (B) was largely refaced c.1900 (RCHMY 4, pl.55). One of the original first-floor terracotta windows of c.1480 remains complete, under a brick arch similar to those on the east front (RCHMY 4, pl.59, left); it has three lights with segmental heads. All the other windows are modern. In the centre of this elevation is a small projecting gable, probably of early 18th-century date, in which is reset a fragment of a 17th-

Fig. 86 John Browne's view of the main entrance, 1817. The drawing shows the infilled windows and alterations to the brickwork with Browne's customary close attention to detail. It also shows the wear on the stonework, in contrast to Half-penny's idealised view (see Fig.75).

century carved stone frieze. In front of the western part of this elevation is the base of a fragment of the abbey precinct wall, standing only one course above the ground (see Norton 1994, 272, fig.8). Norton believes that a medieval interval tower may have stood on the site of the projecting gable.

The west end of the southern cross-wing is almost freestanding. The lower part is of limestone ashlar with a moulded 13th-century plinth and contains a 17th-century three-light window. The walling above is of brick with stone dressings.

A gabled projection was built in the north-east corner of the eastern courtyard c.1590, the lower part forming a porch in front of the existing screens passage. The walling of the medieval building around the eastern courtyard is mainly of brick of c.1480 but includes areas of stonework on the ground floor which may be of 13th-century date, though it does not include the moulded 13th-century plinth; 13th-century stone has been re-used in the upper storey. Incomplete fragments of diaper pattern in the walls of the main range indicate that the brickwork is much disturbed and rebuilt. On the west side of the hall range are the arched heads of two first-floor openings which may have led to an external two-storey gallery; stone corbels for carrying the roof of such a gallery remain.

In the south wing an upper window of five transomed lights may be of the mid-16th century. In the main range and the eastern part of the south wing a string course over the upper windows is of c.1570 and changes in its level indicate the positions of windows at that time. They had brick jambs plastered to simulate stonework and this plaster can be seen flanking an 18th-century window.

The north side of the north wing (C) is now largely masked by later buildings. During repair work in the 1960s it was seen that this late 15th-century wall stands on the base of a 13th-century wall. A 15th-century bay window, now partially masked, is of ashlar with four cinquefoil-headed lights at first-floor level.

The medieval kitchen (D) projects northwards from the north wing. The ground-floor walls are of ashlar with the partial remains of a 13th-century plinth; the upper walls are of 15th-century brickwork with stone quoins. In the north wall a five-light ground-floor window framed in ovolo-moulded stonework was inserted in the late 16th or early 17th century. On the first floor an ovolo-moulded transomed window of c.1610 cuts through plasterwork surviving from a window of c.1570. In the west wall is an ovolo-moulded three-light window of the late 16th century flanked by masonry which supports a rectangular gabled bay above, all probably of c.1580.

Interior of the medieval house

The medieval building was of two storeys but in the 17th century the first floor of the hall range was lowered by about 2ft 6in (0.76m) and a second floor constructed. The current first-floor ceiling cuts across the heads of the 17th-century windows. The present entrance hall of the main range (A) was created c.1610 but now contains a modern oak staircase. The elaborately decorated early 17th-century plaster ceiling in the southern room of this range came from a house in North Street in the 1960s. At the north end of the top storey the upper part of the 15th-century timber-framed cross wall is exposed (RCHMY 4, pl.60, bottom).

The southern cross-wing (B) of c.1480 comprised four rooms on the ground floor. The eastern room has a deep recess in the south wall representing a medieval garderobe. The entire upper floor now forms one large room, open to the roof, but was originally subdivided. There are three fireplaces: the one furthest east is of the late 15th century and has an arched head in moulded brick (RCHMY 4, pl.66, top left); the middle fireplace has moulded jambs of re-used stone and a flat lintel (RCHMY 4, pl.66, bottom left); the third fireplace dates to c.1540–50 and has chamfered stone jambs and an arched brick head. Most of the roof timbers are of c.1480 (RCHMY 4, pl.63, left).

The north cross-wing (C) has a large ground-floor room at the east end with the 15th-century ceiling divided into square panels by moulded beams (RCHMY 4, pl.60, top). The ceilings and ceiling beams in the western part of the range are all of c.1580. In the north wall is a fireplace dating to c.1610, with a stone surround decorated with jewel ornament (RCHMY 4, pl.66, top right). In the south wall is part of a 17th-century doorway (RCHMY 4, pl.72, top). In the west wall is a doorway of c.1610 to the building added beyond (RCHMY 4, pl.61, bottom right). The former kitchen, projecting to the north, has a ceiling of c.1580 and in the east wall is a large fireplace recess, part of which may be of 13th-century date.

On the first floor the ceiling of the east room is divided into square panels by late 15th-century moulded beams. The ceiling at the west end is also carried on late 15th-century beams, though of a different design. The fireplace in the northern wall is adjacent to a medieval window, now blocked.

The western part of the north cross-wing and the upper part of the kitchen wing (D) together form the Huntingdon Room (RCHMY 4, pl.64). Around the walls of the room is a plaster frieze incorporating three motifs (RCHMY 4, pl.65, top): a pomegranate between two wyverns (the crest of Henry Hastings, Earl of Huntingdon); a bull's head between two Hs within a garter under an earl's coronet (for Henry

Fig. 87 *The eastern courtyard by Cave, c.1822. A view looking north, with parts of the north and east ranges. On the right, the entrance door which was later moved to the east front; traces of older window openings are also visible. The inner front was built on the foundations of the original abbot's palace, with many additions and alterations.*

Fig. 88 *The Huntingdon Room by A. Buckle, 1883. This shows Tudor panelling and a large fireplace of c.1579, the voussoirs carved with cartouches, masks and arabesques, and its size indicated by the Elizabethan gentleman leaning casually against the corner. The bear and ragged staff either side of the fireback are the device of Catherine Dudley, wife of the Earl of Huntingdon.*

78

Fig. 89 *Monkhouse's 'Palace of the Stuarts': the inner doorway of the central range, with steps leading up to the Huntingdon Room. An attractive and clearly rendered view, with careful attention to the detail of the stonework. This was one of the 17th-century Strafford doorways described by Hutchinson and Palliser as 'gross' (1980, 153).*

Hastings, created Knight of the Garter in 1570); and a bear and ragged staff (for his wife Catherine, daughter of John Dudley, Duke of Northumberland). In the east wall of the northern part of the room is a magnificent fireplace with carved stone voussoirs and ornamented pilaster jambs (Fig.88). The east end of the southern part of this room is lined with early 17th-century panelling, perhaps re-used, and a recess to the east of the fireplace represents a medieval bay window.

The northern extension of the main hall range of the medieval house (E) is the first post-dissolution addition. It was built between 1560 and c.1570 in re-used ashlar, probably from the abbey, and brick. Stone-built dormer windows were added at the end of the 16th century. An original window of c.1570 remains in the west wall under the stairs. The northernmost room, running into a large semi-octagonal bay window, is lined with 18th-century panelling,

Fig. 90 *Nicholson's view of the south front, along the lane now leading from Exhibition Square to the Museum Gardens, August 1813. Part of the city wall is shown on the left. On the right, the projecting gable with steps is now gone – much of this was altered by Brierley in the late 19th century.*

Figs. 91 and 92 (facing page) *The vaults under the outer west range, here etched by Halfpenny (1807), have often been attributed to the reign of Henry VIII, but actually date from the Presidency of Lord Sheffield in c.1610. The doorway is of re-used 14th-century masonry from the abbey cloisters.*

behind which is the jamb of a blocked window made up with moulded stonework of c.1300. On the first floor the north wall is built largely of re-used 13th-century stone and above the present doorway can be seen the top of an original doorway. In the northernmost room is an original fireplace, and the original seven-bay roof has survived.

The second north range (F) was added along the west side of the main north range c.1610. Recesses in the south-west corner of the southern room represent the garderobes of the adjoining medieval range. The central north block (G) was built in stages: the ground floor, built of coursed masonry, in c.1610; the upper two storeys, mainly of brick, are of the late 17th century.

The central range (H) separates the eastern and western courtyards and at the northern end returns to meet the west end of the medieval north crosswing. It was originally designed c.1610 as a single-storey gallery with a two-storey return to give access from Lord Sheffield's new hall to the council chamber (now the Huntingdon Room). An upper storey was added by Lord Wentworth in 1633; an elaborate new doorway surmounted by Wentworth's arms is of the same date (see Fig.81). The east front of the central range has original windows of c.1610 and 1633. Inside, at the northern end, a semi-circular-headed doorway (Figs.89 and 116) gives access to a stone staircase which was constructed c.1633. In the north wall is a 12th-century stone carved with pelleted interlace. From the upper part of the stair hall a modern doorway leads to the ante-room to the Huntingdon Room. At the eastern end of this is a grand doorway to the former council chamber, the Huntingdon Room (see Fig.76).

The south range (J) forms the southern side of the western courtyard and part of the southern side of the eastern courtyard (Fig.90). It was originally built in the late 16th century but has been largely rebuilt in succeeding centuries. A large buttress added against the east end is near, but not quite on, the line of the abbey precinct wall. The first floor of the block is entered from the eastern court by a modern external stone stairway leading to a round-headed doorway flanked by tapered pilasters surmounted by a moulded frame with a pediment containing the Stuart royal arms (see Fig.80). This was erected by Wentworth c.1635 but is now very weathered.

Lord Sheffield's hall block is of two storeys and built of re-used limestone ashlar. It now contains a dining hall on the upper floor and kitchens below. Some of the first-floor windows retain a few pieces of old stone in the jambs. To the west is a lower two-storey building occupied by the National School. At the far west of this south range is a gatehouse which projects on the southern side. Above the southern arch is a restored 17th-century window. The western jamb of the northern archway is built up against a fragment of a 16th-century building in which there is the moulded jamb of a gateway, with hinge-pins surviving.

Internally, the walls of the modern kitchen below the hall are faced with medieval re-used stone. In the southern wall is a big 17th-century fireplace. In the middle of the first-floor hall there is a domed feature within the roof which was added in the 1720s as a louvre or ventilator, when the hall served as an assembly room. Within the eastern wall of the gatehouse is a 16th-century doorway, probably reset.

The outer west range (K) stands in part on the site of the chapter house of the abbey; a fragment of rough walling near the north end of the eastern front may represent the east wall of the chapter house. This range was erected for Lord Sheffield c.1610. It included a vaulted basement which still survives (Figs.91–2), containing a buttery and cellar. The upper storey was damaged during the siege of 1644 and removed in the 18th century. A drawing by Place of c.1680 (Fig.84) shows only part of the west wall standing, with a big bay window surmounted by an entablature in which the frieze matches that on the east side of the central range. School buildings were erected over the basement in the late 19th century, replaced by new buildings for the University of York in the early 1960s.

The west side of this building is completely masked by the Yorkshire Museum. On the east side the stone wall of the 17th-century building stands c.7ft (2.13m) above ground level. It is of re-used medieval masonry and the windows are mostly original. When the top of the vault was exposed in 1962 it was seen to include much re-used material of the late 12th century, including some carved voussoirs. A doorway at the south end of the northern basement room is of the early 14th century and is re-used from the abbey cloisters (RCHMY 4, pl.74, top left).

This description of the King's Manor will have given the reader just a glimpse of the complexity of the history and development of the building. As Hutchinson and Palliser (1980, 149) comment:

Back to back with the Yorkshire Museum is the most complex and confusing though not the most beautiful of York's secular buildings. It grew intermittently over at least four centuries (probably much longer) and for half that time within its existing boundaries so that architectural development always seems three or four layers deep.

Illustrations

St Mary's Abbey

General views

1. **1680** *A View of the Ruins of the Manor and St Maries Abby, Yorke*

   Francis Place. Pen and ink and wash.
   View from the south-east with part of a wall and window of the King's Manor in the foreground; ruins of the abbey nave and part of the gatehouse in the background.
   Society of Antiquaries of London: Coleraine Collection vii 46 top.
   Reproduced in *The Archaeological Journal* **128** (1971), pl.15.
   See also Illustration 251.

2. **c.1700** *York from opposite St Mary's Tower*

   Francis Place. Pen and ink over black lead. Right-hand part unfinished.
   View looking north-east across the Ouse: part of Marygate, abbey gatehouse, St Olave's Church, west end of abbey church, Manor Yard, York Minster.
   British Museum Department of Prints and Drawings 1850-2-23-832 (LB 4).
   Photostat in York Art Gallery.
   Evelyn Collection A769 (YAYAS Minster Library).

3. **c.1700** *York, St Mary's Abbey*

   Francis Place. Pen and brown ink with grey wash. Inscribed 'Prospect of St Mary's Abbey at York'. On the back, eight lines erased, and below 'No.6 Sept. 4 [16] 98'.
   View looking north-east across the Ouse (with various craft on it) towards the opposite bank. Abbey ruins and St Olave's Church on rising ground, and Manor Yard. Marygate water tower on the left.
   British Museum Department of Prints and Drawings 1850-2-23-841 (LB 8).
   Photostat in York Art Gallery.

4. **n.d.** *Prospect of St Mary's Abbey*

   Francis Place. Pen and ink, roundel on tinted paper.
   View looking east from opposite St Mary's staith: Marygate water tower and the south-east range of the hospitium. York Minster towers in the background.
   York Art Gallery YORAG : 1102 (ix).

5. **1736** *A West View of the Ruins of St Mary's Abby, York* (Figs.55 and 69)

   W.H. Toms. Lithograph.
   View across the river: Marygate water tower, hospitium, water gate and abbey church.
   Drake 1736, 574.
   York Art Gallery YORAG : R2503.
   YAT Collection IV 5 1.

6. **1776** *St Mary's Abbey with a View of the Manor Shore*

   Edward Abbot (?). Wash drawing.
   View across the river showing the abbey gatehouse, St Olave's Church, the abbey church and Multangular Tower.
   Wakefield Art Gallery: Gott Collection 1770/3/7.

7. **1785** *From outside North Street Postern looking East*

   Francis White. Engraving.
   Detail from City and Ainsty plan.
   Abbey precincts: water tower, church nave, hospitium, from across the river. Gateway and St Olave's tower on the left; Lendal Tower on the right.
   YAT Collection TG25.
   RCHMY (NMR) YC 3A.

8. **1797** *St Mary's Abbey and the Minster*

   J.M.W. Turner. Pencil sketch.
   11 x 14¾in (274 x 370mm).
   Marygate water tower and abbey shore in use as a boatyard. Abbey church behind on the left; hospitium and Minster on the right.
   Tate Gallery: Tweed and Lakes sketchbook TB xxv, 70.
   Reproduced in Hill 1996, 147, pl.214.
   See also: Evelyn Collection A681 (YAYAS Minster Library).

9. **1797** *York Minster from the Ouse, near St Mary's Abbey*

   Thomas Girtin. Watercolour.
   14 x 19¼in (340 x 489mm).
   Abbey, water tower and hospitium from across the river. York Minster in the background. Barge moored at the end of Marygate in the foreground.
   Very similar to illustration 8, and possibly taken from Turner's sketch.
   Harewood House Trust.
   Reproduced in Hill 1999, 50, pl.31.

Fig. 93 Abbey from beyond the precinct wall by John Varley. A general view from near the present Museum Street entrance to the Museum Gardens (i.e. from the south-east), showing the lodge, gatehouse and church ruins, with St Olave's Church in the background and the Multangular Tower on the right. This was before the time of the Yorkshire Philosophical Society gardens since cows, a horse, a cart and lean-to sheds can all be seen in front of the abbey ruins.

10. *c.1803   Abbey from the south-east* (Fig.93)

John Varley. Watercolour.
Shows entrance into the abbey grounds through the present Museum Street, with the Multangular Tower on the right and the ruins of the abbey church and gatehouse in the background.
York Art Gallery YORAG : R2502.

11. *1822   At York, 1822*

George Nicholson. Pencil drawing.
Abbey water tower from the river, with abbey nave and tower of St Olave's.
York Art Gallery YORAG : R911.

12. *1825   York, June 23 1825*

George Nicholson. Pencil drawing.
View across the river to the west end of the Minster. Water tower and hospitium in the foreground; St Olave's Church tower, abbey walls and part of the church on the left.
York Art Gallery, Nicholson Sketchbooks YORAG : R2446 (6).

13. *1828   The Manor Shore, York*

F. Nash. Engraving.
Minster Library YK 359.

14. *1829   A General Plan of the Ground occupied by the Abbey of St Mary, York, with the Ruins and Foundations which have been brought to light by the Excavations made in the years 1827 and 1828*

From original drawing by R.H. Sharpe. Lithograph.
Measured plan, scales given.

Wellbeloved 1829, pl.51. Also: Minster Library YK 374.
Revd Robert William Bilton Hornby Collection, *York Antiquities* **2** (Add MS 320), 277.
Evelyn Collection (YAYAS Minster Library), 813, 821.
RCHMY (NMR) negative YC 1034.

15. *1971   Plans of St Mary's Abbey, York*

After R.H. Sharpe. Measured and labelled plans; scale given.
With additions and revised references by A.B. Whittingham.
a) Plan of the complete precinct, opposite p.118.
b) Plan of the church and claustral buildings, p.121.
The Archaeological Journal **128** (1971).

16. *n.d.   St Mary's Abbey: monastic and conventual buildings. Restored view*

S. Sharpe. Pencil and wash drawing, photographed by W. Watson.
'Bird's-eye' view of the 13th-century monastic complex.
Printed in Ridsdale Tate 1929, pl.3.
Also in Benson 1919, 37.
Evelyn Collection E833 (YAYAS Minster Library).

17. *1840   St Mary's Abbey, York: the Abbey Grounds* (Fig.49)

J.S. Prout. Engraving.
View across the river to the abbey shore; hospitium with the abbey church and St Olave's Church in the background and a barge moored at the staith.
Prout 1840, pl.9.
Minster Library YK 360.

18. *c.1840   Bootham Bar area Plan*

Area bounded by Marygate/Bootham/St Leonard's Place.
Evelyn Collection 1756 (YAYAS Minster Library).

19. *1857   Almery Garth*

Measured plan.
Evelyn Collection 1890 (YAYAS Minster Library).

20. *c.1860   The Gardens of the Yorkshire Philosophical Society, York* (Figs.2 and 64)

J. Storey. Coloured lithograph.
14½ x 21½in (372 x 543mm).
'Bird's-eye' view of the whole abbey precinct with the Yorkshire Museum, observatory, gardens, Multangular Tower, remains of St Leonard's Hospital and surrounding streets.
Yorkshire Philosophical Society.
York Art Gallery YORAG : R1552.
Black and white reproduction in Murray *et al* 1990, 40, pl.26.

21. *n.d.   York Cathedral from the Railway Bridge*

Newbald and Stead. Engraving with colour wash.
Marygate, the abbey church, hospitium and Marygate landing, with the Minster in the background.
Minster Library: Revd Robert William Bilton Hornby Collection, *York Antiquities* (Add MS 320), 95.
Also photograph on p.20.

22. *c.1911   St Mary's Abbey, York. Historical Ground Plan*

E. Ridsdale Tate. Measured plan.
Detailed plan of the Gothic church (with Romanesque church superimposed) and cloisters.
Inset, smaller plan of the whole site.
Ridsdale Tate 1929, pl.6.
Benson 1919, 31.
Evelyn Collection E1759 (YAYAS Minster Library).
RCHMY (NMR) negative no.YC1033.

23. *n.d.   York from a Balloon*

Hood. Photograph.
Aerial view of the abbey walls and precinct.
Evelyn Collection Y483 (YAYAS Minster Library).

24. *n.d.   Museum Gardens Landscape*

Unknown. Photograph.
Evelyn Collection A822 (YAYAS Minster Library).

25. *n.d. (early 20th century)   Set of slides of St Mary's Abbey*

Various views, including some showing clear details of masonry.
Evelyn Collection A2872–2890 (YAYAS Minster Library).

26. *1952   Plans and Sections of Excavations by G.F. Willmot*

Sixteen plans and sections, mainly relating to west end of the church nave (south side); south-east and south-west corners of the cloister and possibly the sacristy.
RCHMY (NMR) file 60254: file of accounts of excavations 1827–55, notes by J. Radley, 1977.

27. *1988   Reconstruction of the Abbey as it was in 1539*

Christopher Wilson. Colour drawing.
'Bird's-eye' view from south-west. A useful adjunct to maps and plans.
Yorkshire Museum.
Colour reproduction in Wilson and Burton 1988.

The abbey church

28. *1320   Ebrauc* (Figs.1, 22)

Ink drawing in the margin of a manuscript.
General view of York from the west. The building on the left has been identified by John Harvey (RCHME) as St Mary's Abbey church: two slender towers with spires and a central tower also with a spire covered in herring-bone leadwork. The full drawing also shows the Minster, partly erased, and other towers, spires and houses (see Aylmer and Cant 1977, 175–7).
Drawing in a 14th-century manuscript of Geoffrey of Monmouth's *History of the Kings of Britain*.
British Library MS Royal, 13.A.III fo.16v.
5 x 4in colour negative in YAT Collection.
Also reproduced in Caine 1897, opposite p.7, but here the central tower of the abbey church is shown with triple blind arcading and crocketed pinnacles instead of a spire.

29. *n.d. (13th century)   Stephen, Abbot of St Mary's, York (d.1112)* (Fig.7)

Part of the abbey church shown on the right.
Oxford, Bodleian Library, MS Bodley 39, fo.92.

30. *c.1678 St Mary's Abbey church from South* (Fig.14)

    William Lodge. Drawing (etching by P. Tempest).
    Most of the south arcade is still standing, with triforium. Monastery gatehouse on the left.
    York Art Gallery YORAG : R1949, R2496, and 'after Lodge', R2500.
    Minster Library YK 325.

31. *c.1680 Ruins of St Mary's Abbey church* (Fig.16)

    William Lodge. Pencil, pen and ink and grey wash. 5½ x 9¼in (143 x 249mm).
    View from the south-west. Part of the north triforium and most of the south arcade of the nave is still standing.
    Previously attributed to Francis Place.
    York Art Gallery YORAG : R1854.
    Evelyn Collection 260 (YAYAS Minster Library).

32. *c. 1700 St Mary's Abbey Ruins from Windmill Tower, North side, York*

    Francis Place. Drawing.
    Evelyn Collection A678 (YAYAS Minster Library).
    See also: York Art Gallery YORAG : 1102 (vi).

33. *n.d. St Mary's Abbey ('pillars unique')*

    Francis Place. Drawing.
    Evelyn Collection A261 (YAYAS Minster Library).

34. *n.d. St Mary's Abbey: North Aisle looking East*

    William Lodge. Sketch with wash.
    Shows the north aisle of the church still vaulted and part of the north and south nave arcades.
    York Art Gallery YORAG : R1963.
    Evelyn Collection A816 (YAYAS Minster Library).
    Reproduced in Buttery n.d., 9a.

35. *1719 Part of St Maries nigh York 1719*

    Francis Place. Pen and wash.
    View from the nave of the abbey church (pillar and arches in the foreground) looking south-west towards Lendal Tower, the spire of All Saints North Street and the roof of a summer house near the river.
    York Art Gallery YORAG : R1966 (1102 xi).
    Evelyn Collection 820 (YAYAS Minster Library).

36. *1721 The South View of the Ruins of St Mary's Abbey in York, 1721*

    Samuel Buck. Etching.
    View from the south-west (liturgical south) across the river.
    There are points of interest: arches have been filled in and square windows inserted. Otherwise this looks like a hasty copy (of another unknown illustration), even the river being suspect.
    York Art Gallery YORAG : R2492
    Minster Library YK 324.
    Evelyn Collection A724 (YAYAS Minster Library).

37. *1735 (published) The Ruins of St Mary's Abbey, York* (Fig.15)

    J. Haynes. Lithograph.
    Church nave from the south-west with St Olave's Church on the left. Inset, Multangular Tower, with York Minster in the background.
    Gent 1735, between pp.116 and 117.
    Prints in: York Art Gallery YORAG : R2498.
    Minster Library YK 329, YK 330.

38. *c.1776 East Prospect of Part of the Ruins of St Mary's Abbey*

    Edward Abbot (?). Wash drawing.
    The north wall of the church nave, inner side.
    Wakefield Art Gallery: Gott Collection 1776/3/5.

39. *c.1776 South-East Prospect of the Ruins of St Mary's Abbey*

    Edward Abbot (?). Wash drawing
    View of the church showing the inner side of the north wall, with rather more detail of the east end of the nave than usual.
    Wakefield Art Gallery: Gott Collection 1776/3/6.

40. *1778 St Mary's Abbey, York*

    Thomas Malton. Watercolour.
    The width of the nave is emphasised here, and part of the east end of the nave is shown through the west door. The Minster, behind, is placed rather too far to the right.
    York Art Gallery YORAG : R121.
    RCHMY (NMR) negative YC715.

41. *1778 [St Mary's Abbey] Sept. 1, 1778*

    Drawn by T. Hearne; figures by F. Bartolozzi; engraved by W. Byrne and S. Middiman.
    Inscribed 'To the Honourable Lady Payne, This View of St Mary's Abbey, York, is gratefully Inscribed By her Ladyship's most obedient Servants Thos Hearne and Wm Byrne'.
    York Art Gallery YORAG : R1775.
    Minster Library YK 338.

42. *n.d. (c.1760–90) St Mary's Abbey, York*

    S. Hieronymous Grimm. Wash drawing.
    West end and part of the north wall of the church nave from the inner side, looking north-west.
    York Art Gallery YORAG : R368.

Fig. 94 The west front of the abbey church with the King's Manor in the background, by Joseph Halfpenny, 1782. There is an unknown building on the right, probably an agricultural building, presumably demolished when the Yorkshire Museum was built. This shows the land dropping away to the south of the abbey church – the cloisters were built at a lower level.

43. **1782**   *St Mary's Abbey, York* (Fig.94)

    Joseph Halfpenny. Monochrome wash drawing.
    Outer side of the west end of the church and part of a building on the right with a low archway. Part of the King's Manor is visible in the background. Horses and groom in the foreground.
    York Art Gallery YORAG : R269.

44. **1791**   *St Mary's Abbey 13th June 1791*

    John White Abbot. Watercolour.
    North wall and east end of the church nave from the south-west. Not a great deal of detail; shows use of the abbey grounds as a meadow, with a hayrick stacked against the remains of the nave north aisle.
    York Art Gallery YORAG: R3.

45. **1797**   *York, St Mary's Portal*

    J.M.W. Turner. Pencil sketch.
    11 x 14¾in (274 x 370mm).
    View of the west end of the church nave, with the inner sides of the north and east walls visible.
    Tate Gallery: 'Tweed and Lakes' Sketchbook TB xxxv 71.
    Reproduced in Hill 1996, 147, pl.215.

46. **1798**   *Ruins of St Mary's Abbey*

    Published by F. Jukes? Colour lithograph.
    York Art Gallery YORAG : R2486.

47. **1799**   *St Mary's Abbey, York*

    J. Hornsey. Drawing, engraved by J. Walker for publication in 1801.

Fig. 95 *This wash drawing by Henry Cave (1801) shows the interior of the church nave from the south-east. It is similar to Halfpenny's 1807 engraving (Fig.10) but the timber buildings and piles of logs show the actual state and use of the ruins.*

Not very convincing.
York Art Gallery YORAG : R3970.

48. 1801   *St Mary's Abbey, York*

Unknown artist. Engraving, inscribed 'vol. V, pl.226'.
Minster Library YK 328.

49. 1801   *St Mary's Abbey*

Henry Cave. Watercolour.
Inner side of the west end of the nave north aisle, the centre dominated and partly obscured by a shack/lean-to. Lodge visible in the background at left. Of historical interest; otherwise short on detail.
York Art Gallery YORAG : R3414.
See also: Evelyn Collection 1824 and 1825 (YAYAS Minster Library).

50. 1801   *St Mary's Abbey, Manor Shore 1801* (Fig.95)

Henry Cave. Wash drawing.
Interior of church, seen from the east end of the nave.
York Art Gallery YORAG : R2491.

51. 1805   *St Mary's Abbey, York, 1805*

Paul Sandby Munn. Pencil drawing.
East end of the church nave, seen from the north-east.
York Art Gallery YORAG : R3658.

52. 1807   *St Mary's Abbey* (Fig.10)

Joseph Halfpenny. Etching.
North wall and the west end of the nave from the south-east.
Halfpenny 1807, 27.
Also, single print: York Art Gallery YORAG : R2376.

53. c.1807–08   *St Mary's Abbey, York*

John Sell Cotman. Pencil and watercolour.
16 x 11in (399 x 273mm).
View from the north transept towards the arch at the end of the north aisle. Cotman has isolated the structure from its surrounding buildings, as though in open countryside, and thus simplified it. A few stacks of building material are on the right and a section of dark wall in the background. By concerning himself

with line and light, Cotman has transformed the scene from a work of topography to a work of art.
Birmingham Museums and Art Gallery P11953.
Colour reproduction in Hill 2005, 14, pl.9.

54. *1808   St Mary's Abbey 8 Apr. 1808*

F[rancis] N[icholson]. Possibly by his nephew, George Nicholson.
Evelyn Collection A2552 (YAYAS Minster Library).

55. *1808   St Mary's Abbey Sept. 1808*

George Nicholson. Pencil drawing.
View of the abbey church from the south-east, showing the north wall of the nave on the right; cart shed occupying the centre. Little detail.
York Art Gallery: Nicholson Sketchbooks YORAG: R2446 (48).

56. *1810   Part of St Mary's Abbey, York*

Paul Sandby Munn. Monochrome watercolour.
East end of the nave and part of the north wall of the church from the south-west.
York Art Gallery YORAG : R1478.
See also: Minster Library YK 346 and YK 347.

57. *1810   St Mary's Abbey, York* (Fig.24)

John Sell Cotman. Etching dated Oct. 8 1810.
The north-west pier of the crossing, with an artist (possibly Paul Sandby Munn) sketching in the foreground.
York Art Gallery YORAG : 2002.42.

58. *1811   Detail from Nave Interior*

Henry Cave. Pencil sketch.
York Art Gallery YORAG : 2005.238.

59. *1812   St Mary's Abbey, York*

Paul Sandby Munn. Soft ground etching.
Based on a drawing of 1805 (Etchings of Landscapes, no.3).
As Illustration 51.
York Art Gallery YORAG : R 3968.

60. *1813   Part of St Mary's Abbey*

Henry Cave. Etching.
West end of the abbey church from the south-west.
Cave 1813, pl.39.
York Art Gallery YORAG : R 2320.
Original drawing in York Art Gallery.

61. *1815   St Mary's Abbey, York 1815*

John Coney. Engraving.
View from the south-east showing the full length of the north side of the nave, together with the west end.
Coney 1842, vol.2.
York Art Gallery YORAG : R2429.
Minster Library YK 337.
Minster Library: Revd Robert William Bilton Hornby Collection, *York Antiquities* **2** (Add MS 320), 223.
Evelyn Collection 1810 (YAYAS Minster Library).

62. *1816   Part of St Mary's Abbey, York; from a sketch taken in 1816*

Henry Cave. Lithograph W.F. Wodson.
Detail of blind arcading.
York Art Gallery YORAG : R3969.

63. *1817   Part of St Mary's Abbey, York*

G. Stanley. Engraving.
From Storer 1815–16.
Minster Library YK 350 and 351.

64. *1819   The church from the South-West*

Henry Cave. Aquatint.
Mainly a view of the west end, rather foreshortened and squat.
York Art Gallery YORAG : R2501.
Also a coloured engraving of the same, dated 18 Jan. 1819.

65. *1821   At York: St Mary's Abbey* (Fig.19)

Samuel Prout. Soft ground etching.
West end and part of the north wall from the south-east.
From a series of Views of Rural Cottages in the North of England.
York Art Gallery YORAG : R2756.

66. *1821   At York*

Samuel Prout. Lithograph.
West end of the abbey church; Minster in the background.
York Art Gallery YORAG : R3994.

67. *1825   St Mary's Abbey, York, May 21 1825*

George Nicholson. Pencil drawing.
North transept arch, east end of the nave from the south-west. No great detail.
York Art Gallery: Nicholson Sketchbooks YORAG : R2446 (44).
See also: Evelyn Collection A2582 (YAYAS Minster Library), where given as by F[rancis] N[icholson] but almost certainly by his nephew, George.

68. *1825   St Mary's Abbey, York, May 21 1825*

George Nicholson. Pencil drawing no.45.
View of the north-west corner of the abbey church,

Fig. 96 John Browne is well known for his work on York Minster, and his keen eye for detail is just as evident in his drawings of the abbey. This is a typically precise study, probably made in the 1820s, of the inner face of the nave north wall, clearly delineating the arcading beneath the ruined window.

from the south.
York Art Gallery YORAG : R917.

69.   1827   *St Mary's Abbey, June 12 1827*

George Nicholson. Pencil drawing.
West end of the nave with the Minster behind.
York Art Gallery: Nicholson Sketchbooks YORAG : R2446 (43).

70.   1827   *Part of the church of St Mary's Abbey*

W.H. Bartlett. Steel engraving by Le Keux.
North wall and the east end of the church from the south-west.
From Britton 1828.
York Art Gallery YORAG : R3974.
Minster Library YK 334.
Minster Library: Revd Robert William Bilton Hornby Collection, *York Antiquities* **2** (Add MS 320), 235.
See also: Minster Library YK 335 and Add MS 320, no.233.

71.   n.d.   *South View of St Mary's Abbey, York*

John Browne. Lithograph.
A very clear depiction of the north aisle of the church.
York Art Gallery YORAG : R3980.
See also: Evelyn Collection A8163 (YAYAS Minster Library).

72.   n.d.   *Part of St Mary's Abbey, York* (Fig.96)

John Browne. Pencil drawing.
A clear and careful drawing of the arcading on the inner face of the nave north wall.
York Art Gallery YORAG : R3369.

73.   n.d.   *House incorporating parts of the Abbey* (Fig.71)

John Browne (?). Drawing.
An unusual and particularly interesting drawing. Shows a cottage with three windows and a porch. A large window of ecclesiastical design, possibly from the abbey, has been built into the front.
York Art Gallery YORAG : R3367.

74.   1829   *View of the West Front of the church* (Fig.17)

Frederick Nash. Lithograph.
The west front with children playing in the foreground.
Wellbeloved 1829, pl.52.

75.   1829   *North-West View of the Nave of the church* (Fig.13)

Frederick Nash. Lithograph.
A rare view of the north wall of the church from the outer side, showing the buttress designs. The doorway is shown open; in Halfpenny's 1807 inner view it is blocked (see Fig.10).
Wellbeloved 1829, pl.53.

76.   1829   *One of the Compartments of the North Aisle of the Nave of the church* (Fig.12)

R.H. Sharp. Measured drawing. Lithograph.
Interior (i.e. view from the south).
Wellbeloved 1829, pl.54.

77.   1831   *St Mary's Abbey, York 'sketched on the spot by Miss Atkinson'*

Louis Haghe after Miss Atkinson. Coloured lithograph published by J. and G. Todd, Stonegate, York, and R. Ackerman, Strand, June 25th 1831.
Abbey nave from the south-west.
York Art Gallery YORAG : R2490 (coloured), R3975 (uncoloured).
Minster Library: Revd Robert William Bilton Hornby

Collection, *York Antiquities* **2** (Add MS 320), 23.
See also: 1831 St Mary's Abbey; copy of lithograph of sketch by 'Miss Atkinson'
J.E. Green, monochrome wash drawing.
York Art Gallery YORAG : R268.

78. *1834   St Mary's, York*

George Cuitt, Jr. Etching
West end, with a glimpse of the east end of the nave.
Cuitt 1834, pl.31.
York Art Gallery YORAG : R3030.
Minster Library YK 348.

79. *1836   Ruins of St Mary's Abbey*

H. and W. Brown. Wood engravings.
a) from the south-east, York Art Gallery YORAG : R3973.
b) from the south-west, York Art Gallery YORAG : R3976.
c) from the river (i.e. south-west), York Art Gallery YORAG : R3979.
Brown and Brown 1836 (no page numbers).

80. *1836   St Mary's Abbey from Micklegate Bar Walls*

H. and W. Brown. Wood engraving.
A clear view across to the abbey church from the city wall on the south, showing the whole north side of the church as yet unobstructed by later buildings (eg York Railway Station).
York Art Gallery YORAG : R2978.

81. *1840   St Mary's Abbey, York: West end of the Nave* (Fig.97)

J.S. Prout. Semi-coloured lithograph.
Prout 1840, pl.5.
York Art Gallery YORAG : R3995.
Evelyn Collection A809 (YAYAS Minster Library).

Fig. 97 St Mary's Abbey, York, west end of the nave, by J.S. Prout, 1840. This semi-coloured lithograph gives a very clear and detailed view of the west front, looking through the ruined doorway to the crossing pier. The modern building beyond is probably a house in Marygate built on to the abbey precinct walls.

Fig. 98 *West end of the abbey church by Francis Bedford, 1843. This picture, used as the frontispiece of* Sketches in York, *gives clear detail of the stonework and window.*

82. **1840** *St Mary's Abbey, York: East end of Nave* (Fig.23)

J.S. Prout. Semi-coloured lithograph.
The arch and pier of the crossing, seen from the north-west.
Prout 1840, pl.6.
York Art Gallery YORAG : R3991, R3996.

83. **1840** *St Mary's Abbey*

William Moore. Pencil drawing.
East end of the nave from the north-east.
York Art Gallery YORAG : R337.

84. **1840** *West End of the Abbey*

Edwin Moore. Pencil and ink on green paper.
York Art Gallery YORAG : R3590.

85. **1843** *St Mary's Abbey, West End* (Fig.98)

Francis Bedford, Jr. Semi-coloured lithograph, engraved by Monkhouse.
Bedford n.d. (c.1843), frontispiece.

86. **1843** *St Mary's Abbey, York* (Fig.20)

Francis Bedford, Jr. Semi-coloured lithograph, engraved by Monkhouse.
The abbey church from the south-west
Bedford n.d. (c.1843), pl.10.
Also: York Art Gallery, single prints, R2436, R3977.

87. **1843** *St Mary's Abbey*

a) William Richardson. Watercolour.
North wall of the nave from the south-east with good detail of the stonework. An attractive painting in its own right, recently restored. One of a series of paintings of Yorkshire abbeys.
York Art Gallery YORAG : R3023.
RCHMY negative (NMR) YC310.

b) Ruins of North Aisle, St Mary's Abbey, 1843 (Fig.11)
William Richardson. Coloured lithograph.
As above.
Richardson 1843, vol.I, pl.26.
York Art Gallery YORAG : R1792.

88. 1843   *St Mary's Abbey, West End* (Fig.21)

William Richardson. Watercolour.
Good detail of stonework as well as attractive colouring.
York Art Gallery YORAG : R1793.

89. n.d.   *St Mary's Abbey, York*

Willam Moore. Pencil drawing.
View from inside the west end of the church, looking east; north nave wall on the left, east end of the nave in the centre, King's Manor in the background at right.
York Art Gallery YORAG : R3115.

90. n.d.   *St Mary's Abbey, York*

E. Sharpe. Semi-coloured lithograph by Haworth Fielding.
View of the north-west corner of the church interior, with useful architectural detail.
York Art Gallery YORAG : R3998.

91. 1845   *St Mary's Abbey, York*

W.M. Fox Talbot. Photograph.
North wall of the nave and west end from the south-east.
Science Museum, London: negative no.358/69.

92. n.d.   *St Mary's Abbey, York*

William Monkhouse. Lithograph.
Church nave from the east.
Minster Library: Revd Robert William Bilton Hornby Collection, *York Antiquities* **2**(Add MS 320), 241.

93. n.d. (1846?)   *St Mary's Abbey*

William Moore. Drawing.
East end of the nave.
York Art Gallery YORAG : R3115.

94. n.d. (c.1848) *St Mary's Abbey and the Yorkshire Museum*

William Monkhouse. Lithograph and colour wash.

Fig. 99 *The Ruins of St Mary's Abbey, York, c.1850, by Louis-Jules Arnout. This hand-coloured lithograph is not entirely accurate – the path up to the west end is steeper than this – but the artist has successfully contrasted the Gothic/medieval abbey with the then modern (neo-classical) Yorkshire Museum, as well as contrasting the hard black and white foreground with the softer background, to make an appealing picture.*

View looking north: north wall of the abbey church, St Olave's Church behind on the left, Yorkshire Museum on the right.
Minnster Library: Revd Robert William Bilton Hornby Collection, *York Antiquities* **2** (Add MS 320), 315.

95. *n.d.* *The Ruins of St Mary's Abbey, York*

G. Shepherd. Drawing.
Minster Library YK 345.

96. *n.d.* *St Mary's Abbey, York*

W. Monkhouse. Semi-coloured lithograph.
North aisle and east end from the south-east.
York Art Gallery YORAG : 2499.

97. *c.1850* *The Ruins of St Mary's Abbey, York* (Fig.99)

Louis-Jules Arnout. Hand-coloured lithograph.
11 x 16in (278 x 404mm).
West end of the abbey church in snow; Yorkshire Museum in the background at right. There are inaccuracies, notably the perspective and the gradient of the slope below the church, but the artist has created an interesting work, contrasting the medieval abbey church with the (then) classical/modern museum, and the stark branches in the foreground with the softer lines of the background.
York Art Gallery YORAG : 2002.41.

98. *1853* *Ruins of St Mary's Abbey (Museum Gardens)*

William Pumphrey. Photographs.
Three plates showing the remains of the abbey church.
Pumphrey 1853, pls.32–4, portfolio in York Reference Library.

99. *1867* *St Mary's Abbey*

William Moore. Pencil drawing with white chalk.
Good detail of the doorway at the west end of the church.
York Art Gallery YORAG : R3125.

100. *n.d.* *St Mary's Abbey, York*

William Moore. Pencil drawing.
View looking east from the abbey nave. Minster in the background.
York Art Gallery YORAG : R3115.

101. *1877/78 Museum Gardens, St Mary's Abbey*

G.H.F. Jones. Pen and ink drawings in York Art Gallery.
a) Remains of the west front, YORAG : 2005.547 (Jones 1878, pl.34).

b) East end of the north aisle (Jones 1878, pl.35).
c) From the north-east, YORAG : 2005.548 (Jones 1878, pl.36).
d) Abbey from St Olave's churchyard, YORAG : 2005.546 (Jones 1878, pl.37).

102. *1880* *Part of St Mary's Abbey*

G.H.F. Jones. Watercolour.
Part of the east end of the north aisle.
York Art Gallery YORAG : R364.

103. *1883* *St Mary's Abbey*

A. Brunet-Debaines. Etching.
East end of the nave, from the east.
Lefroy 1883, 10.

104. *1883* *St Mary's Abbey, York*

A. Buckle. Etching.
View of the nave from the east.
Davies 1883, opposite p.3.

105. *1886* *St Mary's Abbey, West Front*

J. England Jefferson. Photomechanical reproductions.
Benson and Jefferson 1886, pl.32.
York Art Gallery YORAG : R3983.

106. *n.d.* *St Mary's Abbey, York*

W.H. Bartlett, figures by Harvey. Watercolour.
North wall and east end of the church nave.
York Art Gallery YORAG : R440.

107. *n.d.* *South-west End of Abbey*

T. Hearne, figures by F. Bartolozzi. Drawing.
West end from the north-west. Multangular Tower in the background at right.
York Art Gallery YORAG : R270.
Evelyn Collection A1781 (YAYAS Minster Library).
See also: *St Mary's Abbey, York*
After T. Hearne. Watercolour.
York Art Gallery YORAG : R1489.

108. *1900* *Chancel and Adjacent Features*

W.H. Brierley. Measured plan, scale given.
Plan of the abbey (mainly the chancel), in relation to other features and buildings.
YPSAR 1900, pl.1.

109. *1902* *St Mary's Abbey, York*

W.H. Brierley. Measured plan, scale given.
Plan of Gothic church, with Romanesque church superimposed.
YPSAR 1902, pl.5.

110. *1902   St Mary's Abbey, York. Plan showing Excavations made during 1901, 18th March 1902*

W.H. Brierley. Measured plan, scale given.
Plan of 1901 excavations superimposed on outline plan of Gothic church.
YPSAR 1902, pl.6.

111. *1902   St Mary's Abbey. York*

W.J. Boddy. Postcard reproduction of a watercolour.
East end of the nave, with part of St Olave's Church on the right.
York Art Gallery YORAG : R2781.

112. *c.1906   St Mary's Abbey. York* (Fig.100)

W.J. Boddy. Watercolour.
View through the west doorway to the north-west pier of the crossing tower.
York Reference Library album.

113. *1906   St Mary's Abbey, York, from South-West* (Fig.101)

E. Ridsdale Tate. Lithograph.
Church nave from an unusual angle. St Olave's Church tower on the left.
York Art Gallery YORAG : R3999.
Ridsdale Tate 1906.

114. *1906   St Mary's Abbey, York. Choir*

W. Watson. Photograph.
East end of the nave, with foundations of the choir in the foreground.
Evelyn Collection A1521 (YAYAS Minster Library).
Reproduced in Auden 1906, opposite p.143.

115. *c.1906–07   St Mary's Abbey*

H. M. Loadman. Photographs.
St Mary's Abbey 1906, details of arches, pls.6a and b.
St Mary's Abbey 1906, pl.8b.
St Mary's Abbey 1906, east end of the nave, pl.16f.
St Mary's Abbey 1905, north side, pl.16g.
St Mary's Abbey 1907, pl.24b.
Loadman n.d.

116. *c.1910   South Elevation of St Mary's Abbey, York (probable appearance before dissolution in 1539)* (Fig.27)

E. Ridsdale Tate. Measured drawing (scale given).
South elevation of the church, omitting the cloisters and sacristy (represented as blank spaces).
RidsdaleTate 1929, pl.2.
Benson 1919, 29.
Evelyn Collection A2166 (YAYAS Minster Library).

117. *c.1910   West Front of St Mary's Abbey (Restored view)* (Fig.18)

E. Ridsdale Tate. Wash drawing.
Reconstruction of the west front of the abbey church as it may have appeared before the dissolution in 1539.
RidsdaleTate 1929, pl.1.
Evelyn Collection A2164 (YAYAS Minster Library).

118. *1912   Excavations of the Choir – St Mary's Abbey (Oct. 1912)*

Photographs.
Views of remaining stonework and excavation trenches.
a) Looking east from the west end of the choir, with the King's Manor and Art Gallery in the background (Fig.25).
b) Viewed from the east.
c) South arcade, pillars rebuilt (February 1913) (Fig.26).
Ridsdale Tate 1929, pl.5.
Evelyn Collection 2196, 2197 and 2198 (YAYAS Minster Library).

119. *n.d.   St Mary's Abbey. Photographs in Evelyn Collection*

a) Old lime tree blown down (church nave from the south-west).
b) North-west end of the north aisle.
c) West end.
d) Nave.
Evelyn Collection A2200, 2203, 2414 and 2415 (YAYAS Minster Library).

120. *n.d.   Abbey church from the West*

Mallow. Photograph.
Evelyn Collection A662 (YAYAS Minster Library).

121. *n.d.   St Mary's Abbey, North-West Aisle*

E. Ridsdale Tate. Reconstruction.
Evelyn Collection A1529 (YAYAS Minster Library).

122. *c.1919–23   Photographs in Evelyn Collection (YAYAS Minster Library)*

a) St Mary's Abbey looking east: nave wall and crossing, A1704.
b) Vine leaf tendrils on west porch (1919), A1534.
c) West end from the hospitium (1921), A1776.
d) St Mary's Abbey by moonlight, A2195.
e) Nave looking east (1923), A2194.
f) Nave looking east, A2173.

123. n.d.   *St Mary's Abbey by Moonlight*

G. Parr. Lithograph.
Pleasant but not notably detailed view from the south-west.
York Art Gallery YORAG : R3989.
See also: *St Mary's Abbey by Moonlight*
Photograph.
Evelyn Collection A2195 (YAYAS Minster Library).

124. n.d.   *Photographs in Evelyn Collection (YAYAS Minster Library)*

a) St Mary's Abbey, choir looking north-west, St Olave's Church in the background, A823.
b) St Mary's Abbey, bowling green, looking towards the Art Gallery, A824.
c) Bases of pillars with inscription, A825.

125. 1970   *'From copperplate', St Mary's Abbey*

L.R.S. Pyrah. Print.
York Art Gallery YORAG : 2004.1.

Fig. 100 *St Mary's Abbey, York, c.1906, by W. Boddy. This postcard reproduction of an original watercolour shows the view looking through the main west doorway of the abbey church from the west to the north-west pier of the crossing tower. It is an unusual viewpoint.*

Fig. 101 *Abbey from the south-west, E. Ridsdale Tate, 7 July 1906. An attractive view from further back than most, with St Olave's Church on the left, the west front, part of the inner face of the north wall and the crossing pier.*

Claustral buildings

126. 1829 *South-East View of the Remains of St Mary's Abbey, York* (Fig.5)

Frederick Nash. Lithograph.
Excavations in progress, 1827–29. Foundations of the chapter house and east range in the foreground, the hall beneath refectory behind. In the background, the hospitium and abbey church.
Wellbeloved 1829, pl.55.
Evelyn Collection 814 (YAYAS Minster Library).
Reproduced in *The Archaeological Journal* **28** (1971), pl.15.

127. 1829 *View of the Ruins Adjoining the South Transept of the church, with the Palace of K. James 2nd and the Tower of the Minster in the Background* (Fig.32)

Frederick Nash. Lithograph.
View of excavations in progress in the chapter house, looking east. King's Manor in the background.
Wellbeloved 1829, pl.56.

Fig. 102 Parts of the buildings of St Mary's Abbey, F. Nash lithograph, measured drawings from Wellbeloved 1829 (pl.58). Detail showing voussoir, possibly depicting the Marriage at Cana, from a set of seven showing scenes from the life of Christ now in the Yorkshire Museum.

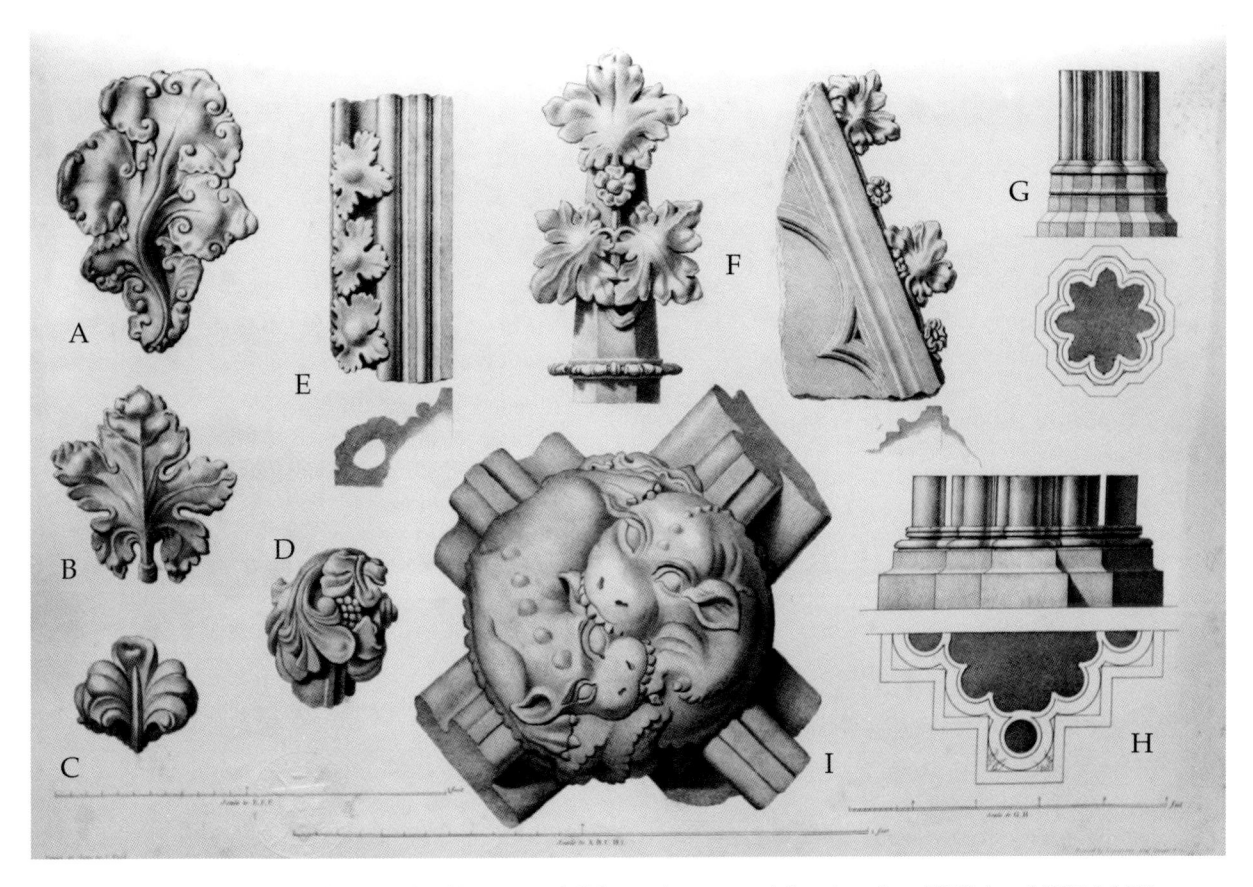

Fig. 103 Parts of the buildings of St Mary's Abbey, F. Nash lithograph, measured drawings from Wellbeloved 1829 (pl.59). A–E: Leaves from carvings in the warming room; F: Part of a crocketed pinnacle from the cloister south walk; G: pillar in the warming room; H: Plan and elevation of pillar from the chapter house; I: Roof boss from the warming room depicting two monsters or sea creatures intertwined and biting each other.

Fig. 104 Details of St Mary's Abbey, York, by W. Richardson. Details of Moses and the apostles, bosses from the warming house and some windows (left, the interior of one compartment of the north aisle of the nave; right, the exterior of one compartment of the north aisle of the nave).

York Art Gallery YORAG : R2506.
Evelyn Collection 815 (YAYAS Minster Library).

128. 1829 *Parts of the Buildings of St Mary's Abbey, York* (Figs.42–3)

Frederick Nash. Lithograph.
Fragments of masonry, now in the Yorkshire Museum, including capitals and mouldings from pillars, two roof-bosses (Virgin Mary and musician), and fireplace from the warming room.
Wellbeloved 1829, pl.57.

129. 1829 *Parts of the Buildings of St Mary's Abbey, York* (Figs.45 and 102)

Frederick Nash. Lithograph.
Fragments of masonry excavated 1827–29, now in the Yorkshire Museum. Includes mouldings, voussoir, parts of capitals, roof boss (Lamb of God) and plan and elevation of buttress from the south walk of the cloister.
Wellbeloved 1829, pl.58.

130. 1829 *Parts of the Buildings of St Mary's Abbey, York* (Figs.44 and 103)

Frederick Nash. Lithograph.
Details of carved masonry excavated 1827–29, now in the Yorkshire Museum. Includes foliage, roof boss (intertwined monsters), and plans and elevations of pillars.
Wellbeloved 1829, pl.59.

131. n.d. (1829?) *Excavations at St Mary's Abbey*

Unknown artist. Lithograph.
View of excavation of the warming room, showing fireplace and fender with carving (see Illustration 128), King's Manor in the background.
Presumably dates from the same time as Nash's drawings in Wellbeloved 1829 (Illustrations 126–30), but not included in that set and possibly by a different hand.
Minster Library: Revd Robert William Bilton Hornby Collection, *York Antiquities* **2** (Add MS 320), 269.

132. *n.d.* *Fragment of St Mary's Abbey. Pillar in vestibule of chapter house*

John Browne. Sepia ink and monochrome.
Detail showing the chevron pattern with exceptional clarity.
Minster Library: Revd Robert William Bilton Hornby Collection, *York Antiquities* **2** (Add MS 320), 271.

133. *1843* *Details of masonry from the abbey* (Fig.104)

W. Richardson. Engraving.
Details of stone carvings including windows, capitals, bosses and statues.
Richardson 1843.

Chapter house and vestibule

134. *1829* *A Sketch of the chapter house portal arch, St Mary's Abbey, York, from the fragments as arranged by D. Chantrell, Archt. Feby 12th 1829*

D. Chantrell. Pencil, lithography by Inchbold.
Minster Library YK 368.

135. *1829* *Chapter House Porch*

Unknown artist. Drawing.
Good detail of stonework.
Evelyn Collection A164 (YAYAS Minster Library).

136. *1840* *St Mary's Abbey, York. Ruins of the Chapter House* (Fig.34)

J.S. Prout. Semi-coloured lithograph.
View looking north towards the church.
Prout 1840, pl.7.
York Art Gallery YORAG : R3992 and R3993.

137. *1853* *The Chapter House, St Mary's Abbey*

William Pumphrey. Photograph.
View includes some useful details of masonry.
Pumphrey 1853, pl.37.
Portfolio in York Reference Library.
Evelyn Collection A1809 (YAYAS Minster Library).

138. *n.d.* *St Mary's Abbey, York – Vestibule of Chapter House 1154–81* (Fig.33)

From Sir Gilbert Scott's Lectures, p.2.
Detailed reconstruction of the arches.
York Art Gallery YORAG : R4002.

139. *n.d.* *Pillars of the Chapter House Vestibule*

Unknown. Photograph.
Minster Library: Revd Robert William Bilton Hornby Collection, *York Antiquities* **2** (Add MS 320), 270.
See also: Vestibule pillars of porch to chapter house.
Photograph.
Evelyn Collection 2199 (YAYAS Minster Library).

140. *n.d.* *Termination of Label Moulding of St Mary's Abbey, York*

Edwin Ridsdale Tate. Drawing.
Old York Sketches, Tracings etc., chiefly by E. Ridsdale Tate, collected by George Benson, p.77 (York Reference Library).

Twelfth-century statues

141. *1736* *Figures on the churchyard Wall, St Lawrence's Church* (Fig.37)

Francis Drake? Engraving.
Side view of two recumbent figures placed end to end, lying on a low wall. Two of the St Mary's Abbey statues, though this was unknown to Drake in 1736.
Drake 1736, p.56, pl.8, no.9.
See also Drake's note on p.60.

142. *1781* *St Lawrence's Church. Figures on the church Yard Wall*

Unknown artist. Grey wash drawing.
Two separate drawings of sculptured figures (St John the Baptist and perhaps St James) from St Lawrence's churchyard wall, originally from St Mary's Abbey chapter house and now in the Yorkshire Museum.
Wakefield Art Gallery: Gott Collection 1781/2/18.
Reproduced in Wilson and Mee 1998, fig.68, p.94.

143. *1829* *Statues Discovered in Excavating a Part of the South Aisle of the Nave of the abbey church* (Fig.36)

S. Sharp. Measured drawings/lithograph.
1. Moses; 2–4 Apostles.
Now part of the St Mary's Abbey display in the Yorkshire Museum.
Wellbeloved 1829, pl.60.

144. *1829* *Details of St Mary's Abbey, York*

Francis Bedford. Lithograph.
Includes four statues and four bosses from the chapter house; plans and elevations of pillars; sketch of capital of west door; part of the exterior elevation of a compartment of the north aisle of the nave.
Minster Library YK 373.

145. *1840* *Fragments of St Mary's Abbey in the Yorkshire Museum* (Fig.38)

J.S. Prout. Semi-coloured lithograph.
Statues and other pieces of carved masonry as for-

99

merly displayed in the Yorkshire Museum.
Prout 1840, pl.8.
York Art Gallery YORAG : R3990.
Minster Library YK 366.

146. *1913 East End of Cloister Walk, prior to dissolution 1539. Restored from fragments found in rockeries* (Fig.41)

E. Ridsdale Tate. Measured drawing.
Reconstruction of the east end of the south cloister.
York Art Gallery YORAG : R2487.
Evelyn Collection 2165 (YAYAS Minster Library).

147. *n.d. Fireplace in the Abbey, now under Yorkshire Museum*

Photograph.
Evelyn Collection A692 (YAYAS Minster Library).

Outer Precincts

148. *1800 A Mortar formerly belonging to St Mary's Abbey, York*

'A.K'. Engraving.
From the infirmary, now in the Yorkshire Museum.
The Gentleman's Magazine, June 1800, pl.2, p.513.
Minster Library YK 367.

149. *n.d. Ancient Brass Mortar belonging to St Mary's Abbey in the Museum of the Yorkshire Philosophical Society*

William Brown. Wood engraving.
York Art Gallery YORAG : R3981.

150. *n.d. Mortar belonging to Abbey Infirmary*

Photograph.
Evelyn Collection A703 (YAYAS Minster Library).

151. *1874 Memorial Cross Slab* (Fig.47)

D.A. Walter. Drawing from rubbing.
Slab of Emma de Benefield, benefactress of the abbey, now in the Yorkshire Museum. Emma may have been the widow of Adam de Ben[ing]field of Morton in Cleveland.
Walter 1874, pl.25.

Hospitium

152. *c.1680 The Ouse at Lendal Ferry*

Francis Place. Engraving.
View from the river near Lendal Tower, looking across to the Manor shore, with the water tower, hospitium, water gate and possibly part of the precinct wall.
Drake 1736, 331.
See also, the same view: *Near the Manor Shore, York* (Fig.68)
William Lodge. Engraving.
York Art Gallery YORAG : R1977

153. *1776 North Prospect of Part of the Ruins of St Mary's Abbey*

Edward Abbot. Wash drawing.
View mainly of the hospitium and water gate.
Wakefield Art Gallery: Gott Collection 1776/3/5.
See also: *East Prospect of the Hospitium*
'F.G.' Watercolour.
Evelyn Collection A1327 (YAYAS Minster Library).

154. *1795 York, from the Manor*

F. Nicholson. Engraving by Walker.
View from the north-east side of the hospitium (shown on the right) looking south-south-east down river.
Minster Library: Revd Robert W. Bilton Hornby Collection, *York Antiquities* **2** (Add MS 320), 77.

155. *1801 The Hospitium, Manor Shore*

Henry Cave. Sketch.
View from the south.
York Art Gallery YORAG : R2708.
See also: Evelyn Collection A2154 (YAYAS Minster Library).

156. *n.d. The Museum Grounds*

Henry Cave. Sketch.
View of the hospitium.
York Art Gallery YORAG : R3417.

157. *n.d. On the Manor Shore, York*

Henry Cave. Watercolour.
View of the hospitium, looking south-west towards the river.
York Art Gallery YORAG : R3411.

158. *n.d. Hospitium*

Henry Cave. Drawing.
Viewed from the south-west (river) side.
Evelyn Collection A163 (YAYAS Minster Library).

159. *n.d. Back of the Hospitium*

Henry Cave. Watercolour.
Arches in the water gate adjoining the hospitium from the south.
York Art Gallery YORAG : R3418.

160. *n.d. (1820s)   At the Manor Shore*

George Nicholson. Pencil drawing.
View of the gable end of the hospitium.
York Art Gallery YORAG : 2005.583.
See also: Evelyn Collection A626 (YAYAS Minster Library).

161. *1825   At St Mary's Abbey*

George Nicholson. Pencil drawing.
The hospitium from the east.
York Art Gallery YORAG : R1402.
Evelyn Collection A625 (YAYAS Minster Library).

162. *1825   At St Mary's Abbey, York, Sept. 2 1825*

George Nicholson. Pencil sketch.
Part of the hospitium.
York Art Gallery: Nicholson Sketchbooks YORAG : R2171 (32).

163a. *c.1825   Gateway of St Mary's Abbey, York*

George Nicholson. Pencil sketch.
Exterior (south-west) view of the arch adjoining the hospitium.

b. Interior of Gateway, St Mary's Abbey, York, Sep. 2 1825

George Nicholson. Pencil sketch.
Arch adjoining the hospitium from the inner side.
York Art Gallery YORAG : R2171 (30) and (31).

c. At St Mary's, June 3rd 1825 (Fig.105)

Probably shows the water gate alongside the hospitium.
York Art Gallery YORAG : 2005.585.

164. *1832   Granary, St Mary's Abbey* (Fig.50)

'W.T.' (after W. Twopenny). Pencil drawing.
North-east and north-west elevations of the hospitium.
York Art Gallery YORAG : R2488.

165. *1832   Columns supporting floor, Granary, St Mary's Abbey* (Fig.51)

'W.T.' (after W. Twopenny). Pencil drawing.
Good detail of stonework and timber panels in the undercroft of the hospitium.
York Art Gallery YORAG : 2005.596.

166. *n.d. (c.1832)   Granary, York*

'W.T.' (after W. Twopenny). Pencil drawing.
Detail of window frame.
York Art Gallery YORAG : 2005.597.

Fig. 105 This rather enigmatic drawing by Nicholson, simply entitled 'At St Mary's', probably shows the water gate alongside the hospitium.

167. *n.d.   Part of St Mary's Abbey* (Fig.54)

Edward Harper. Lithograph by Monkhouse.
The arch adjoining the hospitium, from the inner side. A clear and useful view.
York Art Gallery YORAG : R3986.

168. *1840   St Mary's Abbey; old Hospitium at York, 1840*

William Moore. Pencil drawing.
South-east end wall with considerable detail of the construction timbers.
York Art Gallery YORAG : R3144.
See also: *The Hospitium*
W. Moore, Jr.
Evelyn Collection A1805 (YAYAS Minster Library).

169. *1840   The Hospitium, St Mary's Abbey, York*

J.S. Prout. Sepia lithograph.
Prout 1840, pl.10.
York Art Gallery YORAG : R3997.
Minster Library YK 365.

170. *1840   The Hospitium, April 7, 1840*

J.R. Catley. Watercolour.
View from the east.
York Art Gallery YORAG : R2338.
Also: As above, almost identical, York Art Gallery YORAG : R2337.

171. *1848   St Mary's Abbey, York*

William Moore. Pencil drawing.
The gateway adjoining the hospitium from the inner side (i.e. from the north). Lendal Tower, the spire of All Saints' North Street and North Street Postern in the background. Some useful detail.
York Art Gallery YORAG : R333.

172. 1852 *Part of Wall near to the Hospitium*

William Moore. Sketch.
York Art Gallery YORAG : R3126.
cf York Art Gallery YORAG : R333 (Illustration 171).

173. 1853 *Hospitium of St Mary's Abbey (Museum Gardens)*

William Pumphrey. Photograph.
View of the north-west end.
Pumphrey 1853, pl.36.

174. 1856 *The Hospitium*

W. Moore. Drawing.
Evelyn Collection A1205 (YAYAS Minster Library).

Fig. 106 Photograph of the interior of the lower room of the hospitium by George Benson. This early 20th-century view from the south-east end shows Roman tiles in the foreground and medieval stone work in the background before it was removed to the Yorkshire Museum in 1912. The rows of columns which divide the ground floor into three aisles are clearly shown. (Imagine York Y32_1588, © City of York Council www.imagineyork.co.uk historic images from York's libraries and archives)

175. 1876 *At York, 1876*

William J. Boddy. Watercolour.
Ruined arches adjoining the hospitium.
York Art Gallery YORAG : R31.
Also: as above R26.

176. 1877/78 *The Museum Gardens: The Hospitium*

G.H. Fowler Jones. Pen and ink drawing.
Jones 1878, pl.38.
York Art Gallery YORAG : 2005.545.

177. 1886 *St Mary's Abbey, Old Hospitium, 1886* (Fig.52)

William Moore. Pencil drawing.
York Art Gallery YORAG : R209.
cf 1840 Hospitium, W. Moore, York Art Gallery YORAG : R3144 (Illustration 168), which is similar, though R209 is somewhat larger and clearer.

178. n.d. *Hospitium, St Mary's Abbey*

Paul Braddon. Watercolour.
Hospitium and arch from the north-east.
York Art Gallery YORAG : R454.

179. 1897 *Hospitium Steps and Watergate* (Fig.53)

William J. Boddy. Watercolour.
View from the inner (north-east) side.
Colour reproduction in Boddy 1906.

180. 1900s *The interior of the hospitium* (Fig.106)

George Benson. Photograph.
Interior of the lower room of the hospitium from the south-east end, with Roman tiles in the foreground and medieval stonework in the background before it was removed to the Yorkshire Museum in 1912.
Imagine York, Y32_1588, © City of York Council www.imagineyork.co.uk historic images from York's libraries and archives.

181. 1907 *Hospitium, York Museum Gardens*

William J. Boddy. Watercolour.
Archway and south gable end.
York Art Gallery YORAG : R2750.

182. *Photographs in Evelyn Collection:*

a) n.d. St Mary's Abbey – hospitium from the south-east A2889.
b) 1921 Hospitium: south side A1810.
c) n.d. Hospitium – Upper room A2162.
Evelyn Collection (YAYAS Minster Library).

Precinct walls

Note 1. The order of illustrations follows the walls from the north-east tower (the water tower) on the river bank at the bottom of Marygate clockwise back to the river bank.

Note 2. Artists were as confused over nomenclature as the general public, particularly regarding the towers at each end of Marygate: the tower on the river bank should be Marygate Tower or water tower; that at the junction with Bootham should be St Mary's Tower.

Marygate water tower

183. *1678   York from St Mary's Tower*

Francis Place. Ink and wash.
4¾ x 9¾ in (121 x 145mm).
The water tower in foreground left is shown still crenellated.
York Art Gallery YORAG : R1858.
YAT Collection TG17.
Colour reproduction in Wilson and Mee 2002, fig.57.
Also engravings:

York Art Gallery YORAG : R1859 (inscribed Lodge), reproduced in Drake 1736, 332.
York Art Gallery YORAG : R5081, R5085 (one copy annotated).
York Art Gallery YORAG : R5086, a wider view of the river.
See also: YAT Collection TG9.
Evelyn Collection 136 (YAYAS Minster Library).

184. *c.1700   York from Beyond the Water Tower at St Mary's*

Francis Place. Pen and ink with grey wash.
View looking south-east, similar to Illustration 183.
BM Department of Prints and Drawings: 1850-2-23-834.
Photostat in York Art Gallery.

185. *n.d.   Bottom of Marygate*

Henry Cave. Watercolour.
View downstream, with the water tower on the left.
York Art Gallery YORAG : R59.

Fig. 107 *York Esplanade, showing St Mary's Tower [actually Marygate water tower], by W. Boddy, 1895. View from the river, looking south-east, with the tower and adjoining precinct wall. A barge is moored on the riverbank. This was the abbey landing which caused so much dissension with the city authorities. Beyond is the river esplanade, with the Minster and St Wilfrid's Roman Catholic church behind.*

186. *1813 (published)   St Mary's Tower* (Fig.59)

Henry Cave. Engraving.
Cave describes this as being at the north-east corner of the abbey, but it is the water tower at the north-west corner. It has lost much of its upper part since drawn by Place (Illustration 183).
Cave 1813, pl.28.

187a. *1822   At York, Oct 4th 1822*

George Nicholson. Pencil drawing.
The water tower from the south-west.
York Art Gallery YORAG : R911.

187b. *As above, view from south.*

York Art Gallery YORAG : R913.

188. *1825   Old Tower on the Manor Shore, York, May 16th 1825*

George Nicholson. Pencil sketches.
Marygate water tower:
a) from the west (18).
b) from the north-west (19).
York Art Gallery: Nicholson Sketchbooks R2171 (18) and (19).

189. *1826   Water-Tower, Marygate, York, Jan. 28th 1826*

George Nicholson. Pencil drawing.
View from the south-east side.
York Art Gallery YORAG : R2446.53.

190. *1885   St Mary's Tower and Landing*

G.H. Fowler Jones. Drawing.
View looking north-east up Marygate.
Minster Library: Revd Robert William Bilton Hornby Collection, *York Antiquities* **2** (Add MS 320), 283.

191. *1885   Bottom of Marygate*

T.P. Cooper. Watercolour.
Arch and tower by Marygate Landing from the west.
York Art Gallery YORAG : R756b.

Fig. 108 Inner view of the lodge and part of the entrance arch by George Nicholson, 17 June 1825. This shows the blind arcade still visible today. The lodge has ecclesiastical-style windows and storage areas built on, emphasising the change in use of the abbey and its associated buildings.

192. *1895   York Esplanade showing St Mary's Tower* (Fig.107)

W. Boddy. Postcard reproduction of watercolour.
View from the river of the tower and adjoining wall, with the former abbey landing.
Album in York Reference Library.

The Abbey gateway

193. *c.1700   St Marie's Gate, York*

Francis Place. Ink drawing.
External view of the gatehouse and lodge.
York Art Gallery YORAG : R2213.
Evelyn Collection A2621 (YAYAS, Minster Library).

194. *c.1700   St Marie's Gate, Yorke*

Francis Place. Ink drawing; roundel on tinted paper.
View from the inner side. Inscribed on the reverse 'Att Yorke, ye contrary way'.
York Art Gallery YORAG : R3213 (Fig.60).
Evelyn Collection 600 (YAYAS Minster Library).

195. *n.d.   St Mary's Lodge*

Unknown artist. Pencil drawing.
View from the inner side.
Evelyn Collection A918 (YAYAS Minster Library).

196. *c.1705   St Marye's church, the Abbey Gates and Part of the Abbey. In Civit. Ebor*

James Poole. Wash drawing.
View from the inner side.
The gatehouse is still complete, with crenellation; also shown are St Mary's chapel and St Olave's church, the latter partly obscured by the west end of the abbey.
Oxford, Bodleian Library, MS Tanner 311, fo.169v–170r.
Reproduced in Wilson and Mee 1998, p.142, fig.107.

197. *1801   St Mary's Abbey Gateway* (Fig.61)

Thomas Rowlandson. Pencil, watercolour, pen and ink.
8 x 13¾in (206 x 347mm).
View from the inner side: lodge, gateway (shorn of gatehouse), part of St Olave's, and the west end of the abbey church. Clear and detailed, if not entirely accurate, and an attractive picture in its own right.
York Art Gallery YORAG : R1718.
Colour reproduction in Murray *et al* 1990, p.51, fig.37.
Also: Preliminary sketch for the above
From double page of a sketchbook. Top cropped, but good detail of the lodge.
York Art Gallery YORAG : R 2692.
Colour reproduction in Murray *et al* 1990, p.50, fig.36.
Evelyn Collection A262 (YAYAS Minster Library).

198. *1807   Entrance to St Mary's Abbey* (Fig.62)

Joseph Halfpenny. Etching.
11¾ x 9in (285 x 230mm).
The entrance archway and the lodge from the outer side, with clear detail of the stonework on the north and east faces.
Halfpenny 1807, pl.30.

199. *n.d.   St Mary's Gatehouse and St Olave's Church*

Henry Cave. Pencil and white bodycolour, with blue touching.
View looking north from in front of the hospitium, showing the inner side of the lodge (hiding the gateway) and part of St Olave's Church.
York Art Gallery YORAG : R3416.
Black and white reproduction in Wilson and Mee 1998, p.142, fig.108.

200. *n.d.   Manor Shore Entrance*

Henry Cave. Watercolour.
Looking through the entrance towards Marygate.
York Art Gallery YORAG : R3415.

See also: St Mary's Abbey Gateway (interior view)
Henry Cave.
Evelyn Collection A661 (YAYAS Minster Library).

201. *1817   Entrance to St Mary's Abbey, York (for the Antiquarian Itinerary)*

G. Stanley. Small steel engraving by Roberts.
View from the inner side.
York Art Gallery YORAG : R2495.
Minster Library YK 353.

202. *1825   Pencil Sketches of the Gateway by George Nicholson*

a) At St Mary's Abbey, June 5th 1825

Viewed from the south-west.
York Art Gallery YORAG : R3998.

b) St Mary's Abbey Lodge, June 17th 1825 (Fig.108)

From the inner side, after roof restoration.
York Art Gallery YORAG : R886.

c) At St Mary's Abbey

Entrance and lodge (with inn sign) from Marygate.
Nicholson Sketchbooks York Art Gallery YORAG : R2446 (60).

203. *1827   St Mary's Abbey, 1827*

George Nicholson. Etching.
5 x 8in (127 x 180mm).
Gatehouse and lodge from the outer side.
York Art Gallery YORAG : R2614.
Evelyn Collection A387 (YAYAS Minster Library).
Reproduced in Murray *et al* 1990, p 59, fig.45.

204. *1827   Interior of the Gateway, St Mary's Abbey, June 12th 1827*

George Nicholson. Pencil drawing.
York Art Gallery YORAG : R793.
Evelyn Collection A627 (YAYAS Minster Library).
Also: Tracing by G.H. Fowler Jones, York Art Gallery YORAG : R791.

205. *1827   Gateway of St Mary's Abbey, York*

George Nicholson. Etching.
5 x 8in (127 x 181mm).
The gateway and lodge from the inner side.
York Art Gallery YORAG : R3148.
Reproduced in Murray *et al* 1990, p.58, fig.44.

206. *n.d.   St Mary's Abbey Lodge*

George Nicholson. Small finished drawing.
From the inner side.
York Art Gallery YORAG : R803.

207. *1849   St Mary's Abbey Lodge*

William Moore. Pencil drawing.
View from the inner side.
York Art Gallery YORAG : R3143.

208. *n.d.   St Mary's Abbey: St Mary's Lodge and St Olave's Church*

William Moore. Sketch.
View from the inner side.
York Art Gallery YORAG : R3142.

209. *1853   Entrance to St Mary's Abbey etc, Marygate*

Willam Pumphrey. Photograph.
Archway and lodge from the outer side.
Pumphrey 1853, pl.35.

210. *n.d.   St Mary's Gate, York*

E[dwin] Moore. Pencil drawing.
Inner side of gateway, with detail of the lodge.
York Art Gallery YORAG : R3587.

211. *?1860s   St Mary's Gate – Entrance to Brown Cow*

William Monkhouse. Engraving.
Evelyn Collection A694 (YAYAS Minster Library).

212. *1883   'St Olave's House' Marygate*

H. Waterworth. Watercolour.
Gatehouse of St Mary's Abbey from across the road in Marygate.
York Art Gallery YORAG : 387.

213. *1886   Gateway to St Mary's Abbey*

Photographs.
a) Inner side.
b) Outer side.
Minster Library: Revd Robert William Bilton Hornby Collection, *York Antiquities* **2** (Add MS 320), 268.

214. *n.d.   Marygate Entrance*

Photograph.
From the inner side.
Evelyn Collection A2202 (YAYAS Minster Library).

Walls along Marygate

215.   *n.d.   Marygate*

Henry Cave. Drawing.
Abbey walls on the right.
Evelyn Collection W2153 (YAYAS Minster Library).

216. *1878   Walls from the inside between square tower and Marygate Tower*

William Chapman. Photograph.
Wall fronting the south-eastern side of Marygate.
Evelyn Collection A1559 (YAYAS Minster Library).

217. *n.d.   Photographs of precinct walls in Marygate*

a) St Mary's Abbey: walls used as butts – bullet marks (A1513).
b) Boundary wall and St Olave's Church (A738).
c) Boundary wall in Marygate, inner side (A739)
Evelyn Collection (YAYAS Minster Library).

218. *1895   Marygate and Bootham*

Plan of the streets, including part of the abbey walls.
Evelyn Collection 1895 (YAYAS Minster Library).
RCHM negative (NMR).

Fig. 109 *Old Tower, Marygate, by H. Waterworth. This late 19th-century wash drawing shows a similar view to Cave's (Fig.63), but gives a clearer picture of the houses abutting the tower and wall. The roof was rebuilt in the 19th century. The houses to the left have now gone, leaving the abbey walls exposed.*

107

219. *c.1900 Abbey walls exterior after removal of houses in Marygate* (Fig.57)

   City engineers. Photograph.
   Imagine York Y9_MAR_3673_A, © City of York Council www.imagineyork.co.uk historic images from York's libraries and archives.

220. *c.1933 Inner side of abbey walls with terraced houses* (Fig.58)

   Photograph.
   Taken from the Museum Gardens. It shows the rear of nos. 7–23 Marygate, a row of terraced houses built on to the abbey precinct wall, demolished in 1937–40. Marygate tower can be seen at the right of the picture and the rear of an open-backed turreted tower at left.
   Imagine York 157_A1C_264, © City of York Council www.imagineyork.co.uk historic images from York's libraries and archives.

St Mary's Tower

221. *1813 Tower at the Entrance of Marygate* (Fig.63)

   Henry Cave. Engraving.
   Clear depiction of the door and windows brought from the King's Manor.
   Cave 1813, pl.35.
   Original drawing in York Art Gallery.

222. *1816 Tower in the Walls at York*

   Stanley. Engraving.
   From the *Antiquarian Itinerary* 1817–18.
   Minster Library YK 357 and 358.

223. *1825 Marygate Tower, York, July 11 1825*

   George Nicholson. Pencil drawing.
   The inner side of the tower.
   York Art Gallery YORAG : R936.

224. *n.d. Marygate Tower, York*

   George Nicholson. Pencil drawing.
   View from the corner of Marygate, showing the boulder at the base of the tower, and houses on the right of the tower, in Marygate.
   York Art Gallery YORAG : R908.

225. *1826 Marygate Tower, March 14th 1826*

   George Nicholson. Pencil drawing.
   York Art Gallery: Nicholson Sketchbooks YORAG : R2446 (36).

226. *1827 View from Marygate, looking towards Bootham Bar, July 19th 1827*

   George Nicholson. Pencil drawing.
   St Mary's Tower, in right foreground, is here seen in the context of Bootham and the Bar.
   York Art Gallery YORAG : R1417 (35).
   YAT Collection IV 0 3.
   Evelyn Collection 631 (YAYAS Minster Library).
   RCHMY negative (NMR).

227. *1840 Bootham and Bootham Bar from Marygate Tower*

   H.B. Carter. Watercolour.
   St Mary's Tower in the foreground.
   York Art Gallery YORAG : R44.
   YAT Collection IV 0 4.

228. *c.1848 The Minster and Bootham Bar from the Corner of Marygate*

   W. Bevan. Lithograph by Monkhouse.
   St Mary's Tower from the north-west, in the foreground of the view along Bootham towards the Bar.
   Bevan and Monkhouse c.1848, no plate nunber.

229. *n.d. Tower Hamlet, Marygate, York*

   H. Waterworth. Watercolour roundel.
   St Mary's Tower from the north, with adjoining buildings.
   York Art Gallery YORAG : R2458.
   See also: wash drawing YORAG : R201 and watercolour YORAG : 2007.314 (Fig.109).

230. *c.1893 St Mary's Tower, Bootham*

   Photograph.
   View from the corner of Bootham and Marygate.
   Reproduced in Caine 1893, opposite p.160.
   Also in Caine 1897, opposite p.97.

231. *1898 At York, 1898*

   William J. Boddy. Watercolour.
   St Mary's Tower from Bootham with adjoining buildings, under snow.
   York Art Gallery YORAG : R30.

Walls along Bootham

232. *1860 Marygate Tower and Abbey Walls*

   William Moore. Sketch.
   Inner side of the tower and walls from a viewpoint just inside the north wall of the abbey precinct,

looking west towards the tower.
York Art Gallery YORAG : R3140.

233. *1890s   Men working on the inner side of the abbey precinct wall in Exhibition Square* (Fig.67)

Just off the picture to the right would be the postern tower and Queen Margaret's Arch. On the other side of the wall is the old White Horse Inn.
Imagine York Y9_11092, © City of York Council www.imagineyork.co.uk historic images from York's libraries and archives.

234. *1914   Abbey Wall in Bootham, Oct. 1914*

Photograph.
Walls revealed by house clearing between Queen Margaret's Arch and St Mary's Tower.
Evelyn Collection A1130 (YAYAS Minster Library).

235. *1915   The Abbey Walls from Bootham, AD – ?* (Fig.65)

E. Ridsdale Tate. Pen and black ink, with two sepia photographs.
14 x 36¼in (360 x 921mm).
In 1877 the precinct walls became the property of the Yorkshire Philosophical Society, which had some houses removed and hoped to clear all buildings blocking the view of the walls. Ridsdale Tate's drawing shows the walls as they had once appeared and would again appear after clearance. The view shows the Bootham walls with, from right to left, St Mary's Tower, Towers D and E, and Queen Margaret's Arch. The slight realignment at Tower D has been exaggerated. In the background, also right to left, St Olave's Church, the abbey, the King's Manor, St Wilfrid's (Roman Catholic) Church tower, the Theatre Royal, the De Grey Rooms, Bootham Bar.
Also two photographs (not shown in Fig.65):
a) 1895 shop on left of exposed section of wall.
b) 1914 shop (J. Athery) on right of exposed section.
York Art Gallery YORAG : R3087.
Reproduced in Murray *et al* 1990, p.47, fig.33.

Queen Margaret's Arch

236. *c.1810   Queen Margaret's Arch and Manor Yard*

Henry Cave. Lithograph.
View looking south-west.
Evelyn Collection A178 (YAYAS Minster Library).

237. *n.d.   Queen Margaret's Arch*

Henry Cave. Watercolour.
View from the inner (south) side, showing the gable ends of two houses on the right, now part of Exhibition Square.

York Art Gallery YORAG : R3407.
See also: *n.d. Inside Queen Margaret's Arch*
E. Ridsdale Tate, after Henry Cave. Drawing.
Evelyn Collection W2144 (YAYAS Minster Library).

238. *c.1840–43   Ancient Gateway to the Yorkshire School for the Blind* (Fig.66)

Francis Bedford. Two-toned lithograph by Monkhouse.
9¾ x 7in (244 x 178mm).
Queen Margaret's Arch from the north-east. On the left is a shop (Mrs M.B. Ward), taken down in 1878 for the creation of Exhibition Square; on the right is the postern tower (shop, Edward Bearpark); in the background, through the arch, is the entrance to the King's Manor.
York Art Gallery YORAG : R2889.
Reproduced in Murray *et al* 1990, p.62, fig.49.

239. *c.1880 Gillygate, from the south-west, seen through Queen Margaret's Arch*

Stereographic plate 'collection of Mr Proctor', considerably worn and damaged.
RCHMY negatives (NMR) YC1097 and YC1098.

240. *n.d.   St Margaret's Arch from Blind School before the building of St Leonard's*

Photograph.
Arch from the south-west with buildings adjoining it at right angles on the right.
Evelyn Collection A1724 (YAYAS Minster Library).

241. *1891   At York*

William J. Boddy. Watercolour.
Queen Margaret's Arch from Bootham Bar: a closer view than Illustration 242, and from further east.
York Art Gallery YORAG : R33.

242. *1891   At York*

William J. Boddy. Watercolour.
Similar to Illustration 241, but from further back and further to the west.
York Art Gallery YORAG : R39.

243. *n.d.   The Princess Margaret Archway, Bootham: Entrance to the Blind School*

William J. Boddy. Watercolour.
The arch and tower from the north-west.
York Art Gallery YORAG : R283.

244. *(published) 1906   Bootham Postern*

William J. Boddy. Watercolour and reproduction.
Queen Margaret's Arch from the south.
Boddy 1906.

245. *1934 Blind School Entrance, 1934*

Paul Braddon. Watercolour.
Queen Margaret's Arch from the north-east, showing a shop front in the tower on the right and the King's Manor doorway sketched in the centre background.
York Art Gallery YORAG : R458.

Note 1: Many views of Bootham Bar from Exhibition Square include the Arch and Postern Tower. See Wilson and Mee 2005, illustrations 157–8, 162–4.

Note 2. For views showing remains of the precinct wall along the river shore see:
Place in Drake 1736, 331 (Illustration 152).
Toms in Drake 1736, 574 (Illustration 5).

Fig. 110 The Yorkshire Museum and Roman Multangular Tower, by H. and W. Brown, 1836. This wood engraving enhances the grandeur of the museum by looking at it from a lower viewpoint and allows a contrast with the Multangular Tower on the right.

Post-Dissolution buildings

246. *1836 Three Wood Engravings by H. and W. Brown*

a) The Yorkshire Museum YORAG : R2493 (Fig.72).
b) The Yorkshire Museum and Roman Multangular Tower YORAG : R2415 (Fig.110).
c) Gateway to the Yorkshire Museum YORAG : R2494; also reproduced in Buttery n.d., 54 (Fig.73).
The gateway of c.1830 (William Wilkins), now replaced.
Brown, H. and W. 1836 (not numbered).
York Art Gallery.

The King's Manor

For clarity and ease of description, the buildings are described as though they lie on an east–west axis corresponding to the liturgical east–west of the abbey.

Plans

247. 1685   *A Drawing of His Majesties Manner House at York* (Figs.74 and 82)

Jacob Richards. Measured plan.
Plan of the King's Manor and its grounds. The original was probably made in 1682 when Sir Christopher Musgrave, Lieutenant of Ordnance, was sent to York to check the condition of the military defences of the castle and the city (Browning *et al* 1991, 280–1). The Manor was at that time the residence of the military governor, Sir John Reresby. Richards' plan is a fair copy which, along with plans of the castle and the city defences, accompanied Sir Christopher Musgrave's report.
Staffordshire County Record Office, Stafford: Dartmouth MSS D(W) 1778/ 8/ III/ 02.
York City Archives (YCA) Acc. 165, photostat of the report and maps.
York City Library no.8 in map drawer. Black and white photograph.

248. 1726   *Plan of the Manor House 'as now divided'*

Measured plan with names of occupiers, possibly drawn by one of them.
a) Upper floor.
b) Ground floor.
Evelyn Collection E466 and E467 (YAYAS Minster Library).

249. 1925 (published)   *The Abbot's House: the King's Manor House*

George Benson. Measured plan.
Benson 1925, figs.3 and 4.

250. 1971   *Plan of the King's Manor*

Labelled and measured plan; scale given.
The Archaeological Journal **128** (1971), 139.

Views

251. *c*.1680   *A View of the Ruins of the Manor and St Maries Abbey in York*

Francis Place. Pen, ink and wash.
View from the south with part of a wall and the remains of the west bay of a window in the Manor (part of the west wing, over vaulted cellars). In the background, ruins of the abbey church and part of the gatehouse.
Society of Antiquaries: Coleraine Collection VII, 46, top.
Reproduced in *The Archaeological Journal* **128** (1971), pl.15.
See also Illustration 1.

252. *c*.1700   *Ruins of a Window in the Manor*

Francis Place. Drawing (roundel on tinted paper).
Part of a bay window, with All Saints, North Street, in the background.
York Art Gallery YORAG : 1102 (viii).
Evelyn Collection A767 (YAYAS Minster Library).
Also, copy, York Art Gallery YORAG : R3210 (Fig.84).
This may be the window, part of which is shown in Illustration 254.

253. *c*.1705   *Part of the Ruines of the Mannor, Yorke*

Francis Place. Pencil and wash.
Section of precinct (?) wall on the right, broken on the left to show a tall ruined section of a building with parts of window openings at three levels and vaults and broken arches in front.
York Art Gallery YORAG : 1102 (xiii) 65.
Also, copy, York Art Gallery YORAG : R1965.
Evelyn Collection A596 (YAYAS Minster Library).
Note: Whittingham described this as a north-east view of St Olave's Church being taken down, with the abbot's gate left, and St Mary's chapel, right (Whittingham 1971, 143).

254. *c*.1705   *In the Mannor, York*

Francis Place. Pencil and wash.
On the left, the standing corner of a wall with a classical frieze and on its right the jamb of a large bay window (see Illustration 252). Ruined walls on the right. Described as 'remains ... of a Renaissance palace which we conjecture once stood where now the Yorkshire Museum stands or some feet behind or above the Henry VIII vaults where [formerly] the Department of History of York University [stood]' (*Preview* **18**, January 1965, 646).
Whittingham describes this as 'the south-west corner of the [church] transept with Wentworth's north-west bay [of the Manor] on the left, and his south-west bay in between, in the distance' (Whittingham 1971, 143).
York Art Gallery YORAG : 1102 (xii).
Also, copy, York Art Gallery YORAG : R1967.
Evelyn Collection A597 (YAYAS Minster Library).
Reproduced in Whittingham 1971, pl.17.

Fig. 111 '*From the Manor Yard*', 1717. Place's view is looking north-east from the King's Manor towards Bootham Bar, visible in the background together with a section of the city wall later removed for the building of St Leonard's Place. Part of the abbey wall is still standing; the door and window openings suggest the remains of a building on the right.

255. 1717   *Bootham, from the Manor Yard* (Fig.111)

Francis Place. Watercolour.
A view of the Manor gardens and abbey walls (with blocked windows). In the background, Bootham Bar, Tower 21 of the city defences, and linking wall.
York Art Gallery ('after Place') YORAG : R1961.
Evelyn Collection 599 (YAYAS Minster Library).
YAT Collection IV 2 1.

256. 1718   *At the Mannor, York, 1718* (Fig.83)

Francis Place. Pencil and wash.
Ruin with the large archway of a gate half hidden by ruins on the right. Tall chimney on the left end of the building. Two-light window at first floor level of the far wall still standing. Possibly the warming house under the Yorkshire Museum or the monastic kitchen (*Preview* **18**, January 1965).
York Art Gallery YORAG : R1969.
Evelyn Collection A595 (YAYAS Minster Library).

257. 1718   *At the Mannor, York, 1718*

Francis Place. Pencil, chalk and wash.
The same ruined building as shown in Illustration 256, seen from behind the gable end visible on the left in that picture.
York Art Gallery YORAG : R1964.

Evelyn Collection A594 (YAYAS Minster Library).
See also: *Ruins of King's Manor (window)*
Francis Place.
Evelyn Collection A1670 (YAYAS Minster Library).

258. 1776   *South-West View of the Manor at York Nov. 15th 1776* (Fig.112)

Edward Abbot (?). Wash drawing.
A relatively rare view from this side.
Wakefield Art Gallery: Gott Collection 1776/3/10.
Evelyn Collection A1321 (YAYAS Minster Library) (attributed to J. Beckwith).

259. 1803   *The Back of the Manor House in 1803*

Henry Cave. Pencil drawing.
South-west view (i.e. from the abbey).
York Art Gallery YORAG : R3400.
Evelyn Collection A181 (YAYAS Minster Library).

260. 1807   *Vaults of St Mary's Abbey* (Fig.91)

Joseph Halfpenny. Etching.
7¼ x 9¼in (184 x 248mm).
These vaults are often attributed to Henry VIII, but actually date from Lord Sheffield's Presidency. The Gothic doorway is 14th-century re-used. Halfpenny gives the vault measurements as 129ft (39.3m) long,

23ft (7.0m) wide and 11ft (3.4m) high, divided by a wall 3ft 5in (1.0m) thick. There were two doors and seven windows on one side, none on the other. Each section contained a deep well.
Halfpenny 1807, pl.28.
York Art Gallery YORAG : R2377.

261. 1807 *Vaults of St Mary's Abbey* (Fig.92)

Joseph Halfpenny. Etching.
7¼ x 9¼in (184 x 248mm).
View from the opposite end to Illustration 260.
Halfpenny 1807, pl.29.
York Art Gallery YORAG : R2378.

262. 1807 *Entrance to the Manor* (Fig.75)

Joseph Halfpenny. Etching.
7¼ x 9¼in (184 x 248mm).
South doorway on the east front.
Halfpenny 1807, pl.31.

263. 1807 *Entrance to the Manor with the Strafford's Arms* [sic] (Fig.81)

Joseph Halfpenny. Etching.
7¼ x 9¼in (184 x 248mm).
Entrance to the west range of the eastern courtyard, with the arms of Thomas, Viscount Wentworth, President of the Council in the North, 1628–41. Halfpenny repeats the myth that Wentworth's use of his own arms in the King's Manor was used as an article of impeachment against him in 1641.
Halfpenny 1807, pl.32.

264. 1810 (published) *A Doorway to the Manor House York – an unfinished Plate* (Fig.113)

John Sell Cotman. Etching.
216 x 146mm.
Part of the main entrance, with a wall on the left. A figure (artist?) with a book or folder and bag is emerging from the doorway. Published 1 August 1810, but probably originally drawn in 1803. Part of a portfolio of etchings planned c.1810 including ten Yorkshire subjects, but this one may not have been intended for publication, particularly since the image appears to be the wrong way round. Hill comments that Cotman's 'main purpose in this etching was never antiquarian … it is the figure posed in the doorway that is his principal subject' (Hill 2005, 161–2).
Private collection.
Reproduced in Hill 2005, pl.149.
York Art Gallery YORAG : R3903.

Fig. 112 *This wash drawing of the south-west front by Edward Abbot (1776) is not easily identifiable; one opinion is that it is Sir Arthur Ingram's house, but it doesn't look like it. This face of the King's Manor has been much altered and is now partly hidden by the buildings of the Yorkshire Museum. The image certainly shows the complexity of the building.*

Fig. 113 John Sell Cotman's view of the main entrance is rather more 'artistic' and less accurate than Halfpenny's (Fig.75) or Browne's (Fig.86) (see pediment over coat of arms). It was probably drawn on his visit to York in 1803.

265. 1813 (?) *Manor House, York, Aug 1813 (?)* (Fig.90)

George Nicholson (?). Pencil sketch.
South wall of the Manor shown on the right, city walls on the left (i.e. looking down the lane leading from the present Exhibition Square to Museum Gardens). An unusual viewpoint with interesting details.
York Art Gallery YORAG : R3195a.

266. 1817 *Part of the Palace at York, Aug. 18th 1817*

Henry Cave. Pencil sketch.
View from the west.
York Art Gallery YORAG : R3399.

267. 1817 *Entrance to the King's Manor* (Fig.86)

John Browne. Pencil and bodycolour.
17¼ x 13½in (348 x 345mm).
South doorway on the east front, Jacobean but with royal arms (Stuart) added in the 1630s, recarved and repainted in 1971. Browne's drawing gives excellent detail of the brickwork, showing infilled windows and other alterations.
York Art Gallery YORAG : R1571.
Reproduced in Murray *et al* 1990, fig.49

268. c.1822 *The King's Manor, York*

Henry Cave. Pencil, watercolour and bodycolour with scratching out.
11 x 16½in (280 x 418mm).
View of the eastern courtyard. The doorway on the right was moved c.1830 to the east front. The over-prominent drain-pipe on the right bears the date 1667. In 1822 Cave was drawing-master at the Manor School here.
York Art Gallery YORAG : R45 (Fig.87).
Reproduced in Murray *et al* 1990, fig.55.
Also: 1822 as above, colour lithograph (T. Sutherland).
Inscribed by Cave 'To Miss Tate and the Ladies of the Manor school'.
York Art Gallery YORAG : R2716 and R3909.

269. 1827 *Manor Buildings June 18 1827*

George Nicholson. Pencil drawing no.9.
Corner of the Manor, with steps; a closer view than R3195a (Illustration 265, Fig.90).
York Art Gallery YORAG : R1385.

270. 1827 *Manor Buildings June 15 1827*

George Nicholson. Pencil drawing no.10.
Corner of the Manor.
York Art Gallery YORAG : R923.

271. 1827 *Manor Buildings June 18 1827*

George Nicholson. Pencil drawing no.13.
Side view from the south.
York Art Gallery YORAG : R881.

Fig. 114 (Facing page, top) H. and W. Brown's wood engraving of 1836 shows the same view as Cave's (Fig.87), but it reveals rather more of the north wing to the left of the doorway.

Fig. 115 (Facing page, bottom) This 1836 wood engraving by H. and W. Brown gives a wider view of the east front and thus puts the main entrance in context. The wall on the right (later demolished) was built to separate boys and the girls, who had different entrances to the building when it served as a school.

The Manor House.

The Manor House Porch.

272. *1829   Manor Palace*

   Nathaniel Whittock. Etching on steel by J. Rogers.
   3¾ x 5¾in (98 x 147mm).
   The east front and main entrance. Clear details of blocked windows and other alterations, though some of them are rather different from those depicted by John Browne (Illustration 267, Fig.86).
   York Art Gallery YORAG : R3149.
   Reproduced in Murray *et al* 1990, fig.50.

273. *1836   The Manor House* (Fig.114)

   H. and W. Brown. Wood engraving.
   View of the first courtyard. The doorway on the right was moved c.1830 to the east front.
   Brown and Brown 1836 (no page numbers).

274. *1836   The Manor House Porch* (Fig.115)

   H. and W. Brown. Wood engraving.
   Part of the east front and the main entrance.
   Brown and Brown 1836 (no page numbers).

Fig. 116 *The doorway at the foot of the steps leading to the Huntingdon Room by A. Buckle, 1883.*

275. *1840   Doorway in the King's Manor*

   John Harper. Pencil.
   7¼ x 6½in (184 x 164mm).
   Doorway into the cross-gallery range, inner courtyard, with Wentworth's coat of arms over.
   York Art Gallery YORAG : R1649.
   Reproduced in Murray *et al* 1990, fig.52.

276. *1840   Entrance to the King's Manor*

   John Harper. Pencil and bodycolour.
   8½ x 6¾in (215 x 169mm).
   The north doorway on the east front. The opening dates from c.1480, but the early 17th-century surround was moved here in 1830 from the inner courtyard, where it is shown in Cave's view of 1822 (Illustration 268, Fig.87).
   York Art Gallery YORAG : R1658.

277. *1840   Entrance to the King's Manor* (Fig.78)

   John Harper. Watercolour.
   The principal entrance (south doorway) on the east front.
   York Art Gallery YORAG : R1623.

278. *n.d.   The Yorkshire School for the Blind, established in memory of the late W. Wilberforce Esq. Formerly a Palace of James the 1st built on the site of the House of the Abbot of St Mary's Abbey*

   W. Monkhouse. Lithograph.
   East front and main doorway.
   York Art Gallery YORAG : R3916 and R3150 (Fig.85).

279. *n.d.   Entrance to the Blind School, York*

   A.H. Cates. Lithograph by F. Bedford.
   Cates n.d., title page.
   York Art Gallery YORAG : R3911.
   Minster Library: Revd Robert William Bilton Hornby Collection, *York Antiquities* **2** (Add MS 320), 372.

280. *n.d.   South View of the Entrance to the Manor House, York*

   H.H. Roddance.
   Minster Library YK 385.

281. *c.1840   The Yorkshire School for the Blind*

   William Monkhouse. Lithograph.
   6¾ x 9½in (167 x 238mm).
   The Blind School occupied the Manor from 1833 to 1956. The ground-floor and many other windows were replaced during this time; the wall separates the girls' entrance from the boys'.
   York Art Gallery YORAG : R3150.

Fig. 117 The King's Manor and Minster by Rodwell. An attractive general view of the north range of the Manor in 1887, with the Minster towers in the background.

Fig. 118 A wide-ranging view of the Manor from the north-west side by Ridsdale Tate, 1889. This was described as 'the most picturesque range of buildings in York' by Hutchinson and Palliser 1980 (p.182). From left to right: the Rutland wing with bay window; the Sheffield wing with dormers and mullioned windows; and the Huntingdon wing which re-used 13th-century stone from the abbey.

See also: Minster Library: Revd Robert William Bilton Hornby Collection, *York Antiquities* **2** (Add MS 320), 357.

282. *n.d.   Palace of the Stuarts, York*

William Monkhouse. Watercolour.
North doorway in the east wall. An attractive watercolour with clear detail of the stonework.
York Art Gallery YORAG : R3095.

283. *n.d.   Palace of the Stuarts, York* (Fig.89)

William Monkhouse. Watercolour.
Attractive watercolour of the inner archway and steps leading up to the Huntingdon Room, with good, crisp detail of the stonework.
York Art Gallery YORAG : R3096.

284. *n.d.   Entrance to the Yorkshire School for the Blind*

Unknown artist. Lithographs.
Minster Library: Revd Robert William Bilton Hornby Collection, *York Antiquities* **2** (Add MS 320), 376, 377.

285. *1847   Lord Huntingdon's Room in the King's Manor*

Thomas Waterworth. Etching.
Wall with fireplace and frieze.
From *The Gentleman's Magazine*, 1807, reproduced in Benson 1919, pl.54.

286. *1850   King's Manor. Inner face of Main Courtyard, 1850*

William Moore. Pencil sketch.
Useful detail of windows, blocked archway and steps on the right.
York Art Gallery YORAG : R3113.

287. *1853   Doorway of the Old Palace*

William Pumphrey. Photograph.
Pumphrey 1853, pl.50.

288. *1860   The Blind School, York*

Edwin Moore. Watercolour.
View from the north (abbey side).
York Art Gallery YORAG : R1439.

289. *1860   Blind School, York*

R. Hudson. Engraving dated 31 July 1886.
View from the north, showing Victorian addition (J.B. and W. Atkinson) with bay window and central door.
York Art Gallery YORAG : R3506.

290. *1875   King's Manor House*

A. Buckle. Watercolour.
North-east front and the main entrance.
York Art Gallery YORAG : R1529.

291. *n.d. (c.1880?) Photographs of the King's Manor*

Banqueting room; quadrangle; doorway to Council Chamber (i.e. the Huntingdon Room).
Minster Library: Revd Robert William Bilton Hornby Collection, *York Antiquities* **2** (Add MS 320), 372.

292. *1883   The King's Manor, York*

A. Buckle. Etchings.
Illustrations for Davies 1883:
a) North-east front, Manor House, York, frontispiece.
b) Doorway, King's Manor, York, title page (carvings on main entrance).
c) Manor House, York, from the west, p.5.
d) Entrance to Lord Huntingdon's Room, Manor House, York, p.6 (Fig.76).
e) In Lord Huntingdon's Room, Manor House, York, p.7 (Fig.88).
f) Principal entrance, Manor House, York, p.9.
g) Wentworth (Lord Strafford) Arms, King's Manor, York, p.10.
h) Doorway (unused), Manor House, York, p.12.
i) At the Manor House, York, p.14 (doorway at foot of steps leading to the Huntingdon Room) (Fig.116).
j) Courtyard, Manor House, York, p.17 (view of first courtyard looking south).

293. *1880s?   Manor House, York* (Fig.80)

Robert Rodwell. Engraving.
View of steps to the Banqueting House, with watchman or porter's shelter, before alteration.
York Art Gallery YORAG : R3913.

294. *1887   Manor House, York* (Fig.117)

Robert Rodwell. Engraving.
Attractive view from the west (i.e. from the abbey).
York Art Gallery YORAG : R3917.

295. *1889   The Manor House, York, Sept. 28th 1889* (Fig.118)

E. Ridsdale Tate. Ink drawing.
A wide-ranging view from the west, with excellent detail.
York Art Gallery YORAG : R3176.

296. *1894–95   Palace of the Stuart Kings* (Fig.79)

E. Piper. Etching.
North-east elevation showing both doorways.
Bound in Piper 1895 (no plate numbers).

Fig. 119 *Boddy's watercolour of the King's Manor Blind School Entrance. Boddy has taken a common theme – the east front of the Manor – but painted it from a more unusual angle. The many alterations over the years and the poor state of the brickwork are clearly shown.*

Fig. 120 *The King's Manor from the abbey by Boddy, 1906, showing the north range.*

297. *c.1900   King's Manor; Corner from North-West (detail)*

Herbert Railton. Pencil drawing.
York Art Gallery YORAG : R2778.

298. *1906   King's Manor from North-West*

Herbert Railton. Pencil drawing.
York Art Gallery YORAG : R2779.

299. *n.d.   Entrance to the Banqueting Hall, King's Manor*

E.W. Haslehurst. Watercolour.
Shows the steps leading to a doorway on the left, since removed.
Black and white reproduction in Benson 1906.

300. *1906   King's Manor, Blind School Entrance* (Fig.119)

William J. Boddy. Watercolour.
East elevation and main doorway from the north.
Colour reproduction in Boddy 1906.

301. *1906   King's Manor, now Blind School, from St Mary's Abbey* (Fig.120)

William J. Boddy. Watercolour.
North elevation of the building, much of it Victorian, but with some earlier work visible.
Colour reproduction in Boddy 1906.

302. *1906   The King's Manor, York, and foundations of Choir of St Mary's Abbey, July 10th 1906* (Fig.121)

E. Ridsdale Tate. Drawing.
Northern elevation from beside the foundations of the north aisle of the abbey choir.
York Art Gallery YORAG : R3972.
Also in Benson 1906.

303. *n.d.   King's Manor*

C. Harlow White. Watercolour.
East front.
Evelyn Collection M2215 (YAYAS Minster Library).

304. *n.d.   Abbot Sever's House – plan*

Conjectural – actual remains shown in black.
Evelyn Collection E1882 (YAYAS Minster Library).

Fig. 121 *Ridsdale Tate's 1906 view of the north range, with the foundations of the abbey church choir in the foreground, also shows well the Manor's relationship to the abbey buildings. A more general view than Fig.117, though it provides good detail of the foundations.*

305. *n.d.   Vaults of Henry VIII's Palace*

Photograph.
cf Halfpenny 1807, pls.28 and 29 (Illustrations 260–1, Figs 91–2).
Evelyn Collection A2201 (YAYAS Minster Library).

306. *1921   King's Manor; Wentworth wing and, on right, Huntingdon block*

Photograph. *Country Life.*
Reproduced in *VCHY*, opposite p.161.

307. *1924   The Manor House*

Photograph. F. Frith and Co. Ltd.
North elevation, mainly 19th century, but with earlier work visible.
Morris 1924, opposite p.172.

308. *1961   King's Manor*

Lord Methuen. Watercolour.
East front.
York Art Gallery YORAG : R2202.

Maps and plans showing the entire site

Plans of individual buildings or sites are listed under those sites.

309. *c.1545* *Plan of York* (Fig.3)

Draft by 'J.H.H.' (probably John H. Harvey) from plans in the Public Record Office, MPB 49, 51.
Detail from a somewhat formalised plan of the city, not drawn to scale, thought to have been drawn following an act of 1541 which restricted rights of sanctuary to the precincts of ecclesiastical buildings (Harvey 1993, 68–9). City records refer to payment for such a map drawn by 'the armit [hermit] of the Kyngs Manour', 12 August 1541 (*YCR* **4**, 63). This part of the plan shows the outline of the abbey precincts with walls, main towers, gateway and postern. A path linking Lendal Ferry to Bootham Bar runs between the abbey wall and the city wall.
YAT Collection MP1.
RCHM negative (NMR) DWG no.66.
RCHMY 3, xxviii, fig.1.

310. *1610* *'Yorke' by John Speed* (Fig.4)

A combination of ground plan and perspective view, this is probably the earliest complete plan of the city. Speed's work is usually carefully done, but much of his plan of the abbey precincts is puzzling: it appears to be divided by a wall, and the plan of the abbey ruins is obscure. Speed may have misinterpreted the standing remains of the church and claustral buildings, and the remains of building work done for the visit of Henry VIII in 1541. The precinct wall and its towers are clearly depicted and include the sections on the city and river sides (south-east and south-west), which have now gone.
Speed 1611 (map of West Riding of Yorkshire with inset plan of York).
York City Library: no.1 in map drawer.
YAT Collection MP2.

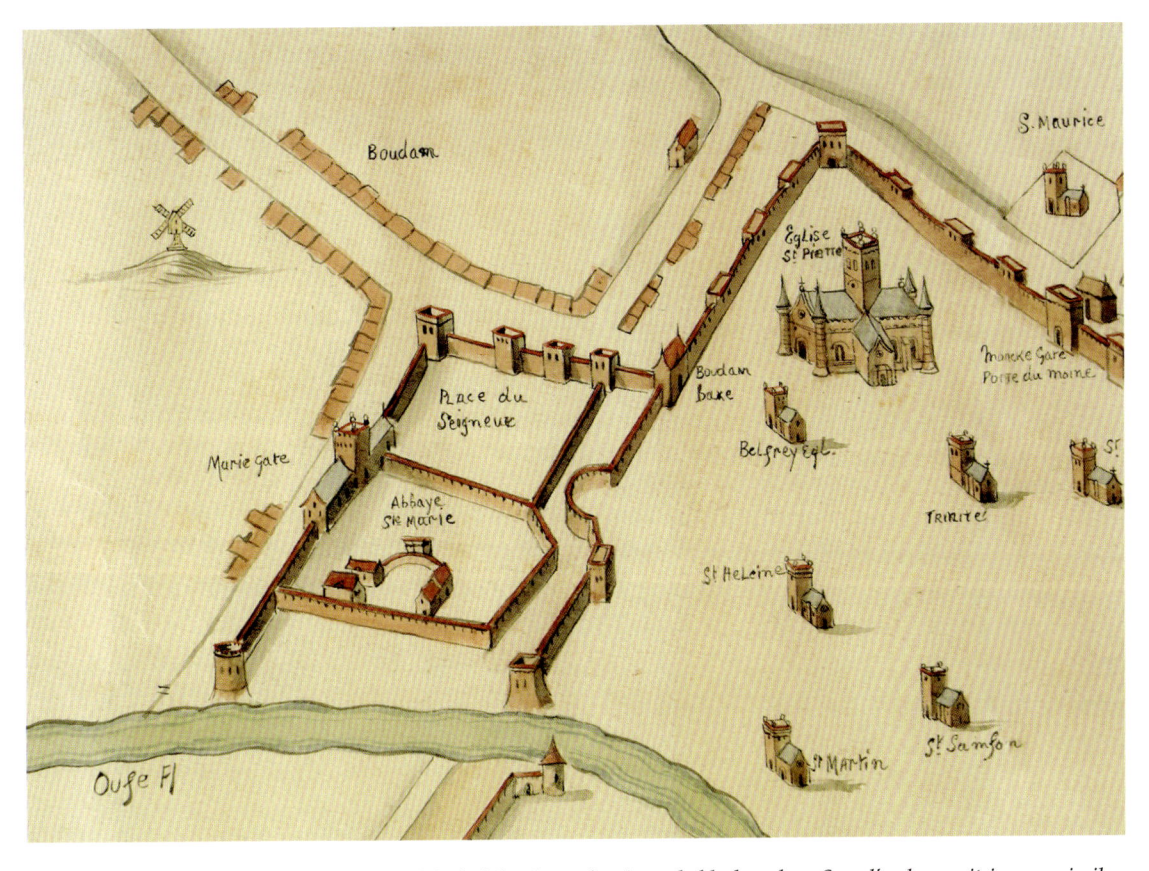

Fig. 122 *Detail from 'Plan de York', 1650. This delightful colour plan is probably based on Speed's plan as it is very similar and the annotation is largely a French translation of Speed's (for example, 'The Lord's Place' becomes 'Place de Seigneur').*

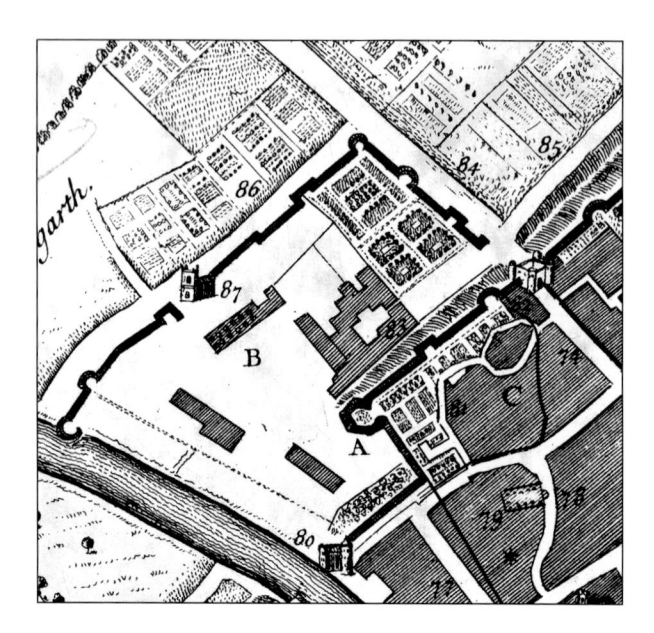

Fig. 123 Drake's plan of 1736 shows the King's Manor in the context of the abbey ruins. It includes buildings in the outer precincts, now gone except for the hospitium, and the line of abbey's river wall. Top left is Almery Garth, formerly the site of the abbot's fishponds.

311. 1650   'Plan de York' (Fig.122)

An attractive coloured plan of the city, more interested in churches than streets. It is largely based on Speed's map (Illustration 310; Fig.4): the same dividing wall is there, and the remains of the abbey buildings are much the same.
York City Library.

312. 1736   A Plan of the City of York (Fig.123)

Francis Drake (?) Measured plan; scale given.
Drake's map of York follows Benedict Horsley's map of 1694 closely, with a few features added. The area of the abbey precincts is shown somewhat stylised; the walls and towers are clearly delineated, as are the city walls and ramparts. By 1736 the river wall had gone but is shown here as a dotted line, along with the path from the water gate to the riverbank. Buildings are indicated as shaded outlines, and include the church (B) with pillars marked, the hospitium with its adjoining buildings and the King's Manor, with gardens to the north-east (83). Outside the precincts to the north-west of Marygate (86) is Almery Garth, formerly open land and fishponds, now under housing and car park.
Drake 1736, 244, fig.14.

313. 1843 (published)   General Plan of the Abbey as disclosed by the excavations made under the direction of the Yorkshire Philosophical Society during the years 1827 and 1828 (Fig.6)

William Richardson. Measured plan; scale given.
Shows the whole of the abbey precinct and buildings, together with the King's Manor.
Richardson 1843, vol.I.

Sources

Borthwick Institute

Faculty Papers contain many architects' plans, elevations and measured drawings. Document research by appointment. Borthwick Institute of Historical Research, University of York, Heslington, York, YO10 5DD. Tel. 01904 321166.

Evelyn Collection, YAYAS

Glass slides and negatives of locations in York, including copies of prints and drawings mainly from originals now in the Art Gallery, and photographs c.1900–35, with later additions, deposited in York Minster Library by the Yorkshire Architectural and York Archaeological Society. Subject index and catalogue. Permission to view from the Keeper of the Evelyn Collection, Mr R.I. Drake, 26 Burtree Avenue, Skelton, York, YO30 3DL. Tel. 01904 470010.

Institute of Advanced Architectural Studies (University of York)

The considerable collection of books of prints is now housed in the Library, King's Manor, Exhibition Square, York, YO1 7EP. Tel. 01904 433969.

Mansion House

Fine collection of oil paintings and watercolours of York views. Viewing by appointment (contact the Civic Secretary). Mansion House, York, YO1 9QL. Tel. 01904 552012.

Merchant Adventurers' Hall

Watercolours, oil paintings, prints and drawings of York views, many on display in the Hall. Merchant Adventurers' Hall, Fossgate, York, YO1 9XD. Tel. 01904 654818.

RCHM

Photographs, some original, some copies of old prints and drawings, with notes, taken by the Royal Commission on the Historical Monuments of England. Filed at the National Monuments Record Centre, Kemble Drive, Swindon, SN2 2GZ. Tel. 01793 414600. General information on listed buildings available from the Listed Buildings Information Service, tel. 0171 208 8221.

Wakefield Art Gallery

The Gott Collection contains prints, drawings and wash drawings of York views produced between 1736 and 1828, notably those by E. Abbot. Wakefield Art Gallery, Wentworth Terrace, Wakefield, West Yorkshire, WF1 3QW. Tel. 01924 305796.

YAT Collection

Photographs of maps, plans and topographical views, mainly from the RCHM collection with later additions. Catalogue, arranged topographically, in the Trust library. York Archaeological Trust for Excavation and Research Ltd, 47 Aldwark, York, YO1 7BX. Tel. 01904 663000.

York City Art Gallery

The Print Room contains the original Evelyn Collection of topographical views, with many later additions. Prints and drawings are filed topographically, paintings under the artist. Viewing by appointment. York City Art Gallery, Exhibition Square, York, YO1 7EW. Tel. 01904 551861.

York City Library: Reference Library and York History Room

Books of prints (see Bibliography, pp.133–6); folios of sketches, maps, plans, collections of old photographs. Central Library, Museum Street, York, YO1 7DS. Tel. 01904 655631.

York Minster Library

Maps and plans, architectural drawings (of York Minster), prints and drawings, photographs, 18th- and early 19th-century newspapers, together with printed books, archives and antiquarian notes relating to local history. Access by appointment with the Archivist, York Minster Library, Dean's Park, York, YO1 7JQ. Tel. 01904 611118. General enquiries 01904 625308. The Library is closed on Fridays.

Yorkshire Museum

The remains of St Mary's Abbey are situated in the Museum Gardens, York. The gardens are open daily from dawn until dusk. Admission to the Museum Gardens is free. The nearby Yorkshire Museum incorporates part of the abbey remains which have been covered over, as well as interpretation of the site and its history. Several objects are also on show, including floor tiles, medieval glass and stone carvings from the abbey. The museum is open from 10am–5pm daily. For up-to-date admission prices see www.yorkshiremuseum.org.uk

The above information is correct at the time of publication.

For further information on collections outside York see Barley 1974.

Select Index of Artists

Abbot, Edward, fl. 1774–76

Produced many coloured wash drawings of buildings in and around York in 1774–76, possibly intended to illustrate a new edition of Drake's *Eboracum* proposed by Thomas Beckwith. These are now in the Gott Collection, Wakefield City Art Gallery; black and white copies of some are in the Evelyn Collection of slides and in the YAT Collection. Some are signed by Abbot; others, similar in style and colouring but more assured, may be by him or by J. Beckwith. Though somewhat naïve, they are very valuable, representing a period otherwise barren in local topographical art; also many show aspects of buildings ignored by other artists.

Arnout, Louis-Jules (1814–1868)

Son of artist Jean-Baptist Arnout. He painted fine views of buildings in various European cities: St Paul's Cathedral and the Bank of England in London; St Mary's Abbey in York; the Louvre and Palais Royal in Paris (1855); the Red Gate in Moscow (1840s); Kazan Cathedral and various palaces in St Petersburg (1840s).

Bedford, Francis, 1816–94

Born in London. Trained as an architect and lithographer. In the early 1840s he worked with William Monkhouse (q.v.) in York and c.1843 published *Sketches in York* and *The Churches of York*. Returned to London, where he worked for several noted lithographers. From 1851 he began to specialise in photography, and in 1862 published a collection of photographs of his travels in the Near East with the Prince of Wales. He was considered one of the finest landscape photographers of the era. Between 1890 and 1892 Bedford exhibited ten views of churches at the Royal Academy, London.

Benson, George, 1856–1935

Architect and antiquary. His publication *York from its Origin to 1925* (3 volumes, 1911, 1919, 1925; reprinted 1968) includes his own plans and elevations of excavations and buildings, and he also published shorter articles. His collection of 'Old York Sketches, Tracings etc., chiefly by Edwin Ridsdale Tate' in York Public Library contains many original drawings of considerable topographical interest. He was Curator of Archaeology and Numismatics at the Yorkshire Philosophical Society's Museum.

Boddy, William James, 1832–1911

Born in Woolwich; settled in York in 1853. Assistant to architects G. Fowler Jones and J.B. and W. Atkinson, then became full-time watercolour artist and teacher at several schools, including St Peter's in York and Ampleforth, until 1908. In 1906, 34 of his watercolours were reproduced in colour in *Historic York* (text by J.S. Fletcher) and local exhibitions of his work were held in 1911 and 1912. Most of his paintings are of well-known views, but some are from unusual angles or give detail not otherwise immediately available. Boddy exhibited at the Royal Academy and the Royal Society of British Artists between 1860 and 1890.

Brown, Henry, 1816–70, and William, 1814–77

Wood engravers, born in York. Published 83 wood-engraved views of York in 1836 as well as several single engravings. Settled in the Netherlands from 1840, becoming successive Heads of the Royal School of Engraving at The Hague. Whilst their small drawings show a lack of concern for accuracy in measurement or perspective, they contain valuable details and the overall impression is often more perceptive than that of more precise draughtsmen.

Brown[e], John, 1792–1877

Born and lived at Walmgate Bar, later moving to Blake Street. Taught drawing and painting, and had a keen interest in history, archaeology and architecture, producing drawings, etchings and some watercolours. In 1827 published a pamphlet on the age of St Margaret's Church porch, illustrated with etchings, and from 1847 a *History of the Metropolitan Church of St Peter* with 150 illustrations, sufficiently accurate to be used for restoration of the Minster after the fire of 1840; he has been described as 'the first Minster Archaeologist'. His drawings, meticulous, clear and detailed, are of immense topographical value.

Buckle, Anthony, 1838–1900

Landscape artist in oils and watercolours, born in Barden, Yorkshire. Studied at York School of Art, then taught there and at the School for the Blind in York at the King's Manor.

Carter, Henry Barlow, 1803–68

Born in Scarborough; served in the Navy, then taught art in Hull and later in Scarborough and travelled in north-eastern England. Retired to Torquay in 1862. Mainly marine and coastal paintings, together with several views of York.

Cave, Henry, 1779–1836

One of York's most important topographical artists. Son of William Cave, engraver. Born in York and lived in Micklegate. Art teacher in several York schools. He produced many drawings, etchings, watercolours and oils of scenes in and around York. In 1810 his *Picturesque Buildings in York* (also entitled *Antiquities of York*) was published, with 2nd and 3rd editions both dated 1813. York City Art Gallery has the etched copper plates and pencil drawings for this work, as well as prints. Cave exhibited work at the Royal Academy between 1814 and 1825. See Cooper 1911.

Cotman, John Sell, 1782–1842

Encouraged to draw when at school in Norwich. Moved to London, found employment with Ackermann and gained the patronage of Dr Munro. Through him got to know Girtin and became a member of the Sketching Club (founded by Girtin) and friend of Paul Sandby Munn. Between 1802 and 1804 Cotman helped Munn to produce drawings for young ladies to use for copying. These included the sketches made when touring together in Yorkshire in 1803. He was an artist ahead of his time in his use of bold colour, simple subject matter and composition, and his preoccupation with pattern and form.

Cuitt Jr., George, 1779–1854

Showed in early life a talent for drawing, and was helped by Sir Laurence Dundas of Aske who sent him to Rome, where he studied for six years. On his return he settled at Richmond in Yorkshire, where he painted both landscapes and portraits. Later moved to Chester. He made etchings of old buildings, especially castles and abbeys in Yorkshire, Chester and North Wales. Published etchings of, among others, Rievaulx Abbey, Kirkstall Abbey, Easby Abbey, St Mary's Abbey and Kirkham Priory, in *Views of Old Buildings in Chester and Yorkshire Abbeys*, 1834.

Drake, Francis, c.1696–1771

Drake was born into an old Yorkshire family, the son of the vicar of Pontefract and canon of York. He was apprenticed at an early age to a surgeon in York and in 1727 the corporation of York appointed him city surgeon. His wife died after only eight years of marriage and he filled his off-duty hours writing a history of York, using manuscripts inherited, borrowed or purchased. The 800-page book was sent to press in 1735 and was published the following year under the title *Eboracum, or The History and Antiquities of the City of York, from its Original to the Present Time; together with the History of the Cathedral Church and the Lives of the Archbishops*. Though now inevitably outdated, *Eboracum* contains much that would otherwise have been forgotten and is particularly valuable on points of topography. Drake devoted much of the rest of his life to historical and antiquarian research.

Halfpenny, Joseph, 1748–1811

Topographical artist and engraver, born in Bishopthorpe, son of the Archbishop's gardener. Trained as a house painter, he later became an art teacher; he also painted some scenery for the Theatre Royal. Freeman of the city 1770. In 1791 and 1792 he travelled in the Lake District and Yorkshire Dales, producing attractive watercolours. He was Clerk of Works to John Carr when the latter was restoring the Minster, and repaired some of the decoration. From scaffolding he drew and in 1795–1800 published *Gothic Ornaments in the Cathedral Church of York*, reprinted 1807, 2nd edition. 1831. His *Fragmenta Vetusta* (1807) contains 35 views of York buildings. Halfpenny's engravings are clear and detailed, but somewhat stiff in execution; for the most part he recorded accurately, though he was happy to omit any part of a scene he considered irrelevant to his purpose, and occasionally sacrificed accuracy in favour of clarity.

Harper, Edward, c.1813–80

Brother of architect and artist John Harper. Together they organised an exhibition of work by living artists held in York in 1836. Edward practised as a solicitor at 6 St Leonard's Place, York, and later in his life moved to Hove in Sussex where he died. He exhibited work at the British Institution in 1859 and 1860.

Harper, John, 1809–42

An architect, born near Blackburn and worked first in London. Moved to York to set up his own practice. Redesigned the façade of the Theatre Royal and designed St Peter's School in Clifton. He was a keen artist and produced many sketches of landscape and architectural subjects. He was praised by his friend William Etty for his 'elegant execution and correct detail'. He died of malaria while on a tour of the Continent.

Haslehurst, Ernest W, 1866–1949

Artist and book illustrator. Born at Walthamstow in Essex, and studied at the Slade School. A keen gardener, nature lover with an interest in scientific instruments. His colour prints (many of which were made into postcards), taken from paintings executed between 1910 and 1915, provide fascinating views of the countryside, villages and towns before the First World War. He painted many of the famous views of historic York. Published from about 1911 to 1940.

Haynes, John, fl. 1728–55

Former schoolmaster and leather engraver, Freeman of York as a saddler 1728. Produced topographical views in York, later in London. In 1730 he illustrated Gent's *History of York*; in 1736 he provided some plates for Drake's *Eboracum*.

Lodge, William, 1649–89

Amateur artist, born in Leeds, educated at Cambridge and Lincoln's Inn, then moved to York, becoming a friend of Francis Place (q.v.) and a member of the 'Virtuosi'. He produced several views of York, most notably the South-West Prospect from the Mount, c.1678. Worked closely with Place on drawings and engravings, and their work is often very similar. Buried at Harewood church.

Lord Methuen, 1886–1974

Born Paul Ayshford in Corsham, Wiltshire. Became 4th Baron Methuen of Corsham Court in 1932. Studied painting under Sir Charles Holmes, later under Walter Sickert in Oxford. First solo exhibition at the Warren Gallery in 1928. Held many solo exhibitions at the Leicester Galleries and showed at the Royal Academy. Elected RA in 1959. Retrospective exhibition in 1972 at the Royal West of England Academy. The Tate Gallery and Victoria & Albert Museum hold his work.

Monkhouse, William, 1813–96

Lithographer and photographer. Born in Ripon, came to York in 1819 (his father was the Dean's gardener). Set up lithography business in Lendal 1840; took on Francis Bedford and together they produced *Sketches in York* and *The Churches of York*. Said to have been one of the first to introduce colour lithography in York. Encouraged by Bedford, he took up photography, joining William Pumphrey (q.v.), then setting up his own business in Lendal.

Moore, Edwin, 1813–93

Son of William Moore Sr, artist, and brother of four other artists. Born in Birmingham, studied with Samuel Prout (q.v.). Lived in York and was a popular teacher at the Friends' School for 50 years. Mainly painted landscapes and showed a delicate sense of colour.

Moore, William, 1817–1909

Brother of Edwin Moore (q.v.). Landscape painter and topographer. Born in Birmingham, studied with H.B. Carter. He lived in Yorkshire, travelled on sketching tours and taught art. York City Art Gallery has a large number of views by members of the Moore family.

Nash, Frederick, 1782–1856

Architectural draughtsman, watercolourist and art teacher, born in Lambeth and attended the Royal Academy Schools. He was appointed architectural draughtsman to the Society of Antiquaries c.1807. He was commissioned to make a series of drawings of the ruins of St Mary's Abbey, York, which he lithographed himself and published in 1829 (see

Fig.5 for an example). He travelled widely and published many drawings from these journeys at home and abroad. He was later elected a member of the Old Watercolour Society and in 1834 moved from London to Brighton where he died.

Nicholson, George, 1787–1878

Born in Malton. His father, George, and uncle, Francis Nicholson, were also artists. Travelled widely and produced watercolours, etchings and drawings, mainly of topographical views. His views of York date mainly from 1806–c.1840. His sketchbooks, now in York City Art Gallery, contain valuable scenes not found elsewhere, and though he occasionally varied the detail in different sketches of the same view, he is generally noted for his accuracy (Hughes 1978). Although Nicholson's artistic output was substantial, he exhibited only four works at the Royal Academy, in 1831–2.

Place, Francis, 1647–1728

Son of a country gentleman in Dinsdale, Co. Durham. Trained as a lawyer in London and later worked with the etcher Wenceslaus Hollar, who influenced him greatly. Amateur artist of considerable ability, producing topographical drawings, 'prospects', watercolours, engravings; experimented with mezzotint and with stoneware pottery. Settled in York in 1675 and from 1692 lived at the King's Manor, where he set up his own printing equipment. Became a member of the York 'Virtuosi'. Took his friend William Lodge (q.v.) on exhausting walking, fishing and painting expeditions, leading to both being arrested (quite unjustly) for suspicious behaviour during the panic over the 'Popish Plot' in 1678. Place's work provides the most important pictorial evidence for the topography of York in the late 17th and early 18th centuries. See Hake 1921; Tyler 1971.

Prout, John Skinner, 1806–76

Watercolour painter, specialising in landscapes and architectural subjects. Born in Plymouth, nephew of Samuel Prout (q.v.). He was largely self-taught. His lithographs, *Antiquities of York*, were published in 1840. Travelled in Australia, Britain and France, then settled in Bristol.

Prout, Samuel, 1783–1852

Painter, draughtsman and writer. In 1801 he met the topographer and antiquarian John Britton, who, impressed with his work, invited him to London the following year to make drawings of antiquarian subjects and copy works of other artists, including Thomas Hearne, William Alexander and J.M.W. Turner.

Pumphrey, William, 1817–1905

Born in Worcester. Became science master at Bootham School, York, 1845. In 1849 he opened a photographic portrait gallery in Coney Street, and in 1853 published *Photographic Views of York and its Environs* (60 views). Other photographs exist, notably the south-west window of the Guildhall, the only record of the 1682 window by Henry Gyles, replaced in 1863. For a list of his photographs see Murray 1986, 23.

Railton, Herbert, 1857–1910

Produced pencil drawings of features on York city walls c.1900. Earlier he produced a fine etching showing what London Bridge and Southwark Cathedral might have looked like c.1500.

Richards, Jacob, fl. 1680s

Produced a coloured plan of the City of York, 1685. Together with plans of the castle and the King's Manor, it accompanies a report of 1682 by Sir Christopher Musgrave, Lieutenant of Ordnance, on the condition of the garrison. They were bound together with plans from other towns in a leather-backed volume which is now in Stafford Record Office.

Richardson, William, 1813–c.1881

Born in York and lived all his life in the city. Trained as an architectural draughtsman. Exhibited at the Royal Academy. Produced watercolours mainly of architectural subjects; his drawings of monasteries were published as a series of 60 lithographs in *The Monastic Ruins of Yorkshire*, 1843.

Ridsdale Tate, Edwin, 1862–1922

Architect and artist, with an interest in history and archaeology. Worked for Gould and Fisher, then in London and Carlisle before returning to York. Built the Tempest Anderson Hall (1912) and the Anchorage at All Saints North Street (1910). Undertook excavations at St Mary's Abbey with W.H. Brook (1912). Many drawings for guidebooks and other sketches. His historical reconstructions of early scenes in York are of considerable interest despite inevitable inaccuracies.

Rowlandson, Thomas, c.1756–1827

English caricaturist, watercolourist, draughtsman and engraver. Although he is commonly thought of as a satirist, most of his drawings are gently humorous, and in some cases objective, records of urban and rustic life. With the exception of a small number of topographical drawings, they are characterised by an abundance of picaresque incidents, and have much in common with the novels of Laurence Sterne and Henry Fielding, which Rowlandson illustrated in 1808 and 1809.

Speed[e], John, 1552?–1629

Cartographer and antiquary, born in Farington, Cheshire. Wrote a *Historie of Great Britaine* in 1611. His maps were published as *The Theatre of the Empire of Great Britaine* (1610–11 and later editions). The plan of York is inset in the map of the West Riding of Yorkshire; buildings are shown as bird's-eye views, and with a few exceptions are detailed, precise and accurately surveyed, providing an invaluable record of the 17th-century city. Sadly, complete copies of the Atlas are now extremely rare, being all too often brutally broken up for the maps to be sold separately.

Storey, John, 1828–88

Topographical and architectural painter in watercolour, lithographer and illustrator. Born in Newcastle-upon-Tyne, he was taught art by Thomas Miles Richardson, Sr. During the 1850s he lived in York, forming an association with the Coney Street lithographer William Bevan. His work was exhibited mainly in Newcastle, where he lived for most of his life.

Toms, William Henry, d.1765

London engraver of maps and topographical prints. Worked for antiquaries such as Sir William Stukely, and also produced many plates for Drake's *Eboracum*. Toms ran a successful engraving business for over 30 years and in 1736 produced a south-west view of the City of York.

Twopenny, William, 1797–1873

Born at Rochester and educated at Oriel College. He was called to the Bar at Lincoln's Inn, 1825, and practised with success in the Temple. He died a bachelor at Upper Grosvenor Street. He was an excellent artist and archaeologist; he issued a folio volume of *Etchings of Ancient Capitals*, and submitted a design for the restoration of the Temple Church. He made a hobby of going to various towns and cities in the United Kingdom depicting ancient buildings, carved doorways, posts and spurs, most of which he left at the British Museum.

Varley, John, 1778–1842

Artist and amateur astrologer, born in Hackney. His father was not keen on John becoming an artist, arguing that 'limning or drawing is a bad trade'. He was patronised by Dr Thomas Monro and also Edward Lascelles, for whom he was commissioned to make drawings of Harewood House. His watercolours were highly regarded and he was an influential teacher. Visited York in 1803 while on a sketching tour of Yorkshire and used material from sketches to produce later paintings. His output was prolific: the 700 watercolours he exhibited at the Old Water Colour Society between 1805 and 1842 probably comprised less than one-tenth of his total production. He produced many views of Ouse Bridge, along with other river-based sketches and paintings of York, and views of the Minster and St Margaret's porch.

Waterworth, H., 1838–86

Studied in York with the lithographers Bevan and Storey (q.v.), and exhibited at York Art Gallery. He made signed and dated views of York between 1877 and 1884. He seems to have lived at Bootham Row, but is not recorded there in the 1881 census.

Wellbeloved, Charles (1769–1858)

Born in London, Wellbeloved became assistant pastor at St Saviourgate Unitarian Chapel in York in 1792, becoming pastor in 1800. He served the church as minister for 66 years, until his death. An antiquary and archaeologist, Wellbeloved wrote *Eburacum; or, York under the Romans* in 1842. He formed the Antiquarian Society, helped organise the Yorkshire Philosophical Society, served as Curator of Antiquities at the Yorkshire Museum, and wrote a history of St Mary's Abbey. In 1827 he undertook to save the Roman wall around the city of York and raised money for its restoration. In 1829 he directed an excavation of St Mary's Abbey before the building of the Yorkshire Museum. Many of Wellbeloved's contributions to his city went beyond scholarship and education. The York Lunatic Asylum was inhumanely and poorly managed until Wellbeloved became the chairman of the committee of governors, 1831–50. He assisted at the Wilberforce School for the Blind. He was a founder of the York Mechanics Institute, whose purpose was to provide education for ordinary people; Wellbeloved himself gave many evening lectures there. He served as director of the York Dispensary, the Savings Bank, the School of Design, and the Art Gallery. After the fire at York Minster in 1829, Wellbeloved successfully campaigned and raised money for its restoration. Wellbeloved's student William Gaskell commented, 'There is scarcely an institution designed for [the benefit of the citizens of York] with which he was not in some way connected, or which he did not help to originate'.

Whittock, Nathaniel, 1791–1860

Born in London, worked in Oxford 1824–29, then in London. He produced many lithographs, notably illustrations for Thomas Allen's topographical work on Yorkshire, 1828–31, and drew 'Bird's Eye View of the City of York' (1856, lithograph 1858).

Glossary

almonry: the place or chamber where alms were distributed to the poor in churches or other ecclesiastical buildings

apse: semicircular or polygonal end of a chancel or chapel

arcade: series of arches supported by columns

ashlar: masonry of large blocks shaped with even faces and square edges

blind arcade: series of arches supported by columns applied to the wall surface instead of being open

corbel: projecting block supporting something above

customary or custumal: the Rule of an Order laid down general principles. Each abbey supplemented this with detailed rules, or customs, relating to administration, daily life and liturgical arrangements

diaper: repetitive surface decoration of lozenges or squares, achieved in brickwork with bricks of two colours

dorter: the communal sleeping area of a monastery; also known as the dormitory

frater: the communal refectory of a monastic establishment

galilee: a small chapel or porch at the western end of a medieval English church

garner: a granary; a building or place where grain is stored

jamb: one of the vertical sides of an opening

lavatorium: a series of basins outside a monastic refectory for the washing of hands

light: compartment of a window defined by the mullions

lintel: horizontal beam or stone bridging an opening

misericord: (in the context of p.35) a room in a monastery set apart for those monks permitted relaxation of the monastic rule (for example, a dispensation from fasting)

mullion: vertical member between window lights

murage: a tax or toll paid for building or repairing the walls of a fortified town

obedientiary: someone in an 'obedient' or subordinate position; a term commonly used in medieval times for the lesser officials of a monastery who were appointed by will of the superior

oblate: a person resident and serving in a monastery but not under vows; a lay religious worker

oeillet: a round opening at the base of a loophole, usually for a cannon muzzle

ordinal: a book of instructions for daily services which gives a good idea of the layout of church furnishings

ovolo: wide convex moulding

plinth: projecting course at the foot of a wall, generally chamfered or moulded at the top

postulant: (sometimes known as a pre-novice) a person preparing to be admitted as a novice into a religious community

presbytery: the part of a church lying east of the choir where the main altar is placed

pulpitum: a stone screen separating the choir from the nave of a major church

quoins: dressed stones at the angles of a building

reredorter: the toilet block of a monastery

retrochoir: the area behind the high altar in a major church

Romanesque: style current in the 11th and 12th centuries; in England often called Norman

rood screen: a screen, either wooden or stone, separating the chancel of the church from the nave

roof boss: an ornamental knob covering the intersection of ribs in a vault or on a ceiling

screens passage: screened-off entrance passage between the main hall and the service rooms

string course: horizontal course or moulding projecting from the surface of a wall

tracery: openwork pattern of masonry in the upper part of an opening

transom: horizontal member separating window lights

triforium: middle storey of a church, its height corresponding to that of the aisle roof

voussoirs: wedge-shaped stones forming an arch

Bibliography

Abbreviations

NMR National Monuments Record

RCHM Royal Commission on Historical Monuments

SS Surtees Society

YCR York Civic Records

YASRS Yorkshire Archaeological Society Record Series

YAYAS Yorkshire Architectural and York Archaological Society

YPS Yorkshire Philosophical Society

YPSAR Yorkshire Philosophical Society Annual Report

St Mary's Abbey

Allen, T., 1829. *A New and Complete History of the County of York* (London)

Auden, G.E. (ed), 1906. *A Handbook to York and District prepared for the 75th Meeting of the British Association for the Advancement of Science, 1906*

AY 1: Rollason, D.W., with Gore, D., and Fellows-Jenson, G., 1998. *Sources for York History to AD 1100* (York: York Archaeological Trust)

Aylmer, G.E., and Cant, R., 1977. *A History of York Minster* (Oxford: Clarendon Press)

Baildon, W.P., 1931. *Notes on the Religious and Secular Houses of Yorkshire*, vol.2, YASRS **81**

Barley, M.W., 1974. *A Guide to British Topographical Collections* (London)

Barnwell, P.S., Cross, C. and Rycraft, A. (eds), 2005. *Mass and Parish in late Medieval England: The Use of York*

Bedford, F., n.d. (c.1843). *Sketches in York* (York)

Benson, G., 1906. *Quaint and Historic York. In and around the old city, from drawings by E. Ridsdale Tate, with notes by G. Benson* (York)

Benson, G., 1911. *York from its Origin to the End of the 11th century* (York)

Benson, G., 1915. 'The Ancient Painted Glass Windows in the Minster and Churches of the City of York' (*YPS Annual Report for 1914*)

Benson, G., 1919. *Later Medieval York: the City and County of the City of York from 1100 to 1603*

Benson, G., 1925. *An Account of the City and County of the City of York: York from the Reformation to the Year 1925*

Benson, G., and Haslehust, E.W., 1911. *York* (London: Blackie & Sons)

Benson, G., and Jefferson, J.E., 1886. *Picturesque York* (York)

Bevan, W., and Monkhouse, W., c.1848. *York Illustrated in a Series of Views*

Blair, J., 2005. *The Church in Anglo-Saxon Society* (Oxford: Oxford University Press)

Boddy, W.J., 1906. *Historic York* (text by J.H. Fletcher)

Bond, J., 2004. *Monastic Landscapes* (Stroud: Tempus)

Bottomley, F., 1995. *The Abbey Explorer's Guide*, 2nd edn (Otley: Smith Settle)

Brady, T., 1854. *York and its Vicinity*

Brierley, W.H., 1900. 'Report on the excavations made in the chancel of St Mary's Abbey church', *YPSAR*, 38–40

Brierley, W.H., 1901. 'Further report on the excavation of the chancel of St Mary's Abbey church', *YPSAR*, 102–3

Brierley, W.H., 1902. 'Report on excavations in St Mary's Abbey during 1902', *YPSAR*, 75–7

Britton, J., 1828. *Picturesque Antiquities of English Cities* (London)

Brown, H., and Brown, W., 1836. *Views of York*

Burton, J., 1988. 'St Mary's Abbey and the City of York', *YPSAR*, 62–73

Burton, J., 1999. *The Monastic Orders in Yorkshire 1069–1215* (Cambridge)

Butler, R.M., 1972. 'A Late 17th century Plan of York', *Antiq J* **52**, 320–9

Buttery, D., n.d. *The Vanished Buildings of York* (York)

Caine, C., 1893. *The Martial Annals of the City of York* (London)

Caine, C. (ed.), 1897. *Analecta Eboracensia by Thomas Widdrington* (London)

Cates, A.H., n.d. *Views in York*

Cave, H., 1813. *Antiquities of York* (London)

Childs, W.R., and Taylor, J. (eds), 1991. *The Anonimalle Chronicle, 1307–1334*, from Brotherton Collection MS 29, YASRS 147 (Leeds)

Coney, J., 1842. *Ecclesiastical Edifices of the Olden Time; a series of Etchings with ground-plans and facsimiles of Hollar's views, of the Cathedral and Conventual churches, Monasteries, Abbeys, Priories and other Ecclesiastical Edifices of England and Wales, vol.2*

Cooper, T.P., 1911. *The Caves of York*

Coppack, G., 1993. *Fountains Abbey* (London: Batsford/English Heritage)

Coppack, G., 2006. *Abbeys and Priories* (Stroud: Tempus)

Coulson, C., 1982. 'Hierarchism in Conventual Crenellation: an Essay in the Sociology and Metaphysics of Medieval Fortification', *Medieval Archaeology* **26**, 69–100

Craster, H.H.E., and Thornton, M.E. (eds), 1933. *The Chronicle of St Mary's Abbey from Bodley MS 39*, SS **148**

Cross, C. and Vickers, N. (eds), 1995. *Monks, Friars and Nuns in sixteenth century Yorkshire*, YASRS **150** (Leeds)

Crossley, F.H., 1949. *The English Abbey; Its Life and Work in the Middle Ages*, 3rd edn (London: Batsford)

Cuitt, G., 1834. *Views of Old Buildings in Chester and Yorkshire Abbeys*

Downman, E.A., 1898. *Ancient church bells in England: their inscriptions, founders' trade marks and measurements*

Drake, F., 1736. *Eboracum: or, the History and Antiquities of the City of York, from its original to the present time. Together with the history of the Cathedral Church and the lives of the Archbishops, etc* (London)

Duffy, E., 1992. *The stripping of the altars: traditional religion in England, c.1400–c.1580* (New Haven: Yale University Press)

Dugdale, W., Dodsworth, R., Stevens, J., and Wright, J., 1817–30. *Monasticon Anglicanum: or, the history of the ancient abbies, and other monasteries, hospitals, cathedral and collegiate churches in England and Wales* (originally published London 1693)

Fletcher, A., 1968. *Tudor Rebellions* (London: Longmans)

Foot, S., 2006. *Monastic Life in Anglo-Saxon England, c.600–900* (Cambridge: Cambridge University Press)

Gent, T., 1730. *The Antient and Modern History of the Famous City of York* (York)

Gent, T., 1735. *Annales Regioduni Hullini, or the History of the Royal and Beautiful Town of Kingston-upon-Hull ... Together with several letters containing some accounts of the antiquities of Bridlington, Scarborough, Whitby, etc* (York)

Hake, H.H., 1921. *Some Contemporary Records relating to Francis Place, Engraver and Draughtsman, with a Catalogue of his Engraved Work*, Walpole Society Pub. 10

Halfpenny, J., 1807. *Fragmenta Vetusta, or the Remains of Ancient Buildings in York* (York)

Harvey, B., 1989. *Living and Dying in England, 1100–1540: the Monastic Experience* (Oxford: Clarendon Press)

Harvey, J., 1965. 'The Fire of York 1137', *Yorkshire Archaeological Journal* **41**, 365–7

Harvey, J., 1988. *Cathedrals of England and Wales* (London: Batsford)

Harvey, P.D.A., 1993. *Maps in Tudor England* (London: Public Record Office)

Hill, D., 1996. *Turner in the North. A Tour through Derbyshire, Yorkshire, Durham, Northumberland, the Scottish Borders, the Lake District, Lancashire and Lincolnshire in the year 1797* (New Haven: Yale University Press)

Hill, D., 1999. *Thomas Girtin, Genius in the North* (Leeds: Harewood House Trust)

Hill, D., 2005. *Cotman in the North: Watercolours of Durham and Yorkshire* (New Haven and London: Yale University Press)

Hughes, J., 1978. *The Nicholson Family* (York: York City Art Gallery)

Hutchinson, J., and Palliser, D.M., 1980. *York* (Edinburgh: J Bartholomew)

Interim: Archaeology in York (Bulletin of the York Archaeological Trust; cited in the text as, for example, *Interim* 12/1, vol.12, part 1)

Jones, G.H. Fowler, 1878. *Sketches in York: from Sketches taken on the spot and from old drawings etc. still existing*

Ker, N.R., 1964. *Medieval Libraries of Great Britain* (London)

Kerr, J., 2009. *Life in the Medieval Cloister* (London)

Knight, C.B., 1944. *A History of the City of York* (York)

Knowles, D., 1963. *The Monastic Order in England: a history of its development from the times of St Dunstan to the fourth Lateran Council, 940–1216*, 2nd edn (Cambridge: Cambridge University Press)

Knowles, D., 1969. *The Religious Orders in England*

Knowles, D., 1976. *Bare ruined choirs: the dissolution of the English monasteries* (Cambridge: Cambridge University Press)

Lawrence, C.H., 1984. *Medieval Monasticism: forms of religious life in Western Europe in the Middle Ages* (London: Longman)

Lefroy, W.C., 1883. *The Ruined Abbeys of Yorkshire ... with etchings and vignettes by A Brunet-Debaines and H Toussaint* (London)

Loadman, H.M., nd. *Collection of York Views*. Album of photographs in York Reference Library

McAleavy, T., 1996. *Life in a Medieval Abbey* (English Heritage)

Morris, J.E., 1924. *York ... with twenty illustrations ... four plans, and a map* (London: Methuen & Co.)

Murray, H., 1986. *Photographs and Photographers of York: the Early Years 1844–79* (York: YAYAS)

Murray, H., 1988. *Nathaniel Whittock's Bird's-Eye View of the City of York in the 1850s* (York)

Murray, H., Riddick, S., and Green, R., 1990. *York through the Eyes of the Artist* (York: York City Art Gallery)

Norton, C., 1994. 'The Buildings of St Mary's Abbey, York, and their Destruction', *Antiq J* **74**, 256–88

Norton, C., 1998. 'The York Fire of 1137: Conflagration or Consecration?', *Northern History* **34**

Palliser, D.M., 1971. *The Reformation in York*, Borthwick Paper **40** (York)

Palliser, D.M., 1979. *Tudor York* (Oxford: Oxford University Press)

Palliser, D.M., 1990. *Domesday York*, Borthwick Paper **78** (York)

Pevsner, N., and Neave, D., 1995. *The Buildings of England. Yorkshire: York and the East Riding* (Harmondsworth: Penguin)

Piper, E., 1895. *Picturesque Old York: A series of twelve etchings by E. Piper R.P.E. Introductory notes by Revd. A.P. Purey-Cust, Dean* (Leeds)

Platt, C., 1984. *The Abbeys and Priories of Medieval England* (London: Secker and Warburg)

Prout, J.S., 1840. *Antiquities of York* (York)

Pumphrey, W., 1853. *Photographic Views of York and its Environs* (York)

Raine, A., 1955. *Mediaeval York: a Topographical Survey based on Original Sources* (London: John Murray)

RCHMY 2, 1972. Royal Commission on Historical Monuments (England), *An Inventory of the Historical Monuments in the City of York. Vol. 2, The Defences* (London: HM Stationery Office)

RCHMY 3, 1972. Royal Commission on Historical Monuments (England), *An Inventory of the Historical Monuments in the City of York. Vol. 3, South-West of the Ouse* (London: HM Stationery Office)

RCHMY 4, 1975. Royal Commission on Historical Monuments (England), *An Inventory of the Historical Monuments in the City of York. Vol. 4, North East* (London: HM Stationery Office)

Richardson, H., 1961. *The Medieval Fairs and Markets of York*, Borthwick Paper **20** (York)

Richardson, W., 1843. *The Monastic Ruins of Yorkshire* (York)

Ridsdale Tate, E., 1906. *Quaint and Historic York. In and Around the Old City, from Drawings by E. Ridsdale Tate, with Notes by George Benson* (York)

Ridsdale Tate, E., 1929. 'The Charm of St Mary's Abbey and the Architectural Museum, York', *YPSAR* 1916 (reprinted 1929), 11–27

Sherbrook, M., 1959. 'The Fall of Religious Houses', in A.G. Dickens (ed), *Tudor Treatises*, YASRS **125**

Speed, J., 1611. *The Theatre of the Empire of Great Britaine: presenting an exact geography of ... England, Scotland, Ireland, etc* (London)

Stanbrook, Abbess of, and Tolhurst, J.B.L., 1936, 1937, 1951. 'The Ordinal and Customary of the Abbey of Saint Mary, York' (St John's College, Cambridge, MS D27). Henry Bradshaw Society **73**, **75**, **84**

135

Steane, J., 2001. *The archaeology of power: England and northern Europe, AD 800–1600* (Stroud: Tempus)

Stopford, J., 2005. *Medieval Floor Tiles of Northern England. Pattern and Purpose: Production between the 13th and 16th centuries* (Oxford: Oxbow)

Storer, J., 1815–16. *The Antiquarian Itinerary, comprising specimens of architecture, monastic, castellated and domestic: with other vestiges of antiquity in Great Britain, accompanied with descriptions*

Stow, J., 1631. *Annales, or, a general Chronicle of England; begun by J. Stow ... continued and augmented ... unto the end of ... 1631, by E. Howes* (London)

Syme, J.S., and Raine, A, 1944. 'Report on recent excavations at St Mary's Abbey in York', *YPSAR*, 32–33.

Torr, J., 1719. *The Antiquities of York City. Collected from the papers of C H, Esqr, with notes and observations ... by J. Torr* (York)

Tyler, R., 1971. *Francis Place, 1647–1728* (York)

VCHY. Tillott, P.M. (ed), 1961 *The Victoria History of the Counties of England: A History of Yorkshire, The City of York* (London: Oxford University Press)

Walbran, J.R. (ed), 1863. *Memorials of the Abbey of St Mary of Fountains I*, SS **42**

Walter, D.A., 1874. *Ancient Memorial Cross Slabs from churches of the City of York and surrounding district* (York)

Wellbeloved, C., 1829. 'Some account of the ancient and present state of the Abbey of St Mary, York, and of the discoveries recently made excavating the ground on which the principal buildings of the Abbey formerly stood', *Vetusta Monumenta* **5** (1835) (plates 51–60 published separately first in 1829) (London: Society of Antiquaries)

Wenham, L.P., 1970. *The Great and Close Siege of York, 1644* (Kineton, Warwick)

Wilkinson, P., 2006. *England's abbeys: monastic buildings and culture* (Swindon: English Heritage)

Wilson, C., 1983. 'The original setting of the Apostle and Prophet figures from St Mary's Abbey, York', in *Studies in Medieval Sculpture*, ed F.H. Thompson, Soc Antiq London occasional paper, new series **3** (London), 100–21

Wilson, C., and Burton, J., 1988. *St Mary's Abbey, York* (York: Yorkshire Museum)

Wilson, B., and Mee, F., 1998. *The Medieval Parish Churches of York: The Pictorial Evidence* (York: York Archaeological Trust)

Wilson, B., and Mee, F., 2002. *'The Fairest Arch in England'. Old Ouse Bridge, York, and its Buildings: The Pictorial Evidence* (York: York Archaeological Trust)

Wilson, B., and Mee, F., 2005. *The City Walls and Castles of York: The Pictorial Evidence* (York: York Archaeological Trust)

Woodward, G.W.O., 1966. *The Dissolution of the Monasteries* (London: Blandford Press)

www.mylearning.org (Free learning resources from museums, libraries and archives in Yorkshire)

YCR. Raine, A. (ed), *York Civic Records*, YASRS (8 vols)

YMB. Sellers, M. (ed), 1912. *York Memorandum Book* I (1376–1419), SS **120**

King's Manor

Browning, A., Geiter, M.K., and Speck, W.A. (eds), 1991. *Memoirs of Sir John Reresby: The complete text and a selection from his letters* (London: Royal Historical Society)

Davies, R., 1883. *The Historie of the King's Mannour House at York, illustrated with etchings by A Buckle* (York)

Reid, R.R., 1921. *The King's Council in the North* (London: Longmans)

RCHMY **4**, 1975. Royal Commission on Historical Monuments (England), *An Inventory of the Historical Monuments in the City of York. Vol. 4, North East* (London: HM Stationery Office)

Whittingham, A.B., 1971. 'St Mary's Abbey, York: an interpretation of its plan', *Archaeol J* **128**, 118–45